William Wordsworth

AN EVALUATION OF HIS POETRY

William Wordsworth

AN EVALUATION OF HIS POETRY

[Edited with Introduction, Author's Information, Complete Text, Summary and Analysis and Study Questions]

Mansi Sachdeva
B.A. English (Hons), Delhi University;
M.A., M. Phil. (English), IGNOU

ANMOL PUBLICATIONS PVT. LTD.
NEW DELHI - 110 002 (INDIA)

ANMOL PUBLICATIONS PVT. LTD.

H.O.: 4374/4B, Ansari Road, Darya Ganj,
New Delhi-110 002 (India)
Ph.: 23278000, 23261597

B.O.: No. 1015, Ist Main Road, BSK IIIrd Stage
IIIrd Phase, IIIrd Block
Bangalore - 560 085 (India)
Visit us at: www.anmolpublications.com

An Evaluation of His Poetry

First Published, 2009

PRINTED IN INDIA

Printed at Mehra Offset Press, Delhi.

Contents

Preface

William Wordsworth was born on April 7, 1770, in Cockermouth, Cumbria, England. He was eight year old, when his mother died. His love for poetry was founded while attending the Hawkshead Grammar School. Wordsworth also made his first attempts at verse. At Hawkshead, Wordsworth's father died and he was left alone with his four siblings orphans. His poetry as well as political sensibilities were influenced a lot during his final semester in St. John's College in Cambridge, as he set out on a walking tour of Europe.

Year 1795 played significant role in the poetic life of Wordsworth, as he met Samuel Taylor Coleridge. In the year 1798, some of the popular Lyrical Ballads were published along with Coleridge. One of the most popular works by Wordsworth is the The Prelude (1850) and is considered as the crowning achievement of English romanticism.

Author

Chapter 1

Introduction

William Wordsworth was born on April 7, 1770, in Cockermouth, Cumbria, England. Wordsworth's mother died when he was eight—this experience shapes much of his later work. Wordsworth attended Hawkshead Grammar School, where his love of poetry was firmly established and, it is believed, he made his first attempts at verse. While he was at Hawkshead, Wordsworth's father died leaving him and his four siblings orphans. After Hawkshead, Wordsworth studied at St. John's College in Cambridge and before his final semester, he set out on a walking tour of Europe, an experience that influenced both his poetry and his political sensibilities. While touring Europe, Wordsworth came into contact with the French Revolution.

This experience as well as a subsequent period living in France, brought about Wordsworth's interest and sympathy for the life, troubles and speech of the "common man". These issues proved to be of the utmost importance to Wordsworth's work. Wordsworth's earliest poetry was published in 1793 in the collections An Evening Walk and Descriptive Sketches. While living in France, Wordsworth conceived a daughter, Caroline, out of wedlock; he left France, however, before she was born. In 1802, he returned to France with his sister on a four-week visit to meet Caroline.

Later that year, he married Mary Hutchinson, a childhood friend, and they had five children together. In 1812, while living in Grasmere, they grieved the loss of two of their children, Catherine and John, who both died that year. Equally important in the poetic life of Wordsworth was his 1795 meeting with the poet, Samuel Taylor Coleridge. It was with Coleridge that Wordsworth published the famous Lyrical Ballads in 1798.

While the poems themselves are some of the most influential in Western literature, it is the preface to the second edition that remains one of the most important testaments to a poet's views on both his craft and his place in the world. In the preface Wordsworth writes on the need for "common speech" within poems and argues against the hierarchy of the period which valued epic poetry above the lyric. Wordsworth's most famous work, The Prelude (1850), is considered by many to be the crowning achievement of English romanticism.

The poem, revised numerous times, chronicles the spiritual life of the poet and marks the birth of a new genre of poetry. Although Wordsworth worked on The Prelude throughout his life, the poem was published posthumously. Wordsworth spent his final years settled at Rydal Mount in England, travelling and continuing his outdoor excursions. Devastated by the death of his daughter Dora in 1847, Wordsworth seemingly lost his will to compose poems. William Wordsworth died at Rydal Mount on April 23, 1850, leaving his wife Mary to publish The Prelude three months later.

A Selected Bibliography

Poetry

An Evening Walk (1793)
Borders (1795)
Complete Poetical Works (1971)
Descriptive Sketches (1793)
Ecclesiastical Sketches (1822)
Intimations of Immortality (1806)
Lines Written Above Tintern Abbey (1798)
Lyrical Ballads (1798)
Memorials of a Tour of the Continent (1822)
Miscellaneous Sonnets (1807)
Peter Bell (1819)

Poems (1977)
Poems I-II (1807)
Selected Poems (1959)
The Excursion (1814)
The Poetical Works (1949)
The Prelude Or Growth of a Poet's Mind (1850)
The Recluse (1888)
The River Duddon (1820)
The Waggoner (1819)
The White Doe of Rylstone (1815)
Upon Westminster Bridge (1801)
Yarrow Revisited (1835)

Prose

Letters of Dorothy and William Wordsworth (1967)
Letters of the Wordsworth Family (1969)
Literary Criticism (1966)
Prose Works (1896)
Prose Works (1974)
The Love Letters of William and Mary Wordsworth (1981)

Essays

Essay Upon Epitaphs (1810)

Chapter 2

Biography of William Wordsworth

William Wordsworth (1770-1850)

British poet, who spent his life in the Lake District of Northern England. William Wordsworth started with Samuel Taylor Coleridge the English Romantic movement with their collection LYRICAL BALLADS in 1798. When many poets still wrote about ancient heroes in grandiloquent style, Wordsworth focused on the nature, children, the poor, common people, and used ordinary words to express his personal feelings. His definition of poetry as "the spontaneous overflow of powerful feelings arising from "emotion recollected in tranquility" was shared by a number of his followers.

"Poetry is the breath and finer spirit of all knowledge; it is the impassioned expression which is in the countenance of all Science." (from Lyrical Ballads, 2nd ed., 1800)

William Wordsworth was born in Cockermouth, Cumberland, in the Lake District. His father was John Wordsworth, Sir James Lowther's attorney - the fifth Baronet Lowther was the most feared and hated aristocrat in all of Cumberland and Westmoreland, "an Intolerable Tyrant over his Tenants and Dependents". However, the magnificent landscape deeply affected Wordsworth's imagination and gave him a love of nature. He lost his mother when he was eight and five years later his father. The domestic problems separated Wordsworth from his beloved and neurotic sister Dorothy, who was a very important person in his life. Dorothy had especially fresh contact to nature from a very early age.

Her thoughts and impression were a valuable source of inspiration for her brother, who also introduced himself as Nature's child. The first time she saw the sea, she burst into tears, "indicating the sensibility for which she was so remarkable," Wordsworth remembered.

With the help of his two uncles, Wordsworth entered a local school and continued his studies at Cambridge University. As a writer Wordsworth made his debut in 1787, when he published a sonnet in The European Magazine. In that same year he entered St. John's College, Cambridge, from where he took his B.A. in 1791. During a summer vacation in 1790, Wordsworth went on a walking tour through revolutionary France. He also traveled in Switzerland.

On his second journey in France, Wordsworth had an affair with a French girl, Annette Vallon, a daughter of a barber-surgeon, by whom he had a illegitimate daughter Anne Caroline. The affair was basis of the poem 'Vaudracour and Julia', but otherwise Wordsworth did his best to hide the affair from posterity. After his journeys, Wordsworth spent several aimless and unhappy years. In 1795 he met Coleridge. Wordsworth's financial situation became better in 1795 when he received a legacy and was able to settle at Racedown, Dorset, with his sister Dorothy.

Encouraged by Coleridge and stimulated by the close contact with nature, Wordsworth composed his first masterwork, Lyrical Ballads, which opened with Coleridge's 'Ancient Mariner.' About 1798 he started to write a large and philosophical autobiographical poem, completed in 1805, and published posthumously in 1850 under the title THE PRELUDE. The long work described the poet's love of nature and his own place in the world order.

"Dust as we are, the immortal spirit grows
Like harmony in music; there is a dark
Inscrutable workmanship that reconciles
Discordant elements, makes them cling together
In one society."

The winter 1798-99 Wordsworth spent with his sister and Coleridge in Germany. There he wrote several works, including the enigmatic 'Lucy' poems. After return he moved Dove Cottage, Grasmere. In 1802 married Mary Hutchinson. They cared for Wordsworth's sister Dorothy for the last 20 years of life - she had lost her mind as a result of physical ailments. Almost all Dorothy's memory was destroyed, she sat by the fire, and occasionally recited her brother's verses.

Wordsworth's second collection, POEMS, IN TWO VOLUMES, appeared in 1807. In the same year Thomas de Quincey met first time Wordsworth and wrote about him and other Lake Poets in several essays. He described revealingly Wordsworth's mean appearance and Dorothy's lack of sex appeal. The frankness of his text, although published in the 1830s and 1840s, was considered indiscreet by later Victorian critics. "... Wordsworth was of a good height (five feet ten), and not a slender man; on the contrary, by the side of Southey, his limbs looked thick, almost in a disproportionate degree. But the total effect of Wordsworth's person was always worst in a state of motion. Meantime, his face - that was one which would have made amends for greater defects of figure." (from Reminiscenes of the English Lake Poets by Thomas de Quincey, 1907)

Wordsworth's path-breaking works were produced between 1797 and 1808. In a letter to Lady Beaumont he said: "Every great and original writer, in proportion as he is great and original, must himself create the taste by which he is to be relished." His poems written during middle and late years have not gained similar critical approval. Wordsworth's Grasmere period ended in 1813 when he moved to Rydal Mount, Ambleside, where he spent the rest of his life. His daughter Catherine and beloved son Thomas had died and his friendship with Coleridge, suffering from addiction, was breaking apart. Coleridge did not visit Grasmere, although he had made a trip to the Lake District.

Wordsworth was appointed official distributor of stamps for Westmoreland. From the age of 50 his creative began to decline, but tree female assistants took care of him, and filled his life with admiration. Wordsworth abandoned his radical faith and became a patriotic, conservative public man. In 1843 he succeeded Robert Southey (1774-1843) as England's poet laureate. Wordsworth died on April 23, 1850. The second generation of Romantics, Byron and Shelley, considered him 'dull.' Later the philosopher Bertrand Russell summed up the poet's career: "In his youth Wordsworth sympathized with the French Revolution, went to France, wrote good poetry, and had a natural daughter. At this period he was called a 'bad' man. Then he became 'good,' abandoned his daughter, adopted correct principles, and wrote bad poetry."

Dorothy Wordsworth (1771-1855) published travel books and journals, such as GRASMERE JOURNALS 1800-03 and THE ALFOXDEN JOURNAL 1798, in which she described the friendship of Wordsworth and Coleridge. After a serious illness in 1829, she was obliged to lead the life of an invalid, which deeply affected her imaginative and mental powers.

Chapter 3

Chronology

WORDSWORTH CHRONOLOGY

1770 Born April 7 to John and Anne (Cookson) Wordsworth, second of five.

1778 Mother dies; William goes to Hawkshead Grammar School.

1783 Father dies.

1787 Goes up to St. John's College, Cambridge.

1789 An Evening Walk.

1790 Walking tour of France, Switzerland, and Germany.

1791 Graduates; goes to France; meets and has an affair with Annette Vallon.

1792 (Illegitimate) daughter Caroline born.

1793 Returns to England to earn money; Anglo-French War prevents his return to France until

1802 Descriptive Sketches.

1794 Reunited with Dorothy.

1795 Inherits legacy of £900. Meets Coleridge.

1797 William and his sister Dorothy move to Alfoxden to be near Coleridge.

1798 Lyrical Ballads.

1798-99 The Wordsworths travel to Germany with Coleridge.

1799 William and Dorothy settle in the Lake district, at Dove Cottage, Grasmere.

1800 Lyrical Ballads revised, Preface added.

1802 visits the Vallons at Calais. After receiving a much-delayed inheritance, marries Mary Hutchinson.

	Sonnets Dedicated to National Independence and Liberty.
1803	Son John born. (Four more children by 1810.)
1805	The Prelude finished. Brother John lost at sea.
1807	Poems in Two Volumes.
1809	The Convention of Cintra.
1810	Quarrel with Coleridge.
1812	Children Thomas and Caroline die.
1813	Moves to Rydal Mount, between Grasmere and Rydal Water; appointed Distributor of Stamps for Westmorland (£400/year).
1814	The Excursion.
1815	The White Doe of Rylstone. Preface to Lyrical Ballads revised.
1819	Peter Bell and The Waggoner.
1820	We Are Seven and The River Duddon (sonnets).
1822	Ecclesiastical Sketches.
1825	Yarrow Revisited, and Other Poems. 1828 tours the Rhineland with Coleridge.
1839	Oxford confers honorary Doctor of Civil Law degree.
1842	Poems, Chiefly of Early and Late Years. 1843 named Poet Laureate.
1847	Daughter Dora dies.
1850	Dies (April 23). The Prelude.

Chapter 4

About Dorothy Wordsworth

Dorothy Wordsworth (1771-1855)

English prose writer, the younger sister of poet William Wordsworth, famous for her diaries and 'recollections'. Several of Dorothy Wordsworth's own poems or notes in her journal were included in various editions of her brother's poetical works. She published nothing during her lifetime, and spent the last twenty-five years struggling against physical and mental illness. E. de Sélincourt, who published her journals in 1933, has called her "probably... the most distinguished of English writers who never wrote a line for the general public."

"She did not cultivate the graces which preside over the person and its carriage. But, on the other hand, she was a person of very remarkable endowments intellectually... Her knowledge of literature was irregular, and thoroughly unsystematic. She was content to be ignorant of many things; but what she knew and had really mastered lay where it could not be disturbed - in the temple of her own most fervid heart." (Thomas De Quincey in Reminiscenes of the Lake Poets, 1961)

Dorothy Wordsworth was born in Cockermouth, Cumberland. She was the third of five children. Her childhood Dorothy spent with various relatives. Ann Cookson of Penrith, her mother, died when Dorothy was six. "I know," she later wrote, "that I received much good that I can trace back to her". Dorothy's father, John Wordsworth, an attorney, died when she was just twelve. He died intestate, his affairs in chaos, and Dorothy was removed from boarding-school. At the age of 15 she went to her grandparents in Penrith and met her brothers again. However, she was not to see much of them before she was 23. From 17 to 22 she lived at Forncett Rectory, Norfolk, where her mother's brother, William Cookson, took her in. She enjoyed her life in Norfolk more than at her grandmother's house. She read, wrote, and improved herself in French. After the winter of 1793/4 she continued to stay in various other places.

Wordsworth began writing in about 1795 when she shared a house in Dorset with her brother. At Alfoxden, Somerset, she became friends with the poet Samuel Taylor Coleridge, and traveled with him and William in Germany (1798-99), where they lived in lodgings in Goslar. Coleridge spent a good deal of time at the University city of Göttingen. For the journey she bought a notebook, which she used for her daily affairs. It contained among others things lists of the clothes, from shirts and nightcaps to fur items, that she would need in the cold winter, and also list of groceries - bread, milk, sugar, and rum. In Alfoxden she started her first journal, and then kept several other journals of travels and expeditions. Her thoughts and writings were an important source of stimulation for Coleridge and William. "Tho we were three persons," Coleridge wrote, "it was but one soul." Sarah Coleridge's role in this artistic circle was not central - she was considered dull, but she raised the children and took care of her opium-addicted husband, who eventually abandoned his patient wife.

With her brother Dorothy occasionally played a curious game - they lay down next to each other outdoors, pretending to be in their graves. Some biographers have speculated about their strong attraction to each other, considering it sexual. William's poems, such as 'Lines' and 'To My Sister', don't give any hint of this, but do express his happiness, when she accompanies him on the walking trips: "My sister! ('tis a wish of mine) / Now that our morning meal is done, / Make haste, your morning task resign; / Come forth and feel the sun." (from 'To My Sister')

In 1799 Dorothy settled with her brother in Dove Cottage, Grasmere, in the Lake District. It was her first real home since her mother died. In 1802 William married Mary Hutchinson, who was Dorothy's best friend. The marriage was happy but Dorothy was too hysterical to attend the wedding. A few days before the marriage she wrote to her friend: "I have long loved Mary Hutchinson as a Sister, and she is equally attached to me this being so, you will guess that I look forward with perfect happiness to the Connection between us, but happy, as I am, I half dread that concentration of all tender feelings, past, present, and future will come up me on the wedding morning."

When Thomas De Quincey met William at Grasmere in 1807, he also made the acquaintance of Dorothy. In the household also lived Mrs. Wordsworth, two children, and at that time one servant. According to De Quincey, Dorothy's face was of Egyptian brown, "rarely, in a woman of English birth, had I seen a more determinate gypsy tan. Her eyes were not soft, as Mrs. Wordsworth's, nor were they fierce or bold; but they were wild and startling, and hurried in their motion." Quincey was impressed by the Lake District: its small fields, miniature meadows, and solitude.

Dorothy's influence on William was, according to Quincey, the way she "humanized him by the gentler charities". Dorothy remained in Grasmere, the Lake District, until 1813, when she moved to nearby Rydal. In 1829 she became ill and was obliged to lead the life of an invalid. From 1835 she developed arteriosclerosis and for the remaining 20 years she suffered from mental problems, possibly originating in thiamin deficiency. She often played with a bowl of soapsuds and hid from visitors. Dorothy Wordsworth died in Rydal Mount on January 25, 1855.

Dorothy Wordsworth started to keep her journal in the late 1790s, recording walks, visits, conversations, and above all the world of nature. The journals were not intended for publication. Suppressing her ambitions of becoming a writer, and devoting herself to domestic duty, she once said: "I should detest the idea of setting myself up as an author." Instead she wrote to "give Wm Pleasure by it". Her brother's poems, such as 'Beggars' and 'Daffodils', use her precise descriptions of the countryside and life in Dove Cottage. Dorothy's ALFOXDEN

JOURNAL 1798 and GRASMERE JOURNALS 1800-03 were published posthumously.

The first notebook of the Grasmere Journal was not empty - it also contained lists and accounts of her stay in Goslar. Among her other works are visit to hamburgh and a journey to... Goslar 1798-99, the memoir recollections of a tour made in scotland (1804), journal of a tour made in scotland (1803), an excursion on the banks of ullswater 1805, journal of a tour on the continent (1820), which included her irritated views of william on their journey in switzerland, an excursion up scawfell pike (1818), and journal of a tour in the isle of man (1828).

Chapter 5

Some Major Events

The Influence of Rousseau

WORDSWORTH'S surprise and resentment would surely have been provoked had he been told that, at half a century's distance and from an European point of view, his work would seem, on the whole, though with several omissions and additions, to be a continuation of the movement initiated by Rousseau. It is, nevertheless, certain that it might be described as an English variety of Rousseauism, revised and corrected, in some parts, by the opposite influence of Edmund Burke.

In Wordsworth, we find Rousseau's well-known fundamental tenets: he has the same semi mystical faith in the goodness of nature as well as in the excellence of the child; his ideas on education are almost identical; there are apparent a similar diffidence in respect of the merely intellectual processes of the mind, and an equal trust in the good that may accrue to man from the cultivation of his senses and feelings. The differences between the two, mainly occasional and of a political nature seem secondary by the side of these profound analogies. For this reason, Wordsworth must be placed by the general historian among the numerous "sons of Rousseau," who form the main battalion of romanticism; though, if we merely regard the ideas he expressed and propagated, his personality may, thereby, lose some of its originality and distinctness.

But, resemblance does not necessarily mean repetition and imitation. Moreover, men's ideas are their least individual possessions. The manner in which a man, and, above all, a poet, becomes possessed of his creed, the stamp he puts upon it, are the things that really matter. Now, Wordsworth formed his thoughts and convictions in the light of the circumstances of his own life, where-by they assumed a reality wanting in those of many of his contemporaries. If he thought like others, he always thought by himself.

He gives us the impression that, had he lived alone on a bookless earth, he would have reached the same conclusions. His deep influence on a limited, but incomparably loyal, number of readers owes less to his beliefs than to his minute, persevering analysis of every step he made towards them. He appeals to our confidence by his constant recourse to his personal experience. He prides himself on being the least inventive of great poets. He belittles fancy. It is true that he claimed imagination as his supreme gift, but, at the same time, he bestowed on the word imagination a new meaning, almost entirely opposed to the ordinary one.

He gave the name to his accurate, faithful and loving observation of nature. In his loftier moods, he used "imagination" as a synonym of "intuition," of seeing into, and even through, reality, but he never admitted a divorce between it and reality. The gift of feigning, of arbitrarily combining the features of a legend or story, which had long been held to be the first poetical prerogative, was almost entirely denied him, and he thanked God for its absence. His hold over many thoughtful and, generally, mature minds is due to his having avowedly, and often, also, practically, made truth his primary object, beauty being only second. Those who had ingenuously turned to his poems for the mere charm of verse were grateful to him inasmuch as they had received, in addition, their first lessons in philosophy.

They had gone to him for pleasure and they came back with a train of reflection that followed them through the round of their daily tasks. They were taught by him a new way of looking at men and nature. Wordsworth achieved this result by dint of one-sided pressure, by tenaciousness of aim. Not that his ideas remained the same from beginning to end. Few men, on the contrary, changed more thoroughly. His mind may be represented as continuously shifting along a half circle, so that, finally, he stood at the opposite end of the diameter. The young revolutionist evolved into a grey-haired conservative, the semi-atheist and pantheist into a pattern of conformity. But, all the time, he kept true to his fixed centre, the search for the greatest good. His very contradictions point to one engrossing pursuit. His life was an unbroken series of slow movements which brought him from one extreme to the other, though his eyes were ever bent in the same direction. Because he never ceased to have the same object in view, he was himself imperfectly conscious of the change in his position.

Wordsworth's Childhood

Wordsworth was born in 1770 at Cockermouth, in the north of the lake country, the second child of a fairly prosperous attorney-at-law and of Anne Cookson, daughter of a Penrith mercer. Seen from the outside, without the optimistic prism of The Prelude, his childhood does not seem to have been any more privileged, while his youth appears decidedly more vexed and troubled, than those of the common run of men. The child, surely, had pleasant hours with his brothers and sister while playing about the terrace of the family garden which overlooked the Derwent, or when bathing in the river. There were bitter hours, however, when he was taken to his mother's family at Penrith, where harsh grandparents often treated the little ones "with reproach and insult." William was particularly unruly and, in consequence, had most to bear from the Cooksons. Hence, we hear of acts of defiance and even of a childish attempt at suicide.

When he was eight years old, his mother died, and, parting from his father, who never recovered his cheerfulness after his bereavement, Wordsworth was sent to Hawkshead grammar school. A very homely one-room house in a very poor village is the place where he was taught. He lodged with one of the old village dames, who, however kind they might be to boys, could only give them coarse and scanty fare. For his companions, he chiefly had farmers' sons, destined for the church, who brought with them the rough manners of their home life. In spite of the delight he found in games, open air life and rambles about hill and lake, it must be admitted that Hawkshead was a very mixed paradise.

Then came his father's death, when the boy was thirteen. The orphan's condition was precarious. Almost all the money left by his father was in the hands of Sir James Lowther, to whom Wordsworth's father had been steward, and Sir James would never hear of paying it back so long as he lived, nor could he be compelled to reimburse. It is true that enough remained to allow William to pursue his studies, and a boy does not take money questions much to heart. But there were wretched holidays at Penrith, in his grandparents' sullen home.

Of the frequent distress of the children in that house, we have a vivid picture in the earliest letters of little Dorothy, the poet's only sister, written in the last year spent by William at Hawkshead. Dorothy, whose sweet, affectionate nature cannot be suspected of unjustified complaints, could scarcely bear the loveless constraint she had to undergo. No more could her brothers: "Many a time have William, John, Christopher and myself shed tears together of the bitterest sorrow." "We have no father to protect, no mother to guide us," and so forth.

His Wanderings

From Hawkshead, Wordsworth went to Cambridge in October, 1787, and remained there at St. John's College till the beginning of 1791. He took little interest either in the intellectual or social life of the university. He never opened a mathematical book and thus lost all chance of obtaining a fellowship. Even his literary studies were pursued irregularly, without any attention being paid to the prescribed course. He did not feel any abhorrence of the students' life, which, at that time, consisted of alternate sloth and wildness.

He first shared in it, but soon grew weary of it and lived more or less by himself. In his university years, his only deep enjoyments were the long rambles in which he indulged during vacations. Meanwhile, discussions with his uncles must, at times, have made life rather distasteful to him. He had no money in prospect. All his small patrimony had been spent on his university education; yet he showed himself vacillating and reluctant when required to make choice of a career. None was to his taste.

The army, the church, the law, tutorial work, were all contemplated and discarded in turn. He showed no strong bent except for wandering and writing poetry. He was, indeed, a young man likely to make his elders anxious. In July, 1790, just at the time when he ought to have been working hard for his approaching examinations, he took it into his head to start for the Alps with a fellow student, on foot, equipped much like a peddler—an escapade without precedent. As soon as he had taken his B.A., without distinction, he set fortune at defiance, and settled in London for a season, doing nothing in particular, "pitching a vagrant tent among the unfenced regions of society." After this, other wanderings and abortive schemes of regular work followed for more than three years, till he threw aside all idea of a fixed career and settled down to resolute poverty.

Such apparent restlessness and indolence could not but be attended by many a pang of remorse. He suffered from his growing estrangement from his relations. He was ill satisfied with himself and uneasy about the future, and these feelings (perhaps darkened by some passages of vexed love) found an outlet in his juvenile poems, all of which are tinged with melancholy.

It seems strange that such a childhood and youth should, afterwards, have furnished him with the optimistic basis of The Prelude. Beyond doubt, this poem was meant to be a selection of all the circumstances in his early life that told for joy and hope. Hence, a heightening of bright colours, and a voluntary omission of more somber hues, in the picture he made of his youth. But the contrast between the dry facts of his early life and his rapture over the same period is, also, owing to a deeper truth. The joy he celebrates in The Prelude springs from sources hidden from all eyes, scarcely suspected by the child himself. Whatever shadows might pass over his days, abundant strength and happiness lay beneath the surface. He was not callous to grief, but, somehow, felt all the time that grief was transient, hope permanent, in his breast. His enjoyment of nature gave him those intense delights which are usually unnoticed in the tale of a life. So did his already passionate love of verse. Thus, The Prelude is all true, though it does not present us with the whole truth.

Of the young man's passion for nature, his early poems, both published in 1793, furnish direct proof. They are the most minute and copious inventories of the aspects he saw, of the noises he heard, in his native lakes (An Evening Walk) or in his wanderings through Switzerland (Descriptive Sketches). Such acuteness and copiousness of observation were only possible in the case of a devotee. However contorted and knotty the verse may be, however artificial the diction, the poet's fervour is as manifest here as in the most eloquent of his subsequent effusions. Though he follows in the train of a succession of descriptive poets, he outdoes them all in abundance of precise touches.

The French Revolution

But his practice of descriptive poetry was interrupted for several years, at the very time when he was giving the finishing touch to these poems. The influence of the French revolution on this part of his life cannot be overrated. Characteristically, he was rather late in becoming an adept. He uttered no paean on the fall of the Bastille. To move him, it was necessary that his senses should be aroused.

Now, the revolution turned her most enticing smile towards him. It so happened that he had first landed at Calais on the eve of the federation of 1790; so, the unparalleled mirth of that time seemed a festivity prepared for his welcome. The glee and hopefulness of the season turned into a charming benevolence, which he tasted with all the relish of a student on a holiday trip. Then came his prolonged stay in France, chiefly at Orleans and at Blois, from November, 1791, to December, 1792, in times already darkened by civil mistrust and violence. But, chance would have it that he should be eyewitness to heart stirring scenes, such as the enlisting of volunteers and the proclamation of the republic. Above all, he had the good fortune to make friends with one of the true heroes of the day, Captain Michel Beaupuy, whose chivalric nature and generous enthusiasm for the new order warmed the young Englishman. Exquisite is the portrait drawn of Beaupuy in The Prelude.

The fine traits of his character are all confirmed by what has since become known of his career, with this reservation, that, through an irresistible tendency to idealise, Wordsworth may have toned down some of the features. Beaupuy was the revolutionary apostle described by the poet, but there was less of the philosopher and more of the soldier in his composition. It is clear from his letters and diaries that he was an ingenuous and soldier-like reasoner, and, also, that he could utter an oath or two when in a passion. Anyhow, he found Wordsworth a bewildered foreigner and left him a determined revolutionist, one might almost say a French republican. A spirit of revolt and indignation against all social iniquities pervaded Wordsworth for years, together with a sympathy, which never left him, for the poorer and humbler members of the community.

When he came back to England, he drew near the Jacobins without becoming one of them; but he was a decided reformer. Alienated from his own country when she went to war with France, he heartily hated king, regent and ministry. His letter to the bishop of Llandaff and his poem Guilt and Sorrow (or Incidents on Salisbury Plain) are the best testimonies of his feelings. Society appeared to him responsible for the wretchedness, and even the crimes, of individuals—his pity went to vagrants and murderers. His abhorrence of war was shown in insistent and gruesome pictures of war scenes.

When the French revolution passed into the Terror, and especially when the republic changed a defensive into an aggressive war, Wordsworth lost his trust in immediate social reform. He turned more and more to abstract meditation on man and society, chiefly under the guidance of William Godwin—a period of dry intellectualism that went against the grain. He suffered from the suppression of his feelings, from being momentarily deaf to "the language of the sense."

Besides, his analysis of men's motives soon convinced him that the evils he fought against were not so much the results of social forms as of something inherent in man's nature.

A man of commanding intellect may be wantonly cruel and vicious; he may use all the powers of logic for his detestable ends; reason is non-moral; the wicked "spin motives out of their own bowels." Hence, a wellnigh absolute, though transient, pessimism, which vented itself in his play The Borderers. If the traditional bonds of morality are relaxed, the fixed rules of our actions or the intuitive guidance of the feelings repudiated, then full scope is given to bold, intelligent, bad men; then are the well-meaning blinded and betrayed to abominable deeds. Then is the Terror possible. Scarcely any hope of betterment is left. The kind-hearted Girondin Marmaduke will be an easy prey to the villainous Montagnard Oswald.

Dorothy Wordsworth

When he wrote this tragedy, Wordsworth had already put an end to his solitary, wandering life and settled at Racedown in Dorsetshire with his sister Dorothy (autumn of 1795). There, they both lived a frugal life, on the meagre income from a legacy of £900 left to the poet by a dying friend. This settlement was the crowning of a long-cherished scheme. Brother and sister were passionately attached to each other. Dorothy's letters make their mutual love known to us and let us into depths of Wordsworth's nature, scarcely revealed by his poems. She speaks of "a vehemence of affection" in him that his readers might not suspect, so careful he usually was, in Hazlitt's words, "to calm the throbbing pulses of his own heart by keeping his eye ever fixed on the face of nature." By this discipline, did he, in those years, slowly conquer his besetting thoughts of despondency.

Wordsworth and Dorothy were equally fond of natural scenery. Their delight in each other and their daily rambles were the first agents in the young disillusionised republican's recovery. Dorothy made him turn his eyes again to the landscape and take an interest in the peasants near their home.

But the poet's mind remained gloomy for a time, as is shown by his pastoral The Ruined Cottage (or The Story of Margaret), which afterwards found its place in the first book of The Excursion.

A heart-rending narrative, if read without the comforting comments of the pedlar afterwards added to it, a perfect poem, too, such as Wordsworth never surpassed, it points out both the exceeding tenderness often met with in the hearts of the poor and the cruelty of fate aggravated by the existing social order. No doctrine, poetic or philosophical, is perceptible in this poem of simple, chastened beauty. It does not give any token of the message with which Wordsworth was soon to think himself entrusted.

Friendship with Coleridge

His sense of a message only became clear to him after he had, in the summer of 1797, removed from Racedown to Alfoxden, so as to live in daily converse with Coleridge, who was then dwelling at Nether Stowey, in Somersetshire. Till then, the two poets had only exchanged a few visits, after the end of 1795, the first results of which had merely been to encourage Wordsworth to poetical composition. He had felt raised and exhilarated by Coleridge's entire, almost extravagant, admiration for his Salisbury Plain and Borderers. But, when they had become close neighbours and intimate friends, Coleridge's innate transcendentalism began to affect Wordsworth.

It is impossible to define exactly the share of each in the elaboration of those poetical and moral tenets which they seemed, for a time, to hold in common, unconscious of the deep differences between them. Yet, on the whole, one may say that Wordsworth's share consisted in his more precise observations of nature and common life. Coleridge, "with the capacious soul," influenced his friend by his metaphysical gifts, "the power he possessed of throwing out in profusion grand, central truths from which might be evolved the most comprehensive systems." An omnivorous reader, with an inclination towards mystic doctrines, Coleridge talked eloquently to Wordsworth on Plato and the neo-Platonists, Berkeley's idealism, the pantheistic system and serene necessitarianism of Spinoza, the intuitional religion of the theosophists—a new world to one who had not yet gone beyond the rationalism of the eighteenth century and who always found his most congenial food in the associationism of Hartley.

Now, Wordsworth, without binding himself to any one master, was to take hints from all in building up his own doctrine. But he was not an intellectual dilettante; all he absorbed from without had to be reconciled to his personal experience and turned to a practical aim. He would show men the way to wisdom and happiness. He would, from his country retreat, give out his views of nature, man and society. He justified this lofty ambition to himself because he was conscious, personally, of having issued out of error into truth, out of despondency into hopefulness. He thought he knew the reasons why most men in his generation had fallen into pessimism and misanthropy.

He now believed in the restorative power of nature, in the essential goodness of a man's heart when unadulterated by the pride of intellect, in the greatness of the senses which could drink in infinite joys and profound lessons of wisdom. Thus did he plan his Recluse, as early as March, 1798, "the first great philosophical poem in existence," as Coleridge anticipated, which was to employ his highest energies for seventeen years. Though never completed, the monument exists in fragments of imposing magnitude—the first book of The Recluse, properly so called, written in 1800; The Prelude, written between 1798 and 1805, an autobiography meant as the ante-chapel to the huge gothic cathedral; and The Excursion, which, though it includes passages composed as early as 1797, was not finished before 1814.

Such intervals of time account better than any other reason for the incompleteness of the edifice, for the poet's ideas changed so much while he was engaged upon his work that no systematic presentation of doctrine, as was first intended, could possibly be achieved. Only the initial impulse remained—the poet's sense of a duty put on him from on high, his earnest wish to benefit his fellow men morally and to make them happier. The reasons for his optimism might and did vary; but the optimistic attitude was preserved to the end, securing the unity of the poet's career.

Lyrical Ballads

But, during his stay with Coleridge in Somersetshire, Wordsworth did not only lay the foundations of his Recluse. The same intercourse gave birth to less ambitious and more immediate verse, to the famous Lyrical Ballads of 1798, a small volume of short poems by Coleridge and himself. It is well known how, after some fruitless attempts at collaboration, the two friends agreed to divide the field of poetry.

To the share of Coleridge fell such subjects as were supernatural, or, at any rate, romantic, which he was to inform with a human interest and a semblance of truth. Wordsworth's part was to be the events of everyday life, by preference in its humblest form; the characters and incidents of his poems "were to be such as will be found in every village and its vicinity where there is a meditative and feeling mind to seek after them, or to notice them when they present themselves." Thus did Coleridge sing The Ancient Mariner, while Wordsworth told the tales Goody Blake and Simon Lee. Nothing can better show Wordsworth's minute realism, how necessary it was to him to hold a little of his mother earth within his fingers. His homely ballads are so many humble practical illustrations of the philosophy he was at this very time promulgating in lofty blank verse, for instance, in his lyrical hymn of thanks to nature, Tintern Abbey.

The ballads have "a something corporeal, a matter-of-factness," which Coleridge could not help lamenting. They are not only clad in humble garb, but, to a certain extent, are more scientific than poetic in their aim. There survived so much of Wordsworth's former rationalism that he almost gave the precedence to psychology over poetry in these experiments. The preface of the 1800 edition of the Ballads really looks like the programme of a man of science. He is inspired by a wish to know more, and make more known, of the human heart.

He goes so far as to call poetry "the history and science of the feelings."

Perfect unity is not characteristic of this period so much as a gladsome energy exerted in several directions. "He never wrote with such glee." His new reading of nature and of man fills him with delight—together with the life he now leads between the most wonderful of friends and the most devoted of inspired sisters. He had such superfluous joy that "he could afford to suffer with those he saw suffer," that he was "bold to look on painful things." He believed in "the deep power of joy," by means of which "we see into the life of things." He made joy the chief attribute of poetry, proclaimed poets "the happiest of men." He rejoiced in his own boldness, found vent for his surviving republicanism in a sweeping, democratic reform of poetical style—putting down the time-honoured hierarchy of words, abolishing the traditional distinction between high and low, in subjects and diction.

These trustful feelings, this spontaneous optimism, expressive of his unimpaired vitality, sustained him throughout the years from 1798 to 1805, during which period his best and most original poetry was written, whether at Alfoxden, or in Germany, where he stayed with his sister from September, 1798, to April, 1799, or in the glorious humility of Dove cottage, at Grasmere, in the lake country, where he settled with Dorothy in the last days of the century and where Coleridge was again his frequent visitant, or in his wanderings over Scotland, with both Coleridge and Dorothy, from August to October 1803. A period of "plain living and high thinking," made famous by great verse.

One may fix on 1805 as the year in, or about, which this period of Wordsworth's poetical life closes. He had now, if not published, at least written, nearly all that is supreme in his works—his only book of The Recluse, all The Prelude, the best parts of The Excursion, besides many of the best and boldest of his short poems, ballads and sonnets. His great Ode on Immortality was all but finished. Had he died then, in his thirty-sixth year, having lived as long as Byron and much longer than Shelley or Keats, he would have left a fame almost as high as he was to attain, though of a different character. His freshness of thought and style being taken together, his works would have stamped him as one of the most daring among the poets of his day.

The sedate and sometimes conventional moralising which has been associated with his name comes into existence in his later productions. But it should be added that, for ten years, he was to achieve, in a new direction, some verse that "one would not willingly let die."

Outward events and the circumstances of his own life had something to do with the change that took place in him about 1805. Politically, it was caused by the beginning of the French empire, the crowning of Napoleon by the pope, "a sad reverse for all mankind"; hence, the final overthrow of Wordsworth's sympathies for the revolution, the decisive proof (so he thought) that his former ideal was false and treacherous. This led him to suspect more and more all that, in his ideas, still savoured of revolt; it caused him to rally more closely round the principles of order and repent his former wishes of social change. The grey tints of mistrust slowly overlaid the glowing enthusiasms of yore. It is true that Wordsworth's feelings were roused, chiefly by the Spanish war, to a patriotic fervour that found expression in many a vigorous sonnet and even turned him into a pamphleteer.

His eloquent and ponderous Convention of Cintra (1809) shows the fighting spirit that was in him. But it had the inconvenience of leading him from verse to prose, from poetry to dialectics, and thus generated an oratorical habit that was to infect many parts of his Excursion.

Wordsworth's Marriage

Then, in his very home, there happened changes that, whether fortunate or sad, impressed on his soul new habits and tendencies. As early as 1802, he had married a Westmorland girl, Mary Hutchinson, in whom he found one of the greatest blessings of his life. The quieting influence of this meek Mary, by degrees, though not at once, was added to, or even took the place of, the more impulsive and exciting companionship of Dorothy. Mrs. Wordsworth's nature told for submission and repose. Besides, the mere fact of his being married checked gradually, though it did not suppress altogether, what might be called the guiltless Bohemianism of his youth.

The duties and cares of the father of a large family grew upon him. Five children were born to the pair between 1803 and 1810, two of whom were to die almost simultaneously in 1812. As early as 1806, the increase of his family had led to a temporary then to a definitive, abandonment of the narrow Dove cottage, to which clung many of his most poetical memories.

Before robbing him of two of his children, death had already struck Wordsworth a blow that went near his heart, one that ever after saddened his life—the loss of his brother John, a sailor shipwrecked in February, 1805. How deeply he was affected by it is known, not only by his poems, but from the letters of the Grasmere household and the journal of Dorothy. There was another cause of grievous sorrow in the state of "the brother of his soul," Coleridge, now a prey to opium and drink, whose growing distress of body and mind was, for years, a depressing, heart-rending sight for his friend, and whose endless idle laments haunted Wordsworth's sleep as well as his waking thoughts.

To which clung many of his mostWhether absent or present, Coleridge had become an increasing source of anxiety to Wordsworth. Wordsworth's infinite patience and forbearance, in these circumstances, cannot be too highly praised. But nothing availed. The friends had to part in 1810, Coleridge betaking himself to London. More painful than all the rest, Coleridge, in one of his irresponsible moods, turned in anger against Wordsworth. An estrangement followed which was never wholly healed, and which left a lifelong scar in Wordsworth's heart.

Yet, the change in Wordsworth's poetry had still deeper causes than all these. Though he had little of Coleridge's self-abandonment, he could not help feeling a decay of his strictly poetical powers—of that imagination and joy on which, till then, he had erected the structure of his verse. When Coleridge had written his ode Dejection in 1802, Wordsworth could immediately retort with his optimistic Leech-Gatherer. But, now, he, also, felt the wane of his "shaping spirit of imagination." The earth no longer offered him the splendour it had for him in his youth.

A glory had departed from the earth. He had, very early, felt the fading of that glory, but had long checked the onset of the unimaginative years to come by fondly dwelling on the memories of his childhood. In 1805, he had so copiously drawn from the treasurehouse for his Prelude that the store was becoming exhausted. He understood the meaning of the depression of his vital spirits: he was travelling further away from the springs of energy, drawing nearer to old age and death. This is a sad thought to all men—it was doubly so to him who had rested all his faith on the freshness of the senses and feelings, and on their gladsome guidance.

Ode to Duty

In want of comfort, he turned to duty. Wordsworth's Ode to Duty (1805), produced at the turning-point of his career, is full of import and significance. It throws a light both on the years that went before and on those that were to follow. It also reveals an aspect of the poet's nature not usually apparent. It is common to speak of him as one of the teachers of duty, and to refer to this ode (or to its title) as a proof. Now, he distinctly resigns himself to the control of duty because, at his time of life, a man can do no better. He abjures with regret the faith that, till then, had been his and in which duty had no place, the dear belief that joy and love can guide man to all good—or, rather, he does not renounce it, but still mutters a hope that better days may come when, joy and love reigning supreme, duty can be dispensed with. As for himself, he would still cling to the same creed if he preserved spirit enough to bear the shocks of change and enjoy his "unchartered freedom." He retires into the arms of duty as a weary warrior of old might end his days in the quiet shelter of a monastery.

He still feels an uncertain convert: "Thee I now would

serve more strictly, if I may." The "stern lawgiver," at first sight, inspires him with more fear than love. He only reconciles himself with the "awful Power" when he has realised that duty wears a smile on her face, that she is beautiful, that, after all, she may be identical with love and joy: Flowers laugh before thee on their beds, And fragrance in thy footing treads; Thou dost preserve the Stars from wrong, And the most ancient Heavens through thee are fresh and strong— a noble stanza, the loftiest of a poem signalised by the almost plaintive appeal that is heard throughout and by the longing, lingering look cast behind.

The Ode to Duty seems to have been written just before the death of his brother John. He expressly says that he is still "untried," and moved by "no disturbance of soul." When the trial came that darkened the world for him, Wordsworth made it his chief task to struggle against grief. He resolutely bade farewell to "the heart that lives alone, housed in a dream." He welcomed "fortitude and patient cheer." He called his former creed an illusion. His themes now, more exclusively than before, will be the sorrows and tragedies of life. But he must find "blessed consolations in distress." He must tell of "melancholy Fear subdued by Faith." The consequence is that his exploration of human woes will, henceforth, be guarded and cautious. He now lacks the bold spirit of youth that can haunt the worst infected places without giving a thought to the danger of contagion.

He is the depressed visitor of the sick, who must needs beware, and be provided with preservatives. He could no longer offer such harrowing pictures of misery as those to be found in his Ruined Cottage or even (in spite of the abrupt conclusion) in his admirable Michael (1800). His diminished vitality makes it necessary for him to ward off dejection.

The Excursion

Argument is the process used at wearisome length in The Excursion. This noble poem may be described as a long sermon against pessimism, scarcely disguised by a story. Though different speakers are introduced, their speeches are mere ventriloquism. Wordsworth, as the optimistic Pedlar, or Wanderer, assails Wordsworth as the Solitary, or the late enthusiast of the French revolution, now dispirited. He uses all his eloquence to raise this other self to his own serene mood. The Excursion too often reminds us of the debates between God and Satan at one time set forth in churches for the edification of the people, the rule being that Satan should have the worst of the controversy.

It is the same with Wordsworth's Solitary, who is presented to us in unfavourable colours; his morals are not of the best. And, when he vents his misanthropy, he does not seem to be quite so fearless, cogent and impressive an exponent of his own views as he might have been. We cannot help thinking that, if the author of Cain had been entrusted with the part, he would have made it many times more telling. The worthy pedlar's triumph would not have been so easily achieved.

The White Doe of Rylstone

The other manner in which Wordsworth now fought against grief is illustrated by his White Doe of Rylstone (1807). In this poem, he renounced argument and called imagination to his aid. He found his subject in the romantic past, in an old tale of war and bloodshed, the tragedy of a catholic rebel killed with all his sons in a revolt against queen Elizabeth. Only one daughter survived, Emily, who, many years after pillage and ruin had passed over the paternal estate, drew comfort from the visitings of a white doe bred by her in her happy days. The doe is a symbol of the past, the lovely phantom of buried memories. Her first apparition gives the lady "one frail shock of pain"; but the pain soon passes into a holy, mild and grateful melancholy, Not sunless gloom or unenlightened, But by tender fancies brightened.m. The awful tragedy has thus been transformed by length of time and strength of habit into something both beautiful and sweet. This is as it should be with the deepest of human woes.

This graceful symbol makes the end of the poem one of the most lovely passages in Wordsworth's poetry. Yet the poem, as a whole, is languid, and even the moral impression is felt to be less convincing than it might have been. The reason is that the poet never dares courageously to cope with despair. He can paint with free energy neither the fate of the rebels, the clang of arms and shocks of death, nor even the pangs and sorrows of Emily. During the battle which is to end in the death of her father and brothers, she, represented as a protestant in a catholic family, is seen awaiting the issue without even daring to express a wish for either side.

When an old man offers to secure a hiding-place for her kindred if vanquished, she declines the offer and declares herself "with her condition satisfied." Later, before she has seen the white doe, she must already have found springs of comfort, for she is strangely said to be "sustained by memory of the past." Such reticence in the picture of desolation much enfeebles the effect of the poem. How much more striking it would have been if it had begun with dark, valiant scenes of tragic fate; if Emily's despair had been made so evident that we should feel for her the want of supernatural comfort, the necessity of the coming in of the white doe.

Laodamia

Wordsworth, in this period, often defeats his own object by refusing to describe the power of evil or woe to the full. He stirs a protest in the reader's mind, incites him to complete the half-drawn picture of misery. Or else, the strain of his muscles in the fight against grief, his repeated assaults and his tricks to elude the grasp of the great adversary, often leave the reader more distressed than he would be by open pessimistic outpourings. Indeed, the greatness of Wordsworth, in these years, lies in his stubborn refusal to confess himself overcome. There is pathos in his optimism, as in the sight of a strong man that will not weep though timely tears might do him good. His stoic poem Laodamia (1814) is a proof of this. The Olympian serenity advocated in it makes us feel—and painfully feel—the distance between the summit where gods dwell and the lower ground inhabited by men. Well for the gods to disprove "the tumult of the soul!" Well for the Elysian fields to be a place where there are No fears to beat away—no strife to heal— The past unsighed for, and the future sure!

But poor Laodamia is merely human and lives on this earth of ours. She cannot "meekly mourn" for her lost hero. She dies of a broken heart, and it seems hard that she should be punished for it as for meditated suicide.

Is this the conclusion of optimism? How hard, inhuman and, one might add, despairing! The poem is great and pathetic, because Wordsworth, all the time, sympathises with Laodamia, feels for her tender weakness, is at heart more like her than like the heroic, dishumanised Protesilaus. But it can scarcely be called a comforting poem. The same might be said of the other verse of this period in which Wordsworth insists on proclaiming both the grandeur and difficulty of hopefulness, when, for instance, he calls hope The paramount duty that Heaven lays For its own honour on man's suffering heart. We perceive how lofty is the peak—and, also, how hard the climbing.

Sonnets; Later Years

The rest of Wordsworth's career (1814–50) adds comparatively little to his best verse. No works of magnitude are to be found in it, the most considerable being collected memorials of one or other of the many tours he made either in the British Isles or on the continent, or series of sonnets, like The River Duddon (1820), and Ecclesiastical Sonnets (1822). Though several of these sonnets or short pieces are as exquisite as any in the former volumes, these gems are now far between, and no new departure is perceptible. The days of original thought and spontaneous creation are over. Perhaps the most lyrical burst of the period is the poem entitled Composed upon an Evening of extraordinary splendour and beauty, in 1818, which breathes his former enthusiasm for the aspects of nature; yet it is to be noticed that an "extraordinary" magnificence is now needed to revive youthful ecstasies that used to feed on what was common in the beauty of things.

The character of his later verse is other than this. Scandalised by the fame of Byron and the success of the new cynical and pessimistic poetry, Wordsworth exaggerates his own sermonising tendencies. There is now a fixed and rigid attitude, a sort of optimistic trick, in the poems which extol the minute joys of life and endeavour to tone down its sorrows. He does his best to convert himself to Anglicanism, which, however, he celebrates with more copiousness than real warmth. His Ecclesiastical Sonnets are the Anglican counterpart, on a much narrower basis, of Châteaubriand's Génie du Christianisme. In politics, his evolution has become complete to the point of appearing a recantation.

He pursues against liberalism the campaign upon which, for liberal reasons, he had entered against Napoleon. He seems to find everything for the best in Europe after the French emperor's overthrow. He approves and upholds the Holy Alliance and opposes, with might and main, every attempt at reform in his own country. He protests against the too advanced instruction which the liberals desire to impart to girls in the lake district, against the spread of mechanics' institutes, against the emancipation of Irish catholics, against the abolition of slavery by parliament, against the abolition of capital punishment, against parliamentary reform, and so forth. The one change he supports is the extension of copyright, which affects his own interests as a writer.

That he was sincere in all his opinions, and that he had strong arguments for his absolute conservatism, cannot be doubted. No apostasy is to be laid to his charge. The evolution of his ideas, which made his old age diametrically opposed to his youth, can be traced, step by step, accounted for by outward circumstances and earnest meditations. Yet we cannot help feeling that, all the same, it is a progress from poetry to prose, from bold imaginings to timorousness, from hope to mistrust, from life to death.

In the meantime, his worldly prosperity and his public reputation were steadily increasing. From the gladsome frugality of the Grasmere days he passed into ease and comfort, thanks to his appointment, in 1813, as stamp distributor for Westmorland, which enabled him to remove to Rydal Mount in 1814. There, he was to live till his death, courted by members of the nobility and higher clergy, visited by a growing number of pilgrims, sincere admirers and mere tourists. His fame, which was at a low ebb at the beginning of that period, partly on account of the ridicule thrown on his poems by reviewers, partly because the public turned in preference to Scott and Byron, gradually rose after 1820, till it culminated in a triumphant reception at Oxford in 1839, a state pension bestowed on him in 1842 and the laureateship in 1843. Before the close of his life in 1850, Wordsworth could feel assured that he had become one of the great poetical influences of the age.

It is inevitable that, when retracing Wordsworth's career, one should insist on the main streams of thought which flowed through his mind. The temptation to look upon him as a prophet is great, and, thus, in any estimate of him, to give chief prominence to the more or less systematic philosophy woven by him out of experience. True, few poets blended philosophy and poetry more intimately together. Yet, the two remain distinct; they are things of a different order. They were in conflict more than once; so, our estimate of Wordsworth's poetical genius should not be reduced to an appreciation of his moral code.

The Ruined Cottage

He was a great poet when, in 1797, he wrote The Ruined Cottage—he never outdid that pastoral and, indeed, only once or twice again reached such perfection. Yet (if we set aside the words of comfort and resignation wherein, years after, it was wrapt up), in itself, the tale is most distressing and desolate. Wordsworth's usual optimism is not to be found in it. It implies a protest against the iniquity of society and the harshness of fate. It is one of Wordsworth's masterpieces, but, in a moral sense, can scarcely be called Wordsworthian. The last of the Lucy poems—though written in 1799—is in even more striking contrast to Wordsworth's known teaching It is one of the most desperate sobs that ever escaped from the heart of a forlorn lover. No glimpse of hope pierces through his vision of the tomb: No motion has she now, no force;

She neither hears nor sees;
Rolled round in earth's diurnal course,
With rocks, and stones, and trees.

Surely, Wordsworth would have condemned such a fit of blank despair in any other poetry than his own. Yet, he never wrote with more essential strength, and many of his admirers must needs regard this quatrain as, perhaps, the most condensed example of his poetical greatness.

What has been said of his moral doctrine applies, also, to his theory of poetical style. It is now agreed that Wordsworth wrote some of his most beautiful poems in entire opposition to his principles of diction. He had laid it down as a rule that the poet should use the simple language of peasants, merely freed from its errors. Yet, even when he interpreted the feelings of cottagers and made them speak in their own names, he often broke this rule in the most glaring manner. The example pointed out by Myers is so conclusive that it would be idle to look for another one. It is taken from The Affiction of Margaret, a pathetic monologue in which a poor widow, who used to keep a shop, laments over the disappearance of her son, and pictures to herself the dangers and sufferings to which he may have been exposed. Not a single phrase in the beautiful stanza "Perhaps some dungeon hears thee groan" but is raised to the highest pitch of lyrical force and subtlety.

Without recurring to such extreme cases, in which we have the poet at war with the systematic thinker, we must admit that, in many of his finest poems, the characteristics of his thought and doctrine are least evident—whether he gives way to a disturbing melancholy, which he usually condemns, as in The two April Mornings or The Fountain, or where he imparts to us an impression of nature on which he hangs no moral, as in The Green Linnet or Yew-trees. The four yew-trees of Borrowdale, "joined in one solemn and capacious grove," constitute one of his most impressive pictures. But no philosophy is tagged to the description, which is self-sufficient. There, you have Wordsworth's power laid bare, founded on his imaginative vision of natural aspects, yet not passing from this to a moral lesson.

If this dark, powerful piece of painting had been handed down to us without the author's name, it is not certain that anyone would have ascribed it to Wordsworth; or, if so, it would have been on account of the Westmorland names found in it; for, the bold allegories, the strange sonorous mythology, would have made many a critic hesitate. These instances tend to prove that his poetry is not identical with his habitual teaching, that it sometimes revolts against it, that it may here and there go beyond it. Of this conclusion, we ought not to lose sight, even when we pass on to the examination of such verses as are both beautiful in themselves and stamped as Wordsworth's manifest creations, to which no exact parallels can be found in any other poet.

His Poetry of Nature

His chief originality is, of course, to be sought in his poetry of nature. But it is not the mere fact of his being a poet of nature that makes him unique. There had been many poets of nature before, more were to come after, him. It is not even the minute, precise, loving observation of her aspects that gives him his pre-eminence. Certainly, he was one of the most truthful describers when his task was to describe; though, for accuracy or subtlety of outward detail, he may have been equalled, nay, surpassed, by other poets who, at the same time, were botanists or naturalists, writers as different from each other as were Crabbe and Tennyson. Of flowers, insects and birds, the latter two knew, perhaps, more than Wordsworth. His undisputed sovereignty is not there. It lies in his extraordinary faculty of giving utterance to some of the most elementary, and, at the same time, obscure, sensations of man confronted by natural phenomena. Poetical psychology is his triumph. Apart from the philosophical or moral structure which he endeavours to raise on data furnished him by his sensations, these sensations are, in themselves, beautiful and new. By new, we mean that he was the first to find words for them, for they must have been as old as mankind.

There was a Boy

There was a Boy is one of the most striking instances of

this. The "gentle shock of mild surprise" felt by the lad who did not catch in due time the answer of the owls to his own hootings, the sudden revelation to him of the fair landscape while he hung listening, his thrill of delight at seeing "the uncertain heavens received into the bosom of the steady lake"—these were additions to man's knowledge and enjoyment of his common sensations. The absolute truth of the analysis impresses one simultaneously with its beauty. The emotion is, surely, subtle, but, at the same time universal, and we have it here expressed once and for ever.

No psychologist can expect to go further than this, no poet to hit on words more apposite and more harmoniously combined so as to make this little mystery of the soul palpable. When Coleridge read the poem in a letter from his friend, he said that, if he had met with these lines in a desert of Africa, he would have cried out "Wordsworth" at once. Here, we have, without doubt, one of the essentials of Wordsworth's poetry.

The same character is to be found in Nutting, where we are told of "the intruding sky," that struck with remorse the boyish nut-gatherer after he had torn the boughs of a virgin bower; or, again, in Skating-scene, where the poet describes the strange appearance of the surrounding hills, which, to the skater who has just stopped short after gliding at full speed, still seem to wheel by "as if the earth had rolled with visible motion her diurnal round." Here we have a mere illusion of the senses, but one of the existence of which, as of its weirdness and beauty, no doubt can be entertained.

Wordsworth and Shelley

One English poet only can be compared with Wordsworth here: Shelley, whose senses were endowed with an unusual, almost a superhuman, gift of insight. He, too, was to enrich our knowledge of sensation by his verse. His sensitiveness goes into things even deeper than Wordsworth's. He can see further through the screen, even spy "the warm light of life." But few, if any, can follow him to the end, or remember having themselves experienced his wonderful ecstasies. He is alone. On the contrary, Wordsworth has no abnormal and hypertrophied sensitiveness. It was the common healthy sensibility of mankind which he found himself sharing. He merely reveals to us what everyone has felt, or may feel any day.

Michael

There may be a poetry of nature less obvious than that founded on a multitudinous notation of her detailed aspects, less subtle than the analysis of exquisite sensations, but, perhaps, of more breadth and grandeur. Hazlitt has said that one could infer that Wordsworth's poetry "was written in a mountainous country, from its bareness, its simplicity, its loftiness and its depth." It is not, indeed, by description that the characters of nature are most deeply caught and expressed; it is by incorporation, so to say, when the image of the outward world, instead of being directly presented, is reflected in the feelings and shines through the most indifferent words; thus deeply had the scenery among which he spent his days penetrated into Wordsworth's mind and soul.

If we had to praise him as the poet of mountains, we might, of course, choose the noble descriptive pages that abound in his volumes; but, rather than to these, rather than to the famous mountain scenes in his Excursion—which are too conscious—we should turn to a poem like Michael, where scenery, characters and style form a perfect harmony of lines and tints that could not have existed without a secret process of assimilation. Lofty and bare, indeed, is this pastoral; few flowers grow on the heights where old Michael meant to build his sheepfold. The land is unadorned.

It has no other features than the sheer lineaments of its sweeps and pastures or its steep rocks, over which are spread by turns the naked sky and the winter mists. All this, together with the bracing air, you feel from the first to the last line, not less when the poet gives you the speech of his ancient "statesman" or a glimpse of his stern mind, than when he paints the landscape itself. Even as the scenery is composed of essentials, so is the old man's character, and so his language. In such passages there is not one word of description, and yet the "pastoral mountains" are constantly conjured up with their raw atmosphere, behind the discoursing shepherd. Every syllable he utters is their emanation.

The Lucy poems

Another summit is reached by the poet when he freely allows his creed of the refining agency of the senses to pass into a sort of waking dream, instead of asserting itself by argument as in The Prelude, or even, as in Tintern Abbey, by lyrical proclamation. Few will deny one of the very first ranks in his verse to the fourth of the Lucy poems, where he tells us how his beloved had been cared for by nature since her tenderest years, how nature had vowed to make her "a Lady of her own," imparting to her "the silence and the calm of mute insensate things," either bidding the storm "mould the maiden's form by silent sympathy," or causing "beauty born of murmuring sound to pass into her face." Here, Wordsworth joins company with the most aerial of poets. He drops to the earth, for once, all that matter-of-factness of which Coleridge complained.

He sets common observation at defiance and simply ignores the objections of common sense, with which he is elsewhere only too prone to argue. Though most thoroughly himself when shaping Lucy's natural education, he gives wings, not feet, to his most cherished belief. We have, in this lyric, "the fine excess" of poetry. Whatever may be said of these country maids who, though brought up under the clouds and stars, and by the side of dancing rivulets, failed to be informed with grace and beauty, Wordsworth has used his privilege as a poet of embodying a vision made, after all, of mysterious possibilities, perhaps of truths in the making.

But nature never engrossed all his thoughts. Many were given to man, chiefly to the feelings of man. He shows the same mastery in his delineation of the hidden germs of feeling as of those of sensation. He, again, excels when describing the moral emotions in the blending of the subtle and the simple, of the strange and the essential. But the beauty of his verse seems, in this case, to come less from intuitive discovery than from long brooding. Fullness and compactness of meaning now characterise his greatest utterances. All readers catch their pathos at once; few, immediately, if ever, their entire signification.

A noticeable instance is the finale of the plain prosaic story Simon Lee, a short stanza full to overflowing of his prolonged meditations on the present iniquity and harshness of society. Poets and moralists have vied in easy railings at man's ingratitude. Shakespeare, among others, is full of such denunciations. Alas! the greater cause for grief is the existence of gratitude, chiefly of excessive gratitude, which implies that there is a scarcity of fellow-feeling, a dearth of benevolence, a lack of mutual neighbourly assistance in this world. That exaggerated thanks should be offered for the merest trifle, for a deed of easy and imperative kindness, betrays daily uncharitableness and opens vistas of the insensibility of existing society; it shows "what man has made of man": I've heard of hearts unkind, kind deeds

With coldness still returning;
Alas! the gratitude of man
Hath oftener left me mourning.

This is one of his many reflections which are more pregnant and sink deeper into the mind and heart than those of almost any other poet.

His Description of the Moral Emotions

From such deep sources do many of his sonnets, chiefly of his political sonnets, draw their rare intensity of moral feeling. It is enough to remind the reader of a few familiar passages: his melancholy on hearing of the extinction of the republic of Venice; his energy of tone when he comforts poor Toussaint Louverture, the liberator of San Domingo, now thrown into a prison; the bitter restrained irony of his "high-minded Spaniard," who resents, more than the devastation of his country, Napoleon's so-called benefits, and so forth. In his more strictly English sonnets, the greatness is not due to novelty of thought. It so happens that almost every idea and emotion expressed by Wordsworth in 1802 and the years following had been more than foreshadowed by Coleridge as early as 1798 in his Ode to France or Fears in Solitude.

But the truly Wordsworthian power of the sonnets is owing to the protracted sojourn of these feelings in his breast before he gave utterance to them, to his long reluctance against their admission, to his repeated inward debates. Hence, instead of Coleridge's extemporised effusions, which have been aptly compared, by Angellier, to the sea-scud which is thrown off by a storm, here we have the distilled elixir. Nearly ten years of vexed thoughts went to the making, in 1803, of the final line of the sonnet to England, where, after enumerating and condemning what he calls her many political crimes, he sighs (with a unique mixture of reproof and tenderness, of grief and repressed pride) at the thought that she, nevertheless, is the least unworthy champion of liberty left in the world:

O grief that Earth's best hopes rest all in thee!

It would be hard to match these ten monosyllables for compactness of historical allusion and complex feeling. Such condensed moral utterances are among the glories of Wordsworth's verse.

Other characteristics ought to be added, regarding his more purely artistic gifts—gifts of verse-writing and style, gifts of composition. But this would land us in endless discussions; for, in these respects, Wordsworth's mastery is surely relative and intermittent. He reaches, at times, so high a degree of excellence that the mere verbal felicity of some of his simplest lines baffles the imitation of the most refined artists:

Perhaps the plaintive numbers flow
For old, unhappy, far-off things,
And battles long ago....

But he frequently mixes the highest poetry with the flatness of unimpassioned, uninspired prose. He also shows himself, in many a period or stanza, devoid of ease, elegance and pliancy. He is more than once awkwardly naïve, clumsily familiar, or, on the contrary, more solemn and pompous than needs be. The talent for construction, niggardly bestowed on the romantic poets of all countries, is particularly weak in him. He could never frame and fashion a considerable poem with due equilibrium of substance and form, of thought and story. In this respect, The Excursion is a memorable failure. As to The Prelude, it owes its permanent interest partly to its admirable passages of poetry, partly to its philosophical or to its autobiographical value, which we feel, as we read, to be merits not strictly poetic. Only in compositions of moderate length, like The Ruined Cottage, Michael, Laodamia did he achieve perfect harmony, and in many of his lyrics and sonnets.

That he often tries to lift us and himself to the poetic mood rather than takes this mood for granted, cannot be denied. Poetry often seems to be his object rather than his possession. He made the training of man to poetry his chief office here below. He leads us warily from the inlands of prose to the shore, marking out the way with unprecedented care; but he is sometimes content with gazing on the element and leaves it to others boldly to sail upon it or plunge into it. The main body of his poems is educative and preparatory. Yet he has left sufficient of absolute verse, heart-searching and beautiful, enough for a Wordsworthian anthology that will remain among the most enduring treasures of romanticism.

Chapter 6

Romanticism

Introduction to Romanticism

Romanticism has very little to do with things popularly thought of as "romantic," although love may occasionally be the subject of Romantic art. Rather, it is an international artistic and philosophical movement that redefined the fundamental ways in which people in Western cultures thought about themselves and about their world.

Historical Considerations

It is one of the curiosities of literary history that the strongholds of the Romantic Movement were England and Germany, not the countries of the romance languages themselves. Thus it is from the historians of English and German literature that we inherit the convenient set of terminal dates for the Romantic period, beginning in 1798, the year of the first edition of Lyrical Ballads by Wordsworth and Coleridge and of the composition of Hymns to the Night by Novalis, and ending in 1832, the year which marked the deaths of both Sir Walter Scott and Goethe. However, as an international movement affecting all the arts, Romanticism begins at least in the 1770's and continues into the second half of the nineteenth century, later for American literature than for European, and later in some of the arts, like music and painting, than in literature.

This extended chronological spectrum (1770-1870) also permits recognition as Romantic the poetry of Robert Burns and William Blake in England, the early writings of Goethe and

Schiller in Germany, and the great period of influence for Rousseau's writings throughout Europe. The early Romantic period thus coincides with what is often called the "age of revolutions"—including, of course, the American (1776) and the French (1789) revolutions—an age of upheavals in political, economic, and social traditions, the age which witnessed the initial transformations of the Industrial Revolution. A revolutionary energy was also at the core of Romanticism, which quite consciously set out to transform not only the theory and practice of poetry (and all art), but the very way we perceive the world. Some of its major precepts have survived into the twentieth century and still affect our contemporary period.

Imagination

The imagination was elevated to a position as the supreme faculty of the mind. This contrasted distinctly with the traditional arguments for the supremacy of reason. The Romantics tended to define and to present the imagination as our ultimate "shaping" or creative power, the approximate human equivalent of the creative powers of nature or even deity. It is dynamic, an active, rather than passive power, with many functions.

Imagination is the primary faculty for creating all art. On a broader scale, it is also the faculty that helps humans to constitute reality, for (as Wordsworth suggested), we not only perceive the world around us, but also in part create it. Uniting both reason and feeling (Coleridge described it with the paradoxical phrase, "intellectual intuition"), imagination is extolled as the ultimate synthesizing faculty, enabling humans to reconcile differences and opposites in the world of appearance. The reconciliation of opposites is a central ideal for the Romantics. Finally, imagination is inextricably bound up with the other two major concepts, for it is presumed to be the faculty which enables us to "read" nature as a system of symbols.

Nature

"Nature" meant many things to the Romantics. As suggested above, it was often presented as itself a work of art, constructed by a divine imagination, in emblematic language. For example, throughout "Song of Myself," Whitman makes a practice of presenting commonplace items in nature—"ants," "heap'd stones," and "poke-weed"—as containing divine elements, and he refers to the "grass" as a natural "hieroglyphic," "the handkerchief of the Lord." While particular perspectives with regard to nature varied considerably—nature as a healing power, nature as a source of subject and image, nature as a refuge from the artificial constructs of civilization, including artificial language—the prevailing views accorded nature the status of an organically unified whole.

It was viewed as "organic," rather than, as in the scientific or rationalist view, as a system of "mechanical" laws, for Romanticism displaced the rationalist view of the universe as a machine (e.g., the deistic image of a clock) with the analogue of an "organic" image, a living tree or mankind itself. At the same time, Romantics gave greater attention both to describing natural phenomena accurately and to capturing "sensuous nuance"—and this is as true of Romantic landscape painting as of Romantic nature poetry. Accuracy of observation, however, was not sought for its own sake. Romantic nature poetry is essentially a poetry of meditation.

Symbolism and Myth

Symbolism and myth were given great prominence in the Romantic conception of art. In the Romantic view, symbols were the human aesthetic correlatives of nature's emblematic language. They were valued too because they could simultaneously suggest many things, and were thus thought superior to the one-to-one communications of allegory. Partly, it may have been the desire to express the "inexpressible"—the infinite—through the available resources of language that led to symbol at one level and myth (as symbolic narrative) at another.

Other Concepts: Emotion, Lyric Poetry, and the Self

Other aspects of Romanticism were intertwined with the

above three concepts. Emphasis on the activity of the imagination was accompanied by greater emphasis on the importance of intuition, instincts, and feelings, and Romantics generally called for greater attention to the emotions as a necessary supplement to purely logical reason. When this emphasis was applied to the creation of poetry, a very important shift of focus occurred.

Wordsworth's definition of all good poetry as "the spontaneous overflow of powerful feelings" marks a turning point in literary history. By locating the ultimate source of poetry in the individual artist, the tradition, stretching back to the ancients, of valuing art primarily for its ability to imitate human life (that is, for its mimetic qualities) was reversed. In Romantic theory, art was valuable not so much as a mirror of the external world, but as a source of illumination of the world within. Among otheı things, this led to a prominence for first-person lyric poetry never accorded it in any previous period. The "poetic speaker" became less a persona and more the direct person of the poet.

Wordsworth's Prelude and Whitman's "Song of Myself" are both paradigms of successful experiments to take the growth of the poet's mind (the development of self) as subject for an "epic" enterprise made up of lyric components. Confessional prose narratives such as Goethe's Sorrows of Young Werther (1774) and Chateaubriand's Rene (1801), as well as disguised autobiographical verse narratives such as Byron's Childe Harold (1818), are related phenomena. The interior journey and the development of the self recurred everywhere as subject material for the Romantic artist. The artist-as-hero is a specifically Romantic type.

Contrasts With Neoclassicism

Consequently, the Romantics sought to define their goals through systematic contrast with the norms of "Versailles neoclassicism." In their critical manifestoes—the 1800 "Preface" to Lyrical Ballads, the critical studies of the Schlegel brothers in Germany, the later statements of Victor Hugo in France, and of Hawthorne, Poe, and Whitman in the United

States—they self-consciously asserted their differences from the previous age (the literary "ancient regime"), and declared their freedom from the mechanical "rules." Certain special features of Romanticism may still be highlighted by this contrast.

We have already noted two major differences: the replacement of reason by the imagination for primary place among the human faculties and the shift from a mimetic to an expressive orientation for poetry, and indeed all literature. In addition, neoclassicism had prescribed for art the idea that the general or universal characteristics of human behaviour were more suitable subject matter than the peculiarly individual manifestations of human activity. From at least the opening statement of Rousseau's Confessions, first published in 1781—"I am not made like anyone I have seen; I dare believe that I am not made like anyone in existence. If I am not superior, at least I am different."—this view was challenged.

Individualism: The Romantic Hero

The Romantics asserted the importance of the individual, the unique, even the eccentric. Consequently they opposed the character typology of neoclassical drama. In another way, of course, Romanticism created its own literary types. The hero-artist has already been mentioned; there were also heaven-storming types from Prometheus to Captain Ahab, outcasts from Cain to the Ancient Mariner and even Hester Prynne, and there was Faust, who wins salvation in Goethe's great drama for the very reasons—his characteristic striving for the unattainable beyond the morally permitted and his insatiable thirst for activity—that earlier had been viewed as the components of his tragic sin. (It was in fact Shelley's opinion that Satan, in his noble defiance, was the real hero of Milton's Paradise Lost.)

In style, the Romantics preferred boldness over the preceding age's desire for restraint, maximum suggestiveness over the neoclassical ideal of clarity, free experimentation over the "rules" of composition, genre, and decorum, and they promoted the conception of the artist as "inspired" creator over that of the artist as "maker" or technical master. Although in both Germany and England there was continued interest in the ancient classics, for the most part the Romantics allied themselves with the very periods of literature that the neoclassicists had dismissed, the Middle Ages and the Baroque, and they embraced the writer whom Voltaire had called a barbarian, Shakespeare. Although interest in religion and in the powers of faith were prominent during the Romantic period, the Romantics generally rejected absolute systems, whether of philosophy or religion, in favour of the idea that each person (and humankind collectively) must create the system by which to live.

The Everyday and the Exotic

The attitude of many of the Romantics to the everyday, social world around them was complex. It is true that they advanced certain realistic techniques, such as the use of "local colour" (through down-to-earth characters, like Wordsworth's rustics, or through everyday language, as in Emily Bronte's northern dialects or Whitman's colloquialisms, or through popular literary forms, such as folk narratives). Yet social realism was usually subordinate to imaginative suggestion, and what was most important were the ideals suggested by the above examples, simplicity perhaps, or innocence. Earlier, the 18th-century cult of the noble savage had promoted similar ideals, but now artists often turned for their symbols to domestic rather than exotic sources—to folk legends and older, "unsophisticated" art forms, such as the ballad, to contemporary country folk who used "the language of commen men," not an artificial "poetic diction," and to children (for the first time presented as individuals, and often idealized as sources of greater wisdom than adults).

Simultaneously, as opposed to everyday subjects, various forms of the exotic in time and/or place also gained favour, for the Romantics were also fascinated with realms of existence that were, by definition, prior to or opposed to the ordered conceptions of "objective" reason. Often, both the everyday and the exotic appeared together in paradoxical combinations.

In the Lyrical Ballads, for example, Wordsworth and Coleridge agreed to divide their labors according to two subject areas, the natural and the supernatural: Wordsworth would try to exhibit the novelty in what was all too familiar, while Coleridge would try to show in the supernatural what was psychologically real, both aiming to dislodge vision from the "lethargy of custom." The concept of the beautiful soul in an ugly body, as characterized in Victor Hugo's Hunchback of Notre Dame and Mary Shelley's Frankenstein, is another variant of the paradoxical combination.

The Romantic Artist in Society

In another way too, the Romantics were ambivalent toward the "real" social world around them. They were often politically and socially involved, but at the same time they began to distance themselves from the public. As noted earlier, high Romantic artists interpreted things through their own emotions, and these emotions included social and political consciousness—as one would expect in a period of revolution, one that reacted so strongly to oppression and injustice in the world. So artists sometimes took public stands, or wrote works with socially or politically oriented subject matter.

Yet at the same time, another trend began to emerge, as they withdrew more and more from what they saw as the confining boundaries of bourgeois life. In their private lives, they often asserted their individuality and differences in ways that were to the middle class a subject of intense interest, but also sometimes of horror. ("Nothing succeeds like excess," wrote Oscar Wilde, who, as a partial inheritor of Romantic tendencies, seemed to enjoy shocking the bourgeois, both in his literary and life styles.) Thus the gulf between "odd" artists and their sometimes shocked, often uncomprehending audience began to widen.

Some artists may have experienced ambivalence about this situation—it was earlier pointed out how Emily Dickinson seemed to regret that her "letters" to the world would go unanswered. Yet a significant Romantic theme became the contrast between artist and middle-class "Philistine."

Unfortunately, in many ways, this distance between artist and public remains with us today.

Spread of the Romantic Spirit

Finally, it should be noted that the revolutionary energy underlying the Romantic Movement affected not just literature, but all of the arts—from music (consider the rise of Romantic opera) to painting, from sculpture to architecture. Its reach was also geographically significant, spreading as it did eastward to Russia, and westward to America. For example, in America, the great landscape painters, particularly those of the "Hudson River School," and the Utopian social colonies that thrived in the 19th century, are manifestations of the Romantic spirit on this side of the Atlantic.

Recent Developments

Some critics have believed that the two identifiable movements that followed Romanticism—Symbolism and Realism—were separate developments of the opposites which Romanticism itself had managed, at its best, to unify and to reconcile. Whether or not this is so, it is clear that Romanticism transformed Western culture in many ways that survive into our own times. It is only very recently that any really significant turning away from Romantic paradigms has begun to take place, and even that turning away has taken place in a dramatic, typically Romantic way.

Today a number of literary theorists have called into question two major Romantic perceptions: that the literary text is a separate, individuated, living "organism"; and that the artist is a fiercely independent genius who creates original works of art. In current theory, the separate, "living" work has been dissolved into a sea of "intertextuality," derived from and part of a network or "archive" of other texts—the many different kinds of discourse that are part of any culture. In this view, too, the independently sovereign artist has been demoted from a heroic, consciously creative agent, to a collective "voice," more controlled than controlling, the intersection of other voices, other texts, ultimately dependent upon possibilities dictated by language systems, conventions, and institutionalized power structures. It is an irony of history, however, that the explosive appearance on the scene of these subversive ideas, delivered in what seemed to the establishment to be radical manifestoes, and written by linguistically powerful individuals, has recapitulated the revolutionary spirit and events of Romanticism itself.

Popular Romantic Poets

The best known Romantic poets were Blake, Wordsworth, Coleridge, Byron, Shelley, and Keats and their poetry was dependent on various features peculiar to their time: a reaction against previous literary styles, arguments with eighteenth century and earlier philosophers, the decline in formal Anglican worship and the rise of dissenting religious sects, and the rapid and unprecedented industrialization of Britain and consequent changes in its countryside.

Above all, however, it was the impact of the French Revolution which gave the period its most distinctive and urgent concerns. Following the Revolution itself, which began in 1789, Britain was at war with France on continental Europe for nearly twenty years while massive repression of political dissent was implemented at home. Against this background much of the major writing of the period, associated with the term Romantic, takes place between 1789 (when the French Revolution began) and 1824 (the death of Byron) and can be seen as a response to changing political and social conditions in one respect or another.

Chapter 7

William Wordsworth – The Romantic Poet

William Wordsworth is the Romantic poet most often described as a "nature" writer; what the word "nature" meant to Wordsworth is, however, a complex issue. On the one hand, Wordsworth was the quintessential poet as naturalist, always paying close attention to details of the physical environment around him (plants, animals, geography, weather).

At the same time, Wordsworth was a self-consciously literary artist who described "the mind of man" as the "main haunt and region of his song." This tension between objective describer of the natural scene and subjective shaper of sensory experience is partly the result of Wordsworth's view of the mind as "creator and receiver both." Wordsworth consistently describes his own mind as the recipient of external sensations which are then rendered into its own mental creations.

(Shelley made a related claim in "Mont Blanc" when he said that his mind "passively / Now renders and receives, fast influencing, / Holding an unremitting interchange / With the clear universe of things around".) Such an alliance of the inner life with the outer world is at the heart of Wordsworth's descriptions of nature. Wordsworth's ideas about memory, the importance of childhood experiences, and the power of the mind to bestow an "auxiliary" light on the objects it beholds all depend on this ability to record experiences carefully at the moment of observation but then to shape those same experiences in the mind over time.

We should also recall, however, that he made widespread

use of other texts in the production of his Wordsworthian (Keats said "egotistical") sublime: drafts of poems by Coleridge, his sister Dorothy's Journals, the works of Milton, Shakespeare, Thomson, and countless others. Wordsworthian "nature" emerges as much a product of his widespread reading as of his wanderings amid the affecting landscapes of the Lake District.

His poems often present an instant when nature speaks to him and he responds by speaking for nature. The language of nature in such instances is, like the language Wordsworth uses to record such events, often cryptic and enigmatic. The owls in the often-quoted "Boy of Winander" passage of The Prelude hoot to a Wordsworthian child who answers first in their owl-language and then with a poem that records only the mirroring image of an "uncertain heaven," the dark sky reflected in a still silent lake. Wordsworth longs for a version of nature that will redeem him from the vagaries of passing moments, but he usually records those natural phenomena that promise only the passing of time and the cyclical transience of natural process. "Nutting" holds us up painfully against the ravaging of a pristine and naturally spiritualized bower.

The Lucy poems tells us that Lucy is back into nature at her death, but that consolation seems small recompense for the humanized "nature" of the loss. The Prelude wants to keep us in touch with a childhood and subsequent adult identity realized within the natural world; at the same time, however, this autobiographical epic leaves adult readers feeling a long way from the "spots of time" of childhood. Nothing in Wordsworth is simple or singular; like Milton, he is a poet who almost resists the possibility of final or definitive interpretation. His view of nonhuman nature is likewise open-ended. Wordsworth's "nature" points us away from the closed world of theocentric symbol-making toward the unstable world of postmodern meaning.

Dorothy Wordsworth vs. William Wordsworth

Thoughts on My Sickbed vs. Tintern Abbey

Both Dorothy Wordsworth and William Wordsworth

focus their poems on Wye, a natural sanctuary of their past where it appears they shared moments of relaxation and pleasure. Their descriptions of their memories contain remnants of beauty and quiet that stayed with them as they aged and were not physically at Wye anymore. However, along with reveling in their glorious past, Dorothy and William suggest pangs of pain and lamentation connected to their memories.

For Dorothy, these negative sentiments seem fueled by her declining health, but William seems to be contemplative, hypothetical, and worried that along with the changing landscape his memory will be forgotten or altered. This slight contrast could be the force behind some subtle, yet discernible, differences between the two texts, which also harbor some similarities rooted in the matching subject of both poems.

Dorothy's, "Thoughts on My Sickbed" fuses life and nature as co-dependents, as does William's piece, right at the onset with the first two lines: "And has the remnant of my life/ Been pilfered of this sunny spring?". She suggests here that her life has within it a "sunny spring", a season of nature, which is in jeopardy. This fear is further emphasized when she cries out against the though that her heart cannot answer the bird's cry. Initially, this has a desolate sentiment surrounding the descriptions of nature, which continues throughout the poem in Dorothy's memories of Wye. She focuses on the loss of their "cottage-hearth no longer our home" rather than the antiquity and beauty of the past which seem to be more her brother's focus. Although, she does comment on her "youthful" days when she had a "joyful heart" and she welcomed the "fresh" seasons. Again, this is what she thinks has been pilfered from her—her "sunny spring" or "fresh season." Her doom, her sickness, hovers over her and taints each image.

The universal language that was characteristic of women writers at this time is apparent not only in Dorothy's writing, but also in William's as well. As Dorothy is "in quest of known and unknown things", William is filled with "elevated thoughts" and "a sense sublime of something." The difference in this universal language is that William uses it to strengthen his discourse on nature and his personal connection—it being his "all and all," while Dorothy maintains a distance from nature and calls out to her brother in response. I found it possible that there might be a more political reading o Dorothy's searching in line 14. Perhaps one could read this line to be addressing the state of education for women, which was a hot topic of the time. Whether or not Dorothy consciously included this as an underlying theme seems irrelevant if her female readers took her work as an impetus to seek out "known and unknown things" for themselves and therefore become more educated.

Looking at similar objects in the two poems, and contrasting the way in which they are portrayed offers some interesting differences to ponder. For example, Dorothy and William's descriptions of Dorothy's eyes are quite contrasting. Dorothy described her eyes as "busy" and William describes them as "wild." Busy connotes searching, interest, and awareness; while wild tends to connote a more chaotic and uncontrolled demeanor. Dorothy's portrayal of herself is, in this sense, more positive and William's much more negative, but both are in line with the common description of women for their sexes respectively at this time. One goal of female writers was to portray women as more than chaotic and unruly nature images. They wanted to emphasize their existence as rational beings, which is what Dorothy does through the language surrounding her eyes. William takes on the more stereotypical portrayal of women by men by putting her eyes on the same plane as a wild animal.

As many female writers, Dorothy hones in on more detailed images of nature than her brother. For example, she describes the "primrose a lamp on its fortress rock, / the silent butterfly spreading its wings," and William sticks to "waters, rolling from their mountain springs." There is a considerable physical size contrast between the images in Dorothy and William's work. Expanded, this contrast highlights another difference. Dorothy relates abstract things like "springtime" to "earthly hope." This image is grounded in the soil of the land; a very real, tangible, and fertile thing, whereas William writes more about the spiritual aspect and contemplative side of his images. William invokes prayer to address his sister, "For thou art with me," and Dorothy seems to just be calling out to her brother and answering his wishes and concerns that he includes in his poem: "I saw the green banks of the Wye…I thought of nature's loveliest scenes, and with memory I was there." She speaks to him and tells him that she has thought of their past together on the banks and it brought her comfort.

However, one cannot neglect to realise the difference in her comfort of the past and her brother's comfort. William's observations of the changing landscape and fading details from his memory mirror his fear of being forgotten. Dorothy, on the other hand, is on her sickbed thinking back to nature to soothe her in her declining health. William's memory and concerns seem more presumptuous and conceited than Dorothy's memories.

The image of flowers also seems to represent different things for the two authors. Dorothy's descriptions of flowers stand to symbolize her overall sentiment in her illness and shadow her state. In the beginning of the poem, spring escapes Dorothy, a time when flowers bloom. She specifically mentions a violet "betrayed by its noiseless breath" contrasted later to the "budding trees.". She does not have the "promise of fruits and the splendid flower" only the flowers that "loving friends" brought as an offering and comfort. These flowers, once representative of life and the carefree days of her past, now represent Dorothy's impending death. They have, in a sense have betrayed her. One can imagine some colorful flowers representing nature's wonder fitting in with the "misty mountain-winds" in William's poem.

William's, "Tintern Abbey" seems to have a more condescending tone to it. He speaks from a more elevated level, a personal place of power where he can contemplate his role in relation to nature and even God, and place his sister within it as he wants. William manipulates a common prayer and implants his sister within it: "For thou art with me." The reader might overlook "thou" being Dorothy. William has put

Dorothy on the same level as the highest power—God. In doing so, it places him in the most powerful role of all three entities in question. Dorothy is his pawn that he can reposition to where he sees fit, and God is something he feels he can remove and control. When this comparison begins, William seems serious, genuine, and thoughtful towards his sister; however, the tone changes from "and this prayer I make, / knowing that Nature never did betray/ the heart that loved her" to "wilt thou remember me," which places the focus right back on him.

The general tone of each poem seem to follow the attitudes that typifies female and male writers of the Romanticism. Dorothy's poem is more distant and universal in the themes it addresses, while at the same time focusing on minute details of small objects; which undoubtedly carry underlying messages. William on the other hand, being the male writer is straightforward in his message. He takes liberty to change prayers and reflect upon his personal importance to others, and focuses on larger objects in his descriptions. I wondered if some of these differences could be due to the fact that Dorothy is writing from literally a more disabled position than her brother, which could be responsible for her more passive and desolate sentiment throughout the poem?

Chapter 8

Historical Background - The Romantic Age

The Great Writers of 1798-1830. The Critical Reviews

As we look back to-day over the literature of the last three quarters of the eighteenth century, here just surveyed, the progress of the Romantic Movement seems the most conspicuous general fact which it presents. But at the, death of Cowper in 1800 the movement still remained tentative and incomplete, and it was to arrive at full maturity only in the work of the great writers of the following quarter century, who were to create the finest body of literature which England had produced since the Elizabethan period. All the greatest of these writers were poets, wholly or in part, and they fall roughly into two groups: first, William Wordsworth, Samuel Taylor Coleridge, Robert Southey, and Walter Scott; and second, about twenty years younger, Lord Byron, Percy Bysshe Shelley, and John Keats.

This period of Romantic Triumph, or of the lives of its authors, coincides in time, and not by mere accident, with the period of the success of the French Revolution, the prolonged struggle of England and all Europe against Napoleon, and the subsequent years when in Continental Europe despotic government reasserted itself and sternly suppressed liberal hopes and uprisings, while in England liberalism and democracy steadily and doggedly gathered force until by the Reform Bill of 1832 political power was largely transferred from the former small governing oligarchy to the middle class.

How all these events influenced literature we shall see as we proceed. The beginning of the Romantic triumph is found, by general consent, in the publication in 1798 of the little volume of 'Lyrical Ballads' which contained the first significant poetry of Wordsworth and Coleridge.

Even during this its greatest period, however, Romanticism had for a time a hard battle to fight, and a chief literary fact of the period was the founding and continued success of the first two important English literary and political quarterlies, 'The Edinburgh Review' and 'The Quarterly Review,' which in general stood in literature for the conservative eighteenth century tradition and violently attacked all, or almost all, the Romantic poets.

These quarterlies are sufficiently important to receive a few words in passing. In the later eighteenth century there had been some periodicals devoted to literary criticism, but they were mere unauthoritative booksellers' organs, and it was left for the new reviews to inaugurate literary journalism of the modern serious type. 'The Edinburgh Review,' suggested and first conducted, in 1802, by the witty clergyman and reformer Sydney Smith, passed at once to the hands of Francis (later Lord) Jeffrey, a Scots lawyer who continued to edit it for nearly thirty years. Its politics were strongly liberal, and to oppose it the Tory 'Quarterly Review' was founded in 1808, under the editorship of the satirist William Gifford and with the cooperation of Sir Walter Scott, who withdrew for the purpose from his connection with the 'Edinburgh.' These reviews were followed by other high-class periodicals, such as 'Blackwood's Magazine,' and most of the group have maintained their importance to the present day.

Samuel Taylor Coleridge.

The poets Wordsworth and Coleridge are of special interest not only from the primary fact that they are among the greatest of English authors, but also secondarily because in spite of their close personal association each expresses one of the two main contrasting or complementary tendencies in the Romantic movement; Coleridge the delight in wonder and mystery, which he has the power to express with marvelous poetic suggestiveness, and Wordsworth, in an extreme degree, the belief in the simple and quiet forces, both of human life and of Nature.

To Coleridge, who was slightly the younger of the two, attaches the further pathetic interest of high genius largely thwarted by circumstances and weakness of will. Born in Devonshire in 1772, the youngest of the many children of a self-made clergyman and schoolmaster, he was a precocious and abnormal child, then as always a fantastic dreamer, despised by other boys and unable to mingle with them. After the death of his father he was sent to Christ's Hospital, the 'Blue-Coat' charity school in London, where he spent nine lonely years in the manner briefly described in an essay of Charles Lamb, where Coleridge appears under a thin disguise. The very strict discipline was no doubt of much value in giving firmness and definite direction to his irregular nature, and the range of his studies, both in literature and in other fields, was very wide.

Through the aid of scholarships and of contributions from his brothers he entered Cambridge in 1791, just after Wordsworth had left the University; but here his most striking exploit was a brief escapade of running away and enlisting in a cavalry troop. Meeting Southey, then a student at Oxford, he drew him into a plan for a 'Pantisocracy' (a society where all should be equal), a community of twelve young couples to be founded in some 'delightful part of the new back settlements' of America on the principles of communistic cooperation in all lines, broad mental culture, and complete freedom of opinion. Naturally, this plan never past beyond the dream stage.

Coleridge left the University in 1794 without a degree, tormented by a disappointment in love. He had already begun to publish poetry and newspaper prose, and he now attempted lecturing. He and Southey married two sisters, whom Byron in a later attack on Southey somewhat inaccurately described as 'milliners of Bath'; and Coleridge settled near Bristol. After characteristically varied and unsuccessful efforts at conducting a periodical, newspaper writing, and preaching as a Unitarian (a creed which was then considered by most Englishmen disreputable and which Coleridge later abandoned), he moved with his wife in 1797 to Nether Stowey in Somersetshire. Expressly in order to be near him, Wordsworth and his sister Dorothy soon leased the neighboring manor-house of Alfoxden, and there followed the memorable year of intellectual and emotional stimulus when Coleridge's genius suddenly expanded into short-lived but wonderful activity and he wrote most of his few great poems, 'The Ancient Mariner,' 'Kubla Khan,' and the First Part of 'Christabel.' 'The Ancient Mariner' was planned by Coleridge and Wordsworth on one of their frequent rambles, and was to have been written in collaboration; but as it proceeded, Wordsworth found his manner so different from that of Coleridge that he withdrew altogether from the undertaking.

The final result of the incident, however, was the publication in 1798 of 'Lyrical Ballads,' which included of Coleridge's work only this one poem, but of Wordsworth's several of his most characteristic ones. Coleridge afterwards explained that the plan of the volume contemplated two complementary sorts of poems. He was to present supernatural or romantic characters, yet investing them with human interest and semblance of truth; while Wordsworth was to add the charm of novelty to everyday things and to suggest their kinship to the supernatural, arousing readers from their accustomed blindness to the loveliness and wonders of the world around us.

No better description could be given of the poetic spirit and the whole poetic work of the two men. Like some other epoch-marking books, 'Lyrical Ballads' attracted little attention. Shortly after its publication Coleridge and the Wordsworth sailed for Germany, where for the greater part of a year Coleridge worked hard, if irregularly, at the language, literature, and philosophy.

The remaining thirty-five years of his life are a record of ambitious projects and fitful efforts, for the most part turned by ill-health and lack of steady purpose into melancholy failure, but with a few fragmentary results standing out brilliantly. At times Coleridge did newspaper work, at which he might have succeeded; in 1800, in a burst of energy, he translated Schiller's tragedy 'Wallenstein' into English blank verse, a translation which in the opinion of most critics surpasses the original; and down to 1802, and occasionally later, he wrote a few more poems of a high order. For a few years from 1800 on he lived at Greta Hall in the village of Keswick (pronounced Kesick), in the northern end of the Lake Region (Westmoreland), fifteen miles from Wordsworth; but his marriage was incompatible (with the fault on his side), and he finally left his wife and children, who were thenceforward supported largely by Southey, his successor at Greta Hall. Coleridge himself was maintained chiefly by the generosity of friends; later, in part, by public pensions.

It was apparently about 1800, to alleviate mental distress and great physical suffering from neuralgia, that he began the excessive use of opium (laudanum) which for many years had a large share in paralyzing his will. For a year, in 1804-5, he displayed decided diplomatic talent as secretary to the Governor of Malta. At several different times, also, he gave courses, of lectures on Shakespeare and Milton; as a speaker he was always eloquent; and the fragmentary notes of the lectures which have been preserved rank very high in Shakespearean criticism.

His main interest, however, was now in philosophy; perhaps no Englishman has ever had a more profoundly philosophical mind; and through scattered writings and through his stimulating though prolix talks to friends and disciples he performed a very great service to English thought by introducing the viewpoint and ideas of the German transcendentalists, such as Kant, Schelling, and Fichte. During his last eighteen years he lived mostly in sad acceptance of defeat, though still much honored, in the house of a London physician. He died in 1834.

As a poet Coleridge's first great distinction is that which we have already pointed out, namely that he gives wonderfully subtile and appealing expression to the Romantic sense for the strange and the supernatural, and indeed for all that the word 'Romance' connotes at the present day. He accomplishes this result partly through his power of suggesting the real unity of the inner and outer worlds, partly through his skill, resting in a large degree on vivid impressionistic description, in making strange scenes appear actual, in securing from the reader what he himself called 'that willing suspension of disbelief which constitutes poetic faith.' Almost every one has felt the weird charm of 'The Ancient Mariner,' where all the unearthly story centers about a moral and religious idea, and where we are dazzled by a constant succession of such pictures as these:

And ice, mast-high, came floating by,
As green as emerald.
We were the first that ever burst
Into that silent sea.
The western wave was all aflame:
The day was well nigh done:
Almost upon the western wave
Rested the broad, bright sun;
When that strange shape drove suddenly
Betwixt us and the sun.

'Christabel' achieves what Coleridge himself described as the very difficult task of creating witchery by daylight; and 'Kubla Khan,' worthy, though a brief fragment, to rank with these two, is a marvelous glimpse of fairyland.

In the second place, Coleridge is one of the greatest English masters of exquisite verbal melody, with its tributary devices of alliteration and haunting onomatopoeia. In this respect especially his influence on subsequent English poetry has been incalculable. The details of his method students should observe for themselves in their study of the poems, but one particular matter should be mentioned.

In 'Christabel' and to a somewhat less degree in 'The Ancient Mariner' Coleridge departed as far as possible from eighteenth century tradition by greatly varying the number of syllables in the lines, while keeping a regular number of stresses. Though this practice, as we have seen, was customary in Old English poetry and in the popular ballads, it was supposed by Coleridge and his contemporaries to be a new discovery, and it proved highly suggestive to other romantic poets. From hearing 'Christabel' read (from manuscript) Scott caught the idea for the free-and-easy meter of his poetical romances. With a better body and will Coleridge might have been one of the supreme English poets; as it is, he has left a small number of very great poems and has proved one of the most powerful influences on later English poetry.

William Wordsworth, 1770-1850.

William Wordsworth was born in 1770 in Cumberland, in the 'Lake Region,' which, with its bold and varied mountains as well as its group of charming lakes, is the most picturesque part of England proper. He had the benefit of all the available formal education, partly at home, partly at a 'grammar' school a few miles away, but his genius was formed chiefly by the influence of Nature, and, in a qualified degree, by that of the simple peasant people of the region. Already as a boy, though normal and active, he began to be sensitive to the Divine Power in Nature which in his mature years he was to express with deeper sympathy than any poet before him. Early left an orphan, at seventeen he was sent by his uncles to Cambridge University.

Here also the things which most appealed to him were rather the new revelations of men and life than the formal studies, and indeed the torpid instruction of the time offered little to any thoughtful student. On leaving Cambridge he was uncertain as to his life-work. He said that he did not feel himself 'good enough' for the Church, he was not drawn toward law, and though he fancied that he had capacity for a military career, he felt that 'if he were ordered to the West Indies his talents would not save him from the yellow fever.' At first, therefore, he spent nearly a year in London in apparent idleness, an intensely interested though detached spectator of the city life, but more especially absorbed in his mystical consciousness of its underlying current of spiritual being. After this he crossed to France to learn the language.

The Revolution was then (1792) in its early stages, and in his 'Prelude' Wordsworth has left the finest existing statement of the exultant anticipations of a new world of social justice which the movement aroused in himself and other young English liberals. When the Revolution past into the period of violent bloodshed he determined, with more enthusiasm than judgment, to put himself forward as a leader of the moderate Girondins. From the wholesale slaughter of this party a few months later he was saved through the stopping of his allowance by his more cautious uncles, which compelled him, after a year's absence, to return to England.

For several years longer Wordsworth lived uncertainly. When, soon after his return, England, in horror at the execution of the French king, joined the coalition of European powers against France, Wordsworth experienced a great shock—the first, he tells us, that his moral nature had ever suffered—at seeing his own country arrayed with corrupt despotisms against what seemed to him the cause of humanity. The complete degeneration of the Revolution into anarchy and tyranny further served to plunge him into a chaos of moral bewilderment, from which he was gradually rescued partly by renewed communion with Nature and partly by the influence of his sister Dorothy, a woman of the most sensitive nature but of strong character and admirable good sense. From this time for the rest of her life she continued to live with him, and by her unstinted and unselfish devotion contributed very largely to his poetic success.

He had now begun to write poetry (though thus far rather stiffly and in the rimed couplet), and the receipt of a small legacy from a friend enabled him to devote his life to the art. Six or seven years later his resources were several times multiplied by an honorable act of the new Lord Lonsdale, who voluntarily repaid a sum of money owed by his predecessor to Wordsworth's father.

In 1795 Wordsworth and his sister moved from the Lake Region to Dorsetshire, at the other end of England, likewise a country of great natural beauty. Two years later came their change (of a few miles) to Alfoxden, the association with

Coleridge, and 'Lyrical Ballads,' containing nineteen of Wordsworth's poems. After their winter in Germany the Wordsworths settled permanently in their native Lake Region, at first in 'Dove Cottage,' in the village of Grasmere. This simple little stone house, buried, like all the others in the Lake Region, in brilliant flowers, and opening from its second story onto the hillside garden where Wordsworth composed much of his greatest poetry, is now the annual centre of pilgrimage for thousands of visitors, one of the chief literary shrines of England and the world.

Here Wordsworth lived frugally for several years; then after intermediate changes he took up his final residence in a larger house, Rydal Mount, a few miles away. In 1802 he married Mary Hutchinson, who had been one of his childish schoolmates, a woman of a spirit as fine as that of his sister, whom she now joined without a thought of jealousy in a life of self-effacing devotion to the poet.

Wordsworth's poetic inspiration, less fickle than that of Coleridge, continued with little abatement for a dozen years; but about 1815, as he himself states in his fine but pathetic poem 'Composed upon an Evening of Extraordinary Splendour,' it for the most part abandoned him. He continued, however, to produce a great deal of verse, most of which his admirers would much prefer to have had unwritten. The plain Anglo-Saxon yeoman strain which was really the basis of his nature now asserted itself in the growing conservatism of ideas which marked the last forty years of his life. His early love of simplicity hardened into a rigid opposition not only to the materialistic modern industrial system but to all change—the Reform Bill, the reform of education, and in general all progressive political and social movements. It was on this abandonment of his early liberal principles that Browning based his spirited lyric 'The Lost Leader.'

During the first half or more of his mature life, until long after he had ceased to be a significant creative force, Wordsworth's poetry, for reasons which will shortly appear, had been met chiefly with ridicule or indifference, and he had been obliged to wait in patience while the slighter work first of Scott and then of Byron took the public by storm. Little by little, however, he came to his own, and by about 1830 he enjoyed with discerning readers that enthusiastic appreciation of which he is certain for all the future. The crowning mark of recognition came in 1843 when on the death of his friend Southey he was made Poet Laureate. The honour, however, had been so long delayed that it was largely barren. Ten years earlier his life had been darkened by the mental decay of his sister and the death of Coleridge; and other personal sorrows now came upon him. He died in 1850 at the age of eighty.

Wordsworth, as we have said, is the chief representative of some (especially one) of the most important principles in the Romantic Movement; but he is far more than a member of any movement; through his supreme poetic expression of some of the greatest spiritual ideals he belongs among the five or six greatest English poets. First, he is the profoundest interpreter of Nature in all poetry. His feeling for Nature has two aspects. He is keenly sensitive, and in a more delicately discriminating way than any of his predecessors, to all the external beauty and glory of Nature, especially inanimate Nature—of mountains, woods and fields, streams and flowers, in all their infinitely varied aspects.

A wonderfully joyous and intimate sympathy with them is one of his controlling impulses. But his feeling goes beyond the mere physical and emotional delight of Chaucer and the Elizabethans; for him Nature is a direct manifestation of the Divine Power, which seems to him to be everywhere immanent in her; and communion with her, the communion into which he enters as he walks and meditates among the mountains and moors, is to him communion with God. He is literally in earnest even in his repeated assertion that from observation of Nature man may learn (doubtless by the proper attuning of his spirit) more of moral truth than from all the books and sages.

To Wordsworth Nature is man's one great and sufficient teacher. It is for this reason that, unlike such poets as Keats and Tennyson, he so often views Nature in the large, giving us broad landscapes and sublime aspects. Of this mystical semi-pantheistic Nature-religion his 'Lines composed above Tintern Abbey' are the noblest expression in literature. All this explains why Wordsworth considered his function as a poet a sacred thing and how his intensely moral temperament found complete satisfaction in his art. It explains also, in part, the limitation of his poetic genius. Nature indeed did not continue to be to him, as he himself says that it was in his boyhood, absolutely 'all in all'; but he always remained largely absorbed in the contemplation and interpretation of it and never manifested, except in a few comparatively short and exceptional poems, real narrative or dramatic power (in works dealing with human characters or human life).

In the second place, Wordsworth is the most consistent of all the great English poets of democracy, though here as elsewhere his interest is mainly not in the external but in the spiritual aspect of things. From his insistence that the meaning of the world for man lies not in the external events but in the development of character results his central doctrine of the simple life. Real character, he holds, the chief proper object of man's effort, is formed by quietly living, as did he and the dales men around him, in contact with Nature and communion with God rather than by participation in the feverish and sensational struggles of the great world.

Simple country people, therefore, are nearer to the ideal than are most persons who fill a larger place in the activities of the world. This doctrine expresses itself in a striking though one-sided fashion in his famous theory of poetry—its proper subjects, characters, and diction. He stated his theory definitely and at length in a preface to the second edition of 'Lyrical Ballads,' published in 1800, a discussion which includes incidentally some of the finest general critical interpretation ever made of the nature and meaning of poetry. Wordsworth declared: 1. Since the purpose of poetry is to present the essential emotions of men, persons in humble and rustic life are generally the fittest subjects for treatment in it, because their natures and manners are simple and more genuine than those of other men, and are kept so by constant contact with the beauty and serenity of Nature. 2. Not only should artificial poetic diction (like that of the eighteenth century) be rejected, but the language of poetry should be a selection from that of ordinary people in real life, only purified of its vulgarities and heightened so as to appeal to the imagination. (In this last modification lies the justification of rime.) There neither is nor can be any essential difference between the language of prose and that of poetry.

This theory, founded on Wordsworth's disgust at eighteenth century poetic artificiality, contains a very important but greatly exaggerated element of truth. That the experiences of simple and common people, including children, may adequately illustrate the main spiritual aspects of life Wordsworth unquestionably demonstrated in such poems as 'The Reverie of Poor Susan,' 'Lucy Gray,' and 'Michael.' But to restrict poetry largely to such characters and subjects would be to eliminate not only most of the external interest of life, which certainly is often necessary in giving legitimate body to the spiritual meanings, but also a great range of significant experiences which by the nature of things can never come to lowly and simple persons.

That the characters of simple country people are on the average inevitably finer and more genuine than those of others is a romantic theory rather than a fact, as Wordsworth would have discovered if his meditative nature had, allowed him to get into really direct and personal contact with the peasants about him. As to the proper language of poetry, no one to-day (thanks partly to Wordsworth) defends artificiality, but most of Wordsworth's own best work, as well as that of all other poets, proves clearly that there is an essential difference between the language of prose and that of poetry, that much of the meaning of poetry results from the use of unusual, suggestive, words and picturesque expressions, which create the essential poetic atmosphere and stir the imagination in ways distinctly different from those of prose.

Wordsworth's obstinate adherence to his theory in its full extent, indeed, produced such trivial and absurd results as 'Goody Blake and Harry Gill,' 'The Idiot Boy,' and 'Peter Bell,' and great masses of hopeless prosiness in his long blank-verse narratives.

This obstinacy and these poems are only the most conspicuous result of Wordsworth's chief temperamental defect, which was an almost total lack of the sense of humour. Regarding himself as the prophet of a supremely important new gospel, he never admitted the possibility of error in his own point of view and was never able to stand aside from his poetry and criticise it dispassionately. This somewhat irritating egotism, however, was perhaps a necessary element in his success; without it he might not have been able to live serenely through the years of misunderstanding and ridicule which would have silenced or embittered a more diffident spirit.

The variety of Wordsworth's poetry deserves special mention; in addition to his short lyric and narrative poems of Nature and the spiritual life several kinds stand out distinctly. A very few poems, the noble 'Ode to Duty,' 'Laodamia,' and 'Dion,' are classical in inspiration and show the finely severe repression and finish of classic style. Among his many hundreds of sonnets is a very notable group inspired by the struggle of England against Napoleon. Wordsworth was the first English poet after Milton who used the sonnet powerfully and he proves himself a worthy successor of Milton. The great bulk of his work, finally, is made up of his long poems in blank-verse. 'The Prelude,' written during the years 1799-1805, though not published until after his death, is the record of the development of his poet's mind, not an outwardly stirring poem, but a unique and invaluable piece of spiritual autobiography. Wordsworth intended to make this only an introduction to another work of enormous length which was to have presented his views of Man, Nature, and Society. Of this plan he completed two detached parts, namely the fragmentary 'Recluse' and 'The Excursion,' which latter contains some fine passages, but for the most part is uninspired.

Wordsworth, more than any other great English poet, is a poet for mature and thoughtful appreciation; except for a very small part of his work many readers must gradually acquire the taste for him. But of his position among the half dozen English poets who have made the largest contribution to thought and life there can be no question; so that some acquaintance with him is a necessary part of any real education.

Robert Southey.

Robert Southey (1774-1843), a voluminous writer of verse and prose who from his friendship with Wordsworth and Coleridge has been associated with them as third in what has been inaptly called 'The Lake School' of poets, was thought in his own day to be their equal; but time has relegated him to comparative obscurity. An insatiate reader and admirable man, he wrote partly from irrepressible instinct and partly to support his own family and at times, as we have seen, that of Coleridge. An ardent liberal in youth, he, more quickly than Wordsworth, lapsed into conservatism, whence resulted his appointment as Poet Laureate in 1813 and the unremitting hostility of Lord Byron. His rather fantastic epics, composed with great facility and much real spirit, are almost forgotten; he is remembered chiefly by three or four short poems—'The Battle of Blenheim,' 'My days among the dead are past,' 'The Old Man's Comforts' (You are old, Father William,' wittily parodied by 'Lewis Carroll' in 'Alice in Wonderland')—and by his excellent short prose 'Life of Nelson.'

Walter Scott.

In the eighteenth century Scotland had contributed Thomson and Burns to the Romantic movement; now, early in the nineteenth, she supplied a writer of unexcelled and marvelous creative energy, who confirmed the triumph of the movement with work of the first importance in both verse and prose, namely Walter Scott. Scott, further, is personally one of the most delightful figures in English literature, and he is probably the most famous of all the Scotsmen who have ever lived.

He was descended from an ancient Border fighting clan, some of whose pillaging heroes he was to celebrate in his poetry, but he himself was born, in 1771, in Edinburgh, the son of an attorney of a privileged, though not the highest, class.

In spite of some serious sicknesses, one of which left him permanently lame, he was always a very active boy, more distinguished at school for play and fighting than for devotion to study. But his unconscious training for literature began very early; in his childhood his love of poetry was stimulated by his mother, and he always spent much time in roaming about the country and picking up old ballads and traditional lore. Loyalty to his father led him to devote six years of hard work to the uncongenial study of the law, and at twenty he was admitted to the Edinburgh bar as an advocate.

Though his geniality and high-spirited brilliancy made him a social centre he never secured much professional practice; but after a few years he was appointed permanent Sheriff of Selkirk, a county a little to the south of Edinburgh, near the English Border. Later, in 1806, he was also made one of the Principal Clerks of Session, a subordinate but responsible office with a handsome salary which entailed steady attendance and work at the metropolitan law court in Edinburgh during half of each year.

His instinct for literary production was first stimulated by the German Romantic poets. In 1796 he translated Burger's fiery and melodramatic ballad 'Lenore,' and a little later wrote some vigorous though hasty ballads of his own. In 1802-1803 he published 'Minstrelsy of the Scottish Border,' a collection of Scottish ballads and songs, which he carefully annotated. He went on in 1805, when he was thirty-four, to his first original verse-romance.

'The Lay of the Last Minstrel.' Carelessly constructed and written, this poem was nevertheless the most spirited reproduction of the life of feudal chivalry which the Romantic Movement had yet brought forth, and its popularity was immediate and enormous. Always writing with the greatest facility, though in brief hours snatched from his other occupations, Scott followed up 'The Lay' during the next ten years with the much superior 'Marmion,' 'The Lady of the Lake,' and other verse-romances, most of which greatly increased both his reputation and his income. In 1813 he declined the offer of the Poet Laureateship, then considered a position of no great dignity for a successful man, but secured the appointment of Southey, who was his friend.

In 1811 he moved from the comparatively modest country house which he had been occupying to the estate of Abbotsford, where he proceeded to fulfill his ambition of building a great mansion and making himself a sort of feudal chieftain. To this project he devoted for years a large part of the previously unprecedented profits from his writings. For a dozen years before, it should be added, his inexhaustible energy had found further occupation in connection with a troop of horse which he had helped to organize on the threat of a French invasion and of which he acted as quartermaster, training in barracks, and at times drilling for hours before breakfast.

The amount and variety of his literary work was much greater than is understood by most of his admirers today. He contributed largely, in succession, to the 'Edinburgh' and 'Quarterly' reviews, and having become a secret partner in the printing firm of the Ballantyne brothers, two of his school friends, exerted himself not only in the affairs of the company but in vast editorial labors of his own, which included among other things voluminously annotated editions of Dryden and Swift. His productivity is the more astonishing because after his removal to Abbotsford he gave a great part of his time not only to his family but also to the entertainment of the throngs of visitors who pressed upon him in almost continuous crowds. The explanation is to be found partly in his phenomenally vigorous constitution, which enabled him to live and work with little sleep; though in the end he paid heavily for this indiscretion.

The circumstances which led him to turn from poetry to prose fiction are well known. His poetical vein was really exhausted when in 1812 and 1813 Byron's 'Childe Harold' and flashy Eastern tales captured the public fancy. Just about as Scott was good naturedly confessing to himself that it was useless to dispute Byron's supremacy he accidentally came across the first chapters of 'Waverley,' which he had written some years before and had thrown aside in unwillingness to risk his fame by a venture in a new field. Taking it up with renewed interest, in the evenings of three weeks he wrote the remaining two-thirds of it; and he published it with an ultimate success even greater than that of his poetry. For a long time, however, Scott did not acknowledge the authorship of 'Waverley' and the novels which followed it (which, however, was obvious to every one), chiefly because he feared that the writing of prose fiction would seem undignified in a Clerk of Session.

The rapidity of the appearance of his novels testified to the almost unlimited accumulation of traditions and incidents with which his astonishing memory was stored; in seventeen years he published nearly thirty 'Waverley' novels, equipping most of them, besides, with long fictitious introductions, which the present-day reader almost universally skips. The profits of Scott's works, long amounting apparently to from ten to twenty thousand pounds a year, were beyond the wildest dream of any previous author, and even exceeded those of most popular authors of the twentieth century, though partly because the works were published in unreasonably expensive form, each novel in several volumes. Still more gratifying were the great personal popularity which Scott attained and his recognition as the most eminent of living Scotsmen, of which a symbol was his elevation to a baronetcy in 1820.

But the brightness of all this glory was to be pathetically dimmed. In 1825 a general financial panic, revealing the laxity of Scott's business partners, caused his firm to fail with liabilities of nearly a hundred and twenty thousand pounds. Always magnanimous and the soul of honour, Scott refused to take advantage of the bankruptcy laws, himself assumed the burden of the entire debt, and set himself the stupendous task of paying it with his pen. Amid increasing personal sorrows he labored on for six years and so nearly attained his object that the debt was actually extinguished some years after his death. But in the effort he completed the exhaustion of his long-overtaxed strength, and, a trip to Italy proving unavailing, returned to Abbotsford, and died, a few weeks after Goethe, in 1832.

As a man Scott was first of all a true and thorough gentleman, manly, open hearted, friendly and lovable in the highest degree. Truthfulness and courage were to him the essential virtues, and his religious faith was deep though simple and unobtrusive. Like other forceful men, he understood his own capacity, but his modesty was extreme; he always insisted with all sincerity that the ability to compose fiction was not for a moment to be compared with the ability to act effectively in practical activities; and he was really displeased at the suggestion that he belonged among the greatest men of the age.

In spite of his Romantic tendencies and his absolute simplicity of character, he clung strongly to the conservatism of the feudal aristocracy with which he had labored so hard to connect himself; he was vigorously hostile to the democratic spirit, and, in his later years, to the Reform Bill; and he felt and expressed almost childish delight in the friendship of the contemptible George IV, because George IV was his king. The conservatism was closely connected, in fact, with his Romantic interest in the past, and in politics it took the form, theoretically, of Jacobitism, loyalty to the worthless Stuart race whose memory his novels have done so much to keep alive. All these traits are made abundantly clear in the extended life of Scott written by his son-in-law, J. G. Lockhart, which is one of the two or three greatest English biographies.

Scott's long poems, the best of them, are the chief examples in English of dashing verse romances of adventure and love. They are hastily done, as we have said, and there is no attempt at subtlety of characterization or at any moral or philosophical meaning; nevertheless the reader's interest in the vigorous and picturesque action is maintained throughout at the highest pitch. Furthermore, they contain much finely sympathetic description of Scottish scenery, impressionistic, but poured out with enthusiasm. Scott's numerous lyrics are similarly stirring or moving expressions of the primal emotions, and some of them are charmingly musical.

The qualities of the novels, which represent the culmination of Romantic historical fiction, are much the same.

Through his bold and active historical imagination Scott vivifies the past magnificently; without doubt, the great majority of English readers know English history chiefly through his works.

His dramatic power, also, at its best, is superb; in his great scenes and crises he is masterly as narrator and describer. In the presentation of the characters there is often much of the same superficiality as in the poems, but there is much also of the highest skill.

The novels may be roughly divided into three classes: first those, like 'Ivanhoe,' whose scene is laid in the twelfth or thirteenth century; second those, like 'Kenilworth,' which are located in the fifteenth or sixteenth; and third, those belonging to England and Scotland of the seventeenth and eighteenth. In the earlier ones sheer romance predominates and the hero and heroine are likely to be more or less conventional paragons, respectively, of courage and tender charm; but in the later ones Scott largely portrays the life and people which he himself knew; and he knew them through and through. His Scottish characters in particular, often especially the secondary ones, are delightfully realistic portraits of a great variety of types. Mary Queen of Scots in 'The Abbot' and Caleb Balderstone in 'The Bride of Lammermoor' are equally convincing in their essential but very personal humanity. Descriptions of scenery are correspondingly fuller in the novels than in the poems and are equally useful for atmosphere and background.

In minor matters, in the novels also, there is much carelessness. The style, more formal than that of the present day, is prevailingly wordy and not infrequently slipshod, though its vitality is a much more noticeable characteristic. The structure of the stories is far from compact. Scott generally began without any idea how he was to continue or end and sent off each day's installment of his manuscript in the first draft as soon as it was written; hence the action often wanders, or even, from the structural point of view, drags. But interest seldom greatly slackens until the end, which, it must be further confessed, is often suddenly brought about in a very inartistic fashion. It is of less consequence that in the details of fact Scott often commits errors, not only, like all historical novelists, deliberately manipulating the order and details of the actual events to suit his purposes, but also making frequent sheer mistakes. In 'Ivanhoe,' for example, the picture of life in the twelfth century is altogether incorrect and misleading. In all these matters scores of more self-conscious later writers are superior to Scott, but mere correctness counts for far less than genius. When all is said, Scott remains the greatest historical novelist, and one of the greatest creative forces, in world literature.

The Last Group of Romantic Poets.

Coleridge, Wordsworth, Southey, and Scott had mostly ceased to produce poetry by 1815. The group of younger men, the last out-and-out Romanticists, who succeeded them, writing chiefly from about 1810 to 1825, in some respects contrast strongly with them. Byron and Shelley were far more radically revolutionary; and Keats, in his poetry, was devoted wholly to the pursuit and worship of beauty with no concern either for a moral philosophy of life or for vigorous external adventure. It is a striking fact also that these later men were all very short-lived; they died at ages ranging only from twenty-six to thirty-six.

Lord Byron, 1788-1824. Byron (George Gordon Byron) expresses mainly the spirit of individual revolt, revolt against all existing institutions and standards. This was largely a matter of his own personal temperament, but the influence of the time also had a share in it, the time when the apparent failure of the French Revolution had thrown the pronounced liberals back upon their own resources in bitter dissatisfaction with the existing state of society.

Byron was born in 1788. His father, the violent and worthless descendant of a line of violent and worthless nobles, was just then using up the money which the poet's mother had brought him, and soon abandoned her. She in turn was wildly passionate and uncontrolled, and in bringing up her son indulged alternately in fits of genuine tenderness and capricious outbursts of mad rage and unkindness. Byron suffered also from another serious handicap; he was born with deformed feet, so that throughout life he walked clumsily—a galling irritation to his sensitive pride. In childhood his poetic instincts were stimulated by summers spent among the scenery of his mother's native Scottish Highlands. At the age of ten, on the death of his great-uncle, he succeeded to the peerage as Lord Byron, but for many years he continued to be heavily in debt, partly because of lavish extravagance, which was one expression of his inherited reckless willfulness.

Throughout his life he was obliged to make the most heroic efforts to keep in check another inherited tendency, to corpulence; he generally restricted his diet almost entirely to such meager fare as potatoes and soda-water, though he often broke out also into periods of unlimited self-indulgence.

From Harrow School he passed to Trinity College, Cambridge, where Macaulay and Tennyson were to be among his successors. Aspiring to be an athlete, he made himself respected as a fighter, despite his deformity, by his strength of arm, and he was always a powerful swimmer. Deliberately aiming also at the reputation of a debauchee, he lived wildly, though now as later probably not altogether so wickedly as he represented.

After three years of irregular attendance at the University his rank secured him the degree of M. A., in 1808. He had already begun to publish verse, and when 'The Edinburgh Review' ridiculed his very juvenile 'Hours of Idleness' he added an attack on Jeffrey to a slashing criticism of contemporary poets which he had already written in rimed couplets (he always professed the highest admiration for Pope's poetry), and published the piece as 'English Bards and Scotch Reviewers.'

He was now settled at his inherited estate of Newstead Abbey (one of the religious foundations given to members of the nobility by Henry VIII when he confiscated them from the Church), and had made his appearance in his hereditary place in the House of Lords; but following his instinct for excitement and for doing the expensively conspicuous thing he next spent two years on a European tour, through Spain, Greece, and Turkey. In Greece he traveled, as was necessary, with a large native guard, and he allowed reports to become current that he passed through a succession of romantic and reckless adventures.

The first literary result of his journey was the publication in 1812 of the first two cantos of 'Childe Harold's Pilgrimage.' This began as the record of the wanderings of Childe Harold, a dissipated young noble who was clearly intended to represent the author himself; but Byron soon dropped this figure as a useless impediment in the series of descriptions of Spain and Greece of which the first two cantos consist. He soon abandoned also the attempt to secure an archaic effect by the occasional use of Spenserian words, but he wrote throughout in Spenser's stanza, which he used with much power.

The public received the poem with the greatest enthusiasm; Byron summed up the case in his well-known comment: 'I awoke one morning and found myself famous.' In fact, 'Childe Harold' is the best of all Byron's works, though the third and fourth cantos, published some years later, and dealing with Belgium, the battle of Waterloo, and central Europe, are superior to the first two. Its excellence consists chiefly in the fact that while it is primarily a descriptive poem, its pictures, dramatically and finely vivid in themselves, are permeated with intense emotion and often serve only as introductions to passionate rhapsodies, so that the effect is largely lyrical.

Though Byron always remained awkward in company he now became the idol of the world of fashion. He followed up his first literary success by publishing during the next four years his brief and vigorous metrical romances, most of them Eastern in setting, 'The Giaour' (pronounced by Byron 'Jower'), 'The Bride of Abydos,' 'The Corsair,' 'Lara,' 'The Siege of Corinth,' and 'Parisina.' These were composed not only with remarkable facility but in the utmost haste, sometimes a whole poem in only a few days and sometimes in odds and ends of time snatched from social diversions.

The results are only too clearly apparent; the meter is often slovenly, the narrative structure highly defective, and the characterization superficial or flatly inconsistent. In other respects the poems are thoroughly characteristic of their author. In each of them stands out one dominating figure, the hero, a desperate and terrible adventurer, characterized by Byron himself as possessing 'one virtue and a thousand crimes,' merciless and vindictive to his enemies, tremblingly obeyed by his followers, manifesting human tenderness only toward his mistress (a delicate romantic creature to whom he is utterly devoted in the approved romantic-sentimental fashion), and above all inscrutably enveloped in a cloud of pretentious romantic melancholy and mystery.

Like Childe Harold, this impossible and grandiose figure of many incarnations was well understood by every one to be meant for a picture of Byron himself, who thus posed for and received in full measure the horrified admiration of the public. But in spite of all this melodramatic clap-trap the romances, like 'Childe Harold,' are filled with the tremendous Byronic passion, which, as in 'Childe Harold,' lends great power alike to their narrative and their description.

Byron now made a strangely ill-judged marriage with a Miss Milbanke, a woman of the fashionable world but of strict and perhaps even prudish moral principles. After a year she left him, and 'society,' with characteristic inconsistency, turned on him in a frenzy of superficial indignation. He shortly (1816) fled from England, never to return, both his colossal vanity and his truer sensitive self stung by the injustice to fury against the hypocrisy and conventionalities of English life, which, in fact, he had always despised. He spent the following seven years as a wanderer over Italy and central Europe.

He often lived scandalously; sometimes he was with the far more fine-spirited Shelley; and he sometimes furnished money to the Italians who were conducting the agitation against their tyrannical foreign governments. All the while he was producing a great quantity of poetry. In his half dozen or more poetic dramas he entered a new field. In the most important of them, 'Manfred,' a treatment of the theme which Marlowe and Goethe had used in 'Faust,' his real power is largely thwarted by the customary Byronic mystery and swagger. 'Cain' and 'Heaven and Earth,' though wretchedly written, have also a vaguely vast imaginative impressiveness.

Their defiant handling of Old Testament material and therefore of Christian theology was shocking to most respectable Englishmen and led Southey to characterize Byron as the founder of the 'Satanic School' of English poetry. More significant is the longest and chief of his satires, 'Don Juan,' [Footnote: Byron entirely anglicized the second word and pronounced it in two syllables—Ju-an.] on which he wrote intermittently for years as the mood took him. It is ostensibly the narrative of the adventures of a young Spaniard, but as a story it rambles on formlessly without approaching an end, and its real purpose is to serve as an utterly cynical indictment of mankind, the institutions of society, and accepted moral principles. Byron often points the cynicism by lapsing into brilliant doggerel, but his double nature appears in the occasional intermingling of tender and beautiful passages.

Byron's fiery spirit was rapidly burning itself out. In his uncontrolled zest for new sensations he finally tired of poetry, and in 1823 he accepted the invitation of the European committee in charge to become a leader of the Greek revolt against Turkish oppression. He sailed to the Greek camp at the malarial town of Missolonghi, where he showed qualities of leadership but died of fever after a few months, in 1824, before he had time to accomplish anything.

It is hard to form a consistent judgment of so inconsistent a being as Byron. At the core of his nature there was certainly much genuine goodness—generosity, sympathy, and true feeling. However much we may discount his sacrifice of his life in the cause of a foreign people, his love of political freedom and his hatred of tyranny were thoroughly and passionately sincere, as is repeatedly evident in such poems as the sonnet on 'Chillon,' 'The Prisoner of Chillon,' and the 'Ode on Venice.' On the other hand his violent contempt for social and religious hypocrisy had as much of personal bitterness as of disinterested principle; and his persistent quest of notoriety, the absence of moderation in his attacks on religious and moral standards, his lack of self-control, and his indulgence in all the vices of the worse part of the titled and wealthy class require no comment. Whatever allowances charity may demand on the score of tainted heredity, his character was far too violent and too shallow to approach to greatness.

As a poet he continues to occupy a conspicuous place (especially in the judgment of non-English-speaking nations) through the power of his volcanic emotion. It was this quality of emotion, perhaps the first essential in poetry, which enrolled among his admirers a clear spirit in most respects the antithesis of his own, that of Matthew Arnold. In 'Memorial Verses' Arnold says of him:

He taught us little, but our soul
Had felt him like the thunder's roll.
With shivering heart the strife we saw
Of passion with eternal law.

His poetry has also an elemental sweep and grandeur. The majesty of Nature, especially of the mountains and the ocean, stirs him to feeling which often results in superb stanzas, like the well-known ones at the end of 'Childe Harold' beginning 'Roll on, thou deep and dark blue Ocean, roll'! Too often, however, Byron's passion and facility of expression issue in bombast and crude rhetoric.

Moreover, his poetry is for the most part lacking in delicacy and fine shading; scarcely a score of his lyrics are of the highest order. He gives us often the blaring music of a military band or the loud, swelling volume of an organ, but very seldom the softer tones of a violin or symphony.To his creative genius and power the variety as well as the amount of his poetry offers forceful testimony.

In moods of moral and literary severity, to summarize, a critic can scarcely refrain from dismissing Byron with impatient contempt; nevertheless his genius and his in part splendid achievement are substantial facts. He stands as the extreme but significant exponent of violent Romantic individualism in a period when Romantic aspiration was largely disappointed and disillusioned, but was indignantly gathering its strength for new efforts.

Percy Bysshe ShelleY, 1792-1832.

Shelley resembles Byron in his thorough-going revolt against society, but he is totally unlike Byron in several important respects. His first impulse was an unselfish love for his fellow-men, with an aggressive eagerness for martyrdom in their behalf; his nature was unusually, even abnormally, fine and sensitive; and his poetic quality was a delicate and ethereal lyricism unsurpassed in the literature of the world. In both his life and his poetry his visionary reforming zeal and his superb lyric instinct are inextricably intertwined.

Shelley, born in 1792, belonged to a family of Sussex country gentry; a baronetcy bestowed on his grandfather during the poet's youth passed from his father after his own death to his descendants. Matthew Arnold has remarked that while most of the members of any aristocracy are naturally conservative, confirmed advocates of the system under which they enjoy great privileges, any one of them who happens to be endowed with radical ideas is likely to carry these to an extreme.

In Shelley's case this general tendency was strengthened by reaction against the benighted Toryism of his father and by most of the experiences of his life from the very outset. At Eton his hatred of tyranny was fiercely aroused by the fagging system and the other brutalities of an English school; he broke into open revolt and became known as 'mad Shelley,' and his schoolfellows delighted in driving him into paroxysms of rage.

Already at Eton he read and accepted the doctrines of the French pre-Revolutionary philosophers and their English interpreter William Godwin. He came to believe not only that human nature is essentially good, but that if left to itself it can be implicitly trusted; that sin and misery are merely the results of the injustice springing from the institutions of society, chief of which are organized government, formal religion, law, and formal marriage; and that the one essential thing is to bring about a condition where these institutions can be abolished and where all men may be allowed to follow their own inclinations. The great advance which has been made since Shelley's time in the knowledge of history and the social sciences throws a pitiless light on the absurdity of this theory, showing that social institutions, terribly imperfect as they are, are by no means chiefly bad but rather represent the slow gains of thousands of years of painful progress; none the less the theory was bound to appeal irresistibly to such an impulsive and inexperienced idealism as that of Shelley.

It was really, of course, not so much against social institutions themselves that Shelley revolted as against their abuses, which were still more flagrantly apparent in his time than in ours. When he repudiated Christianity and declared himself an atheist, what he actually had in mind was the perverted parody of religion mainly offered by the Church of his time; and, as some one has observed, when he pronounced for love without marriage it was because of the tragedies that he had seen in marriages without love. Much must be ascribed also to his sheer radicalism—the instinct to fly violently against whatever was conventionally accepted and violently to flaunt his adherence to whatever was banned.

In 1810 Shelley entered Oxford, especially exasperated by parental interference with his first boyish love, and already the author of some crude prose-romances and poetry. In the university he devoted his time chiefly to investigating subjects not included or permitted in the curriculum, especially chemistry; and after a few months, having written a pamphlet on 'The Necessity of Atheism' and sent it with conscientious zeal to the heads of the colleges, he was expelled. Still a few months later, being then nineteen years old, he allowed himself to be led, admittedly only through pity, into a marriage with a certain Harriet Westbrook, a frivolous and commonplace schoolgirl of sixteen. For the remaining ten years of his short life he, like Byron, was a wanderer, sometimes in straits for money, though always supported, after some time generously enough, by his father.

At first he tried the career of a professional agitator; going to Ireland he attempted to arouse the people against English tyranny by such devices as scattering copies of addresses from his window in Dublin or launching them in bottles in the Bristol Channel; but he was soon obliged to flee the country.

It is hard, of course, to take such conduct seriously; yet in the midst of much that was wild, his pamphlets contained also much of solid wisdom, no small part of which has since been enacted into law.

Unselfish as he was in the abstract, Shelley's enthusiast's egotism and the unrestraint of his emotions rendered him fitful, capricious, unable to appreciate any point of view but his own, and therefore when irritated or excited capable of downright cruelty in concrete cases. The most painful illustration is afforded by his treatment of his first wife. Three years after his marriage he informed her that he considered the connection at an end and abandoned her to what proved a few years of a wretched existence. Shelley himself formed a union with Mary Wollstonecraft Godwin, the daughter of his revolutionary teacher.

Her sympathetic though extravagant admiration for his genius, now beginning to express itself in really great poetry, was of the highest value to him, the more so that from this time on he was viewed by most respectable Englishman with the same abhorrence which they felt for Byron. In 1818 the Shelleys also abandoned England (permanently, as it proved) for Italy, where they moved from place to place, living sometimes, as we have said, with Byron, for whose genius, in spite of its coarseness, Shelley had a warm admiration. Shelley's death came when he was only thirty, in 1822, by a sudden accident—he was drowned by the upsetting of his sailboat in the Gulf of Spezia, between Genoa and Pisa. His body, cast on the shore, was burned in the presence of Byron and another radical, Leigh Hunt, and the ashes were buried in the Protestant cemetery just outside the wall of Rome, where Keats had been interred only a year earlier.

Some of Shelley's shorter poems are purely poetic expressions of poetic emotion, but by far the greater part are documents (generally beautiful also as poetry) in his attack on existing customs and cruelties. Matthew Arnold, paraphrasing Joubert's description of Plato, has characterized him as 'a beautiful and ineffectual angel, beating in the void his luminous wings in vain.' This is largely true, but it overlooks the sound general basis and the definite actual results which belong to his work, as to that of every great idealist.

On the artistic side the most conspicuous thing in his poetry is the ecstatic aspiration for Beauty and the magnificent embodiment of it. Shelley is the poetic disciple, but a thoroughly original disciple, of Coleridge. His esthetic passion is partly sensuous, and he often abandons himself to it with romantic unrestraint. His 'lyrical cry,' of which Matthew Arnold has spoken, is the demand, which will not be denied, for beauty that will satisfy his whole being. Sensations, indeed, he must always have, agreeable ones if possible, or in default of them, painful ones; this explains his occasional touches of repulsive morbidness. But the repulsive strain is exceptional.

No other poetry is crowded in the same way as his with pictures glorious and delicate in form, light, and colour, or is more musically palpitating with the delight which they create. To Shelley as a follower of Plato, however, the beauty of the senses is only a manifestation of ideal Beauty, the spiritual force which appears in other forms as Intellect and Love; and Intellect and Love as well are equal objects of his unbounded devotion. Hence his sensuousness is touched with a real spiritual quality. In his poetic emotion, as in his social ambitions, Shelley is constantly yearning for the unattainable. One of our best critics has observed: 'He never shows his full power in dealing separately with intellectual or moral or physical beauty. His appropriate sphere is swift sensibility, the intersecting line between the sensuous and the intellectual or moral. Mere sensation is too literal for him, mere feeling too blind and dumb, mere thought too cold.... Wordsworth is always exulting in the fullness of Nature, Shelley is always chasing its falling stars.'

The contrast, here hinted at, between Shelley's view of Nature and that of Wordsworth, is extreme and entirely characteristic; the same is true, also, when we compare Shelley and Byron. Shelley's excitable sensuousness produces in him in the presence of Nature a very different attitude from that of Wordsworth's philosophic Christian-mysticism. For the sensuousness of Shelley gets the upper hand of his somewhat shadowy Platonism, and he creates out of Nature mainly an ethereal world of delicate and rapidly shifting sights and sounds and sensations. And while he is not unresponsive to the majestic greatness of Nature in her vast forms and vistas, he is never impelled, like Byron, to claim with them the kinship of a haughty elemental spirit.

A rather long passage of appreciative criticism [Footnote: Professor A.C. Bradley, 'Oxford Lectures on Poetry' is sufficiently suggestive for quotation:

- From the world of [Shelley's] imagination the shapes of the old world had disappeared, and their place was taken by a stream of radiant vapors, incessantly forming, shifting, and dissolving in the 'clear golden dawn,' and hymning with the voices of seraphs, to the music of the stars and the 'singing rain,' the sublime ridiculous theories of Godwin.

In his heart were emotions that responded to the vision—an aspiration or ecstasy, a dejection or despair, like those of spirits rapt into Paradise or mourning over its ruin. And he wrote not like Shakespeare or Pope, for Londoners sitting in a theatre or a coffee-house, intelligence's vivid enough but definitely embodied in a definite society, able to fly, but also able to sit; he wrote, or rather he sang, to his own soul, to other spirit-sparks of the fire of Liberty scattered over the dark earth, to spirits in the air, to the boundless spirit of Nature or Freedom or Love, his one place of rest and the one source of his vision, ecstasy, and sorrow.

He sang to this, and he sang of it, and of the emotions it inspired, and of its world-wide contest with such shapes of darkness as Faith and Custom. And he made immortal music; now in melodies as exquisite and varied as the songs of Schubert, and now in symphonies where the crudest of Philosophies of History melted into golden harmony. For although there was something always working in Shelley's mind and issuing in those radiant vapors, he was far deeper and truer than his philosophic creed; its expression and even its development were constantly checked or distorted by the hard and narrow framework of his creed. And it was one which in effect condemned nine-tenths of the human nature that has formed the material of the world's great poems." [Footnote: Perhaps the finest piece of rhapsodical appreciative criticism written in later years is the essay on Shelley (especially the last half) by Francis Thompson (Scribner).]

The finest of Shelley's poems, are his lyrics. 'The Skylark' and 'The Cloud' are among the most dazzling and unique of all outbursts of poetic genius. Of the 'Ode to the West Wind,' a succession of surging emotions and visions of beauty swept, as if by the wind itself, through the vast spaces of the world, Swinburne exclaims: 'It is beyond and outside and above all criticism, all praise, and all thanksgiving.' The 'Lines Written among the Euganean Hills,' 'The Indian Serenade,' 'The Sensitive Plant' (a brief narrative), and not a few others are also of the highest quality. In 'Adonais,' an elegy on Keats and an invective against the reviewer whose brutal criticism, as Shelley wrongly supposed, had helped to kill him, splendid poetic power, at least, must be admitted.

Much less satisfactory but still fascinating are the longer poems, narrative or philosophical, such as the early 'Alastor,' a vague allegory of a poet's quest for the beautiful through a gorgeous and incoherent succession of romantic wildernesses; the 'Hymn to Intellectual Beauty'; 'Julian and Maddalo,' in which Shelley and Byron (Maddalo) are portrayed; and 'Epipsychidion,' an ecstatic poem on the love which is spiritual sympathy. Shelley's satires may be disregarded. To the dramatic form belong his two most important long poems. 'Prometheus Unbound' partly follows AEschylus in treating the torture of the Titan who is the champion or personification of Mankind, by Zeus, whom Shelley makes the incarnation of tyranny and on whose overthrow the Golden Age of Shelleyan anarchy succeeds.

The poem is a lyrical drama, more on the Greek than on the English model. There is almost no action, and the significance lies first in the lyrical beauty of the profuse choruses and second in the complete embodiment of Shelley's passionate hatred of tyranny. 'The Cenci' is more dramatic in form, though the excess of speech over action makes of it also only a 'literary drama.' The story, taken from family history of the Italian Renaissance, is one of the most horrible imaginable, but the play is one of the most powerful produced in English since the Elizabethan period.

That the quality of Shelley's genius is unique is obvious on the slightest acquaintance with him, and it is equally certain that in spite of his premature death and all his limitations he occupies an assured place among the very great poets. On the other hand, the vagueness of his imagination and expression has recently provoked severe criticism. It has even been declared that the same mind cannot honestly enjoy both the carefully wrought classical beauty of Milton's 'Lycidas' and Shelley's mistily shimmering 'Adonais.' The question goes deep and should receive careful consideration.

John Keats, 1795-1821

No less individual and unique than the poetry of Byron and Shelley is that of the third member of this group, John Keats, who is, in a wholesome way, the most conspicuous great representative in English poetry since Chaucer of the spirit of 'Art for Art's sake.' Keats was born in London in 1795, the first son of a livery-stable keeper. Romantic emotion and passionateness were among his chief traits from the start; but he was equally distinguished by a generous spirit, physical vigour (though he was very short in build), and courage. His younger brothers he loved intensely and fought fiercely.

At boarding-school, however, he turned from headstrong play to enthusiastic reading of Spenser and other great English and Latin poets and of dictionaries of Greek and Roman mythology and life. An orphan at fourteen, the mismanagement of his guardians kept him always in financial difficulties, and he was taken from school and apprenticed to a suburban surgeon. After five years of study and hospital practice the call of poetry proved too strong, and he abandoned his profession to revel in Spenser, Shakespeare, and the Italian epic authors. He now became an enthusiastic disciple of the literary and political radical, Leigh Hunt, in whose home at Hampstead he spent much time. Hunt was a great poetic stimulus to Keats, but he is largely responsible for the flippant jauntiness and formlessness of Keats' earlier poetry, and the connection brought on Keats from the outset the relentless hostility of the literacy critics, who had dubbed Hunt and his friends 'The Cockney [i.e., Vulgar] School of Poetry.'

Keats' first little volume of verse, published in 1817, when he was twenty-one,-contained some delightful poems and clearly displayed most of his chief tendencies. It was followed the next year by his longest poem, 'Endymion,' where he uses, one of the vaguely beautiful Greek myths as the basis for the expression of his own delight in the glory of the world and of youthful sensations.

As a narrative the poem is wandering, almost chaotic; that it is immature Keats himself frankly admitted in his preface; but in luxuriant loveliness of sensuous imagination it is unsurpassed. Its theme, and indeed the theme of all Keats' poetry, may be said to be found in its famous first line—'A thing of beauty is a joy forever.' The remaining three years of Keats' life were mostly tragic. 'Endymion' and its author were brutally attacked in 'The Quarterly Review' and 'Blackwood's Magazine.' The sickness and death, from consumption, of one of Keats' dearly-loved brothers was followed by his infatuation with a certain Fanny Brawne, a commonplace girl seven years younger than himself.

This infatuation thenceforth divided his life with poetry and helped to create in him a restless impatience that led him, among other things, to an unhappy effort to force his genius, in the hope of gain, into the very unsuitable channel of play-writing. But restlessness did not weaken his genuine and maturing poetic power; his third and last volume, published in 1820, and including 'The Eve of St.

Agnes,' 'Isabella,' 'Lamia,' the fragmentary 'Hyperion,' and his half dozen great odes, probably contains more poetry of the highest order than any other book of original verse, of so small a size, ever sent from the press. By this time, however, Keats himself was stricken with consumption, and in the effort to save his life a warmer climate was the last resource. Lack of sympathy with Shelley and his poetry led him to reject

Shelley's generous offer of entertainment at Pisa, and he sailed with his devoted friend the painter Joseph Severn to southern Italy. A few months later, in 1821, he died at Rome, at the age of twenty-five. His tombstone, in a neglected corner of the Protestant cemetery just outside the city wall, bears among other words those which in bitterness of spirit he himself had dictated: 'Here lies one whose name was writ in water.' But, in fact, not only had he created more great poetry than was ever achieved by any other man at so early an age, but probably no other influence was to prove so great as his on the poets of the next generation.

The most important qualities of his poetry stand out clearly: He is, as we have implied, the great apostle of full though not unhealthy enjoyment of external Beauty, the beauty of the senses. He once said: 'I feel sure I should write, from the mere yearning and tenderness I have for the beautiful, even if my night's labors should be burnt every morning and no eye ever rest upon them.' His use of beauty in his poetry is marked at first by passionate Romantic abandonment and always by lavish Romantic richness.

This passion was partly stimulated in him by other poets, largely by the Italians, and especially by Spenser, from one of whose minor poems Keats chose the motto for his first volume: 'What more felicity can fall to creature than to enjoy delight with liberty?' Shelley's enthusiasm for Beauty, as we have seen, is somewhat similar to that of Keats. But for both Spenser and Shelley, in different fashions, external Beauty is only the outer garment of the Platonic spiritual Beauty, while to Keats in his poetry it is, in appearance at least, almost everything. He once exclaimed, even, 'Oh for a life of sensations rather than of thoughts!' Notable in his poetry is the absence of any moral purpose and of any interest in present-day life and character, particularly the absence of the democratic feeling which had figured so largely in most of his Romantic predecessors. These facts must not be over-emphasized, however. His famous final phrasing of the great poetic idea—'Beauty is truth, truth beauty'—itself shows consciousness of realities below the surface, and the inference which is sometimes hastily drawn that he was personally a fiberless dreamer is as far as possible from the truth.

In fact he was always vigorous and normal, as well as sensitive; he was always devoted to outdoor life; and his very attractive letters, from which his nature can best be judged, are not only overflowing with unpretentious and cordial human feeling but testify that he was not really unaware of specific social and moral issues. Indeed, occasional passages in his poems indicate that he intended to deal with these issues in other poems when he should feel his powers adequately matured.

Whether, had he lived, he would have proved capable of handling them significantly is one of the questions which must be left to conjecture, like the other question whether his power of style would have further developed. Almost all of Keats' poems are exquisite and luxuriant in their embodiment of sensuous beauty, but 'The Eve of St. Agnes,' in Spenser's richly lingering stanza, must be especially mentioned.

Keats is one of the supreme masters of poetic expression, expression the most beautiful, apt, vivid, condensed, and imaginatively suggestive. His poems are noble storehouses of such lines as these:

The music, yearning like a God in pain.
Into her dream he melted, as the rose
Blendeth its odour with the violet.
magic casements, opening on the foam
Of perilous seas, in faery lands forlorn.

It is primarily in this respect that he has been the teacher of later poets.

Keats never attained dramatic or narrative power or skill in the presentation of individual character. In place of these elements he has the lyric gift of rendering moods. Aside from ecstatic delight, these are mostly moods of pensiveness, languor, or romantic sadness, like the one so magically suggested in the 'Ode to a Nightingale,' of Ruth standing lonely and 'in tears amid the alien corn.'

Conspicuous in Keats is his spiritual kinship with the ancient Greeks. He assimilated with eager delight all the riches of the Greek imagination, even though he never learned the language and was dependent on the dull mediums of dictionaries and translations. It is not only that his recognition of the permanently significant and beautiful embodiment of the central facts of life in the Greek stories led him to select some of them as the subjects for several of his most important poems; but his whole feeling, notably his feeling for Nature, seems almost precisely that of the Greeks, especially, perhaps, of the earlier generations among whom their mythology took shape. To him also Nature appears alive with divinities. Walking through the woods he almost expects to catch glimpses of hamadryads peering from their trees, nymphs rising from the fountains, and startled fauns with shaggy skins and cloven feet scurrying away among the bushes.

In his later poetry, also, the deeper force of the Greek spirit led him from his early Romantic formlessness to the achievement of the most exquisite classical perfection of form and finish. His Romantic glow and emotion never fade or cool, but such poems as the Odes to the Nightingale and to a Grecian Urn, and the fragment of 'Hyperion,' are absolutely flawless and satisfying in structure and expression.

Summary

One of the best comments on the poets whom we have just been considering is a single sentence of Lowell: 'Three men, almost contemporaneous with each other, Wordsworth, Keats, and Byron, were the great means of bringing back English poetry from the sandy deserts of rhetoric and recovering for her her triple inheritance of simplicity, sensuousness, and passion.' But justice must be done also to the 'Renaissance of Wonder' in Coleridge, the ideal aspiration of Shelley, and the healthy stirring of the elementary instincts by Scott.

Lesser Writers.

Throughout our discussion of the nineteenth century it will be more than ever necessary to pass by with little or no mention various authors who are almost of the first rank. To our present period belong: Thomas Campbell (1777-1844), author of 'Ye Mariners of England,' 'Hohenlinden,' and other spirited battle lyrics; Thomas Moore (1779-1852), a facile but over-sentimental Irishman, author of 'Irish Melodies,' 'Lalla Rookh,' and a famous life of Byron; Charles.

Lamb (1775-1834), the delightfully whimsical essayist and lover of Shakespeare; William Hazlitt (1778-1830), a romantically dogmatic but sympathetically appreciative critic; Thomas de Quincey (1785-1859), a capricious and voluminous author, master of a poetic prose style, best known for his 'Confessions of an English Opium-Eater'; Walter Savage Landor (1775-1864), the best nineteenth century English representative, both in prose and in lyric verse, of the pure classical spirit, though his own temperament was violently romantic; Thomas Love Peacock (1785-1866), author of some delightful satirical and humorous novels, of which 'Maid Marian' anticipated 'Ivanhoe'; and Miss Mary Russell Mitford (1787-1855), among whose charming prose sketches of country life 'Our Village' is best and best-known.

Chapter 9

Complete Text

Lines Left upon a Seat in a Yew-tree

William Wordsworth (1795)

Lines Left upon a Seat in a Yew-tree which stands near the lake of Esthwaite, on a desolate part of the shore, commanding a beautiful prospect.

Nay, Traveller! rest. This lonely Yew-tree stands
Far from all human dwelling: what if here
No sparkling rivulet spread the verdant herb?
What if the bee love not these barren boughs?
Yet, if the wind breathe soft, the curling waves,
That break against the shore, shall lull thy mind
By one soft impulse saved from vacancy.
— — — — — — — — — — — —Who he was
That piled these stones and with the mossy sod
First covered, and here taught this aged Tree
With its dark arms to form a circling bower,
I well remember.—He was one who owned
No common soul. In youth by science nursed,
And led by nature into a wild scene
Of lofty hopes, he to the world went forth
A favoured Being, knowing no desire
Which genius did not hallow; 'gainst the taint
Of dissolute tongues, and jealousy, and hate,
And scorn,—against all enemies prepared,
All but neglect. The world, for so it thought,
Owed him no service; wherefore he at once

With indignation turned himself away,
And with the food of pride sustained his soul
In solitude.—Stranger! these gloomy boughs
Had charms for him; and here he loved to sit,
His only visitants a straggling sheep,
The stone-chat, or the glancing sand-piper:
And on these barren rocks, with fern and heath,
And juniper and thistle, sprinkled o'er,
Fixing his downcast eye, he many an hour
A morbid pleasure nourished, tracing here
An emblem of his own unfruitful life:
And, lifting up his head, he then would gaze
On the more distant scene,—how lovely 'tis
Thou seest,—and he would gaze till it became
Far lovelier, and his heart could not sustain
The beauty, still more beauteous! Nor, that time,
When nature had subdued him to herself,
Would he forget those Beings to whose minds,
Warm from the labours of benevolence,
The world, and human life, appeared a scene
Of kindred loveliness: then he would sigh,
Inly disturbed, to think that others felt
What he must never feel: and so, lost Man!
On visionary views would fancy feed,
Till his eye streamed with tears. In this deep vale
He died,—this seat his only monument.
If Thou be one whose heart the holy forms
Of young imagination have kept pure,
Stranger! henceforth be warned; and know that pride,
Howe'er disguised in its own majesty,
Is littleness; that he, who feels contempt
For any living thing, hath faculties
Which he has never used; that thought with him
Is in its infancy. The man whose eye
Is ever on himself doth look on one,
The least of Nature's works, one who might move
The wise man to that scorn which wisdom holds
Unlawful, ever. O be wiser, Thou!

Instructed that true knowledge leads to love;
True dignity abides with him alone
Who, in the silent hour of inward thought,
Can still suspect, and still revere himself
In lowliness of heart.

Her Eyes Are Wild

William Wordsworth (1798)

I

Her eyes are wild, her head is bare,
The sun has burnt her coal-black hair;
Her eyebrows have a rusty stain,
And she came far from over the main.
She has a baby on her arm,
Or else she were alone:
And underneath the hay-stack warm,
And on the greenwood stone,
She talked and sung the woods among,
And it was in the English tongue.

II

"Sweet babe! they say that I am mad,
But nay, my heart is far too glad;
And I am happy when I sing
Full many a sad and doleful thing:
Then, lovely baby, do not fear!
I pray thee have no fear of me;
But safe as in a cradle, here,
My lovely baby! thou shalt be:
To thee I know too much I owe;
I cannot work thee any woe.

III

"A fire was once within my brain;
And in my head a dull, dull pain;
And fiendish faces, one, two, three,
Hung at my breast, and pulled at me;
But then there came a sight of joy;
It came at once to do me good;

I waked, and saw my little boy,
My little boy of flesh and blood;
Oh joy for me that sight to see!
For he was here, and only he.

IV

"Suck, little babe, oh suck again!
It cools my blood; it cools my brain;
Thy lips I feel them, baby! they
Draw from my heart the pain away.
Oh! press me with thy little hand;
It loosens something at my chest;
About that tight and deadly band
I feel thy little fingers prest.
The breeze I see is in the tree:
It comes to cool my babe and me.

V

"Oh! love me, love me, little boy!
Thou art thy mother's only joy;
And do not dread the waves below,
When o'er the sea-rock's edge we go;
The high crag cannot work me harm,
Nor leaping torrents when they howl;
The babe I carry on my arm,
He saves for me my precious soul;
Then happy lie; for blest am I;
Without me my sweet babe would die.

VI

"Then do not fear, my boy! for thee
Bold as a lion will I be;
And I will always be thy guide,
Through hollow snows and rivers wide.
I'll build an Indian bower; I know
The leaves that make the softest bed:
And, if from me thou wilt not go,
But still be true till I am dead,
My pretty thing! then thou shalt sing
As merry as the birds in spring.

VII

"Thy father cares not for my breast,
'Tis thine, sweet baby, there to rest;
'Tis all thine own!—and, if its hue
Be changed, that was so fair to view,
'Tis fair enough for thee, my dove!
My beauty, little child, is flown,
But thou wilt live with me in love,
And what if my poor cheek be brown?
'Tis well for me, thou canst not see
How pale and wan it else would be.

VIII

"Dread not their taunts, my little Life;
I am thy father's wedded wife;
And underneath the spreading tree
We two will live in honesty.
If his sweet boy he could forsake,
With me he never would have stayed:
From him no harm my babe can take;
But he, poor man! is wretched made;
And every day we two will pray
For him that's gone and far away.

IX

"I'll teach my boy the sweetest things:
I'll teach him how the owlet sings.
My little babe! thy lips are still,
And thou hast almost sucked thy fill.
—Where art thou gone, my own dear child?
What wicked looks are those I see?
Alas! alas! that look so wild,
It never, never came from me:
If thou art mad, my pretty lad,
Then I must be for ever sad.

X

"Oh! smile on me, my little lamb!
For I thy own dear mother am:
My love for thee has well been tried:
I've sought thy father far and wide.

I know the poisons of the shade;
I know the earth-nuts fit for food:
Then, pretty dear, be not afraid:
We'll find thy father in the wood.
Now laugh and be gay, to the woods away!
And there, my babe, we'll live for aye."

We Are Seven

William Wordsworth (1798)

————A simple Child,
That lightly draws its breath,
And feels its life in every limb,
What should it know of death?
I met a little cottage Girl:
She was eight years old, she said;
Her hair was thick with many a curl
That clustered round her head.
She had a rustic, woodland air,
And she was wildly clad:
Her eyes were fair, and very fair;
—Her beauty made me glad.
"Sisters and brothers, little Maid,
How many may you be?"
"How many? Seven in all," she said
And wondering looked at me.
"And where are they? I pray you tell."
She answered, "Seven are we;
And two of us at Conway dwell,
And two are gone to sea.
"Two of us in the church-yard lie,
My sister and my brother;
And, in the church-yard cottage, I
Dwell near them with my mother."
"You say that two at Conway dwell,
And two are gone to sea,
Yet ye are seven!—I pray you tell,
Sweet Maid, how this may be."

Then did the little Maid reply,
"Seven boys and girls are we;
Two of us in the church-yard lie,
Beneath the church-yard tree."
"You run about, my little Maid,
Your limbs they are alive;
If two are in the church-yard laid,
Then ye are only five."
"Their graves are green, they may be seen,"
The little Maid replied,
"Twelve steps or more from my mother's door,
And they are side by side.
"My stockings there I often knit,
My kerchief there I hem;
And there upon the ground I sit,
And sing a song to them.
"And often after sunset, Sir,
When it is light and fair,
I take my little porringer,
And eat my supper there.
"The first that died was sister Jane;
In bed she moaning lay,
Till God released her of her pain;
And then she went away.
"So in the church-yard she was laid;
And, when the grass was dry,
Together round her grave we played,
My brother John and I.
"And when the ground was white with snow,
And I could run and slide,
My brother John was forced to go,
And he lies by her side."
"How many are you, then," said I,
"If they two are in heaven?"
Quick was the little Maid's reply,
"O Master! we are seven."
"But they are dead; those two are dead!
Their spirits are in heaven!"

'Twas throwing words away; for still
The little Maid would have her will,
And said, "Nay, we are seven!"

Lines Composed a Few Miles Above

Tintern Abbey

***William Wordsworth* (1798)**

Lines Composed a Few Miles Above Tintern Abbey,
On revisiting the banks of the Wye during a tour.
July 13, 1798
Five years have past; five summers, with the length
Of five long winters! and again I hear
These waters, rolling from their mountain-springs
With a soft inland murmur.—Once again
Do I behold these steep and lofty cliffs,
That on a wild secluded scene impress
Thoughts of more deep seclusion; and connect
The landscape with the quiet of the sky.
The day is come when I again repose
Here, under this dark sycamore, and view
These plots of cottage-ground, these orchard-tufts,
Which at this season, with their unripe fruits,
Are clad in one green hue, and lose themselves
'Mid groves and copses. Once again I see
These hedge-rows, hardly hedge-rows, little lines
Of sportive wood run wild: these pastoral farms,
Green to the very door; and wreaths of smoke
Sent up, in silence, from among the trees!
With some uncertain notice, as might seem
Of vagrant dwellers in the houseless woods,
Or of some Hermit's cave, where by his fire
The Hermit sits alone.
These beauteous forms,
Through a long absence, have not been to me
As is a landscape to a blind man's eye:
But oft, in lonely rooms, and 'mid the din
Of towns and cities, I have owed to them

In hours of weariness, sensations sweet,
Felt in the blood, and felt along the heart;
And passing even into my purer mind,
With tranquil restoration:—feelings too
Of unremembered pleasure: such, perhaps,
As have no slight or trivial influence
On that best portion of a good man's life,
His little, nameless, unremembered, acts
Of kindness and of love. Nor less, I trust,
To them I may have owed another gift,
Of aspect more sublime; that blessed mood,
In which the burthen of the mystery,
In which the heavy and the weary weight
Of all this unintelligible world,
Is lightened:—that serene and blessed mood,
In which the affections gently lead us on,—
Until, the breath of this corporeal frame
And even the motion of our human blood
Almost suspended, we are laid asleep
In body, and become a living soul:
While with an eye made quiet by the power
Of harmony, and the deep power of joy,
We see into the life of things.
If this
Be but a vain belief, yet, oh! how oft—
In darkness and amid the many shapes
Of joyless daylight; when the fretful stir
Unprofitable, and the fever of the world,
Have hung upon the beatings of my heart—
How oft, in spirit, have I turned to thee,
O sylvan Wye! thou wanderer thro' the woods,
How often has my spirit turned to thee!
And now, with gleams of half-extinguished thought,
With many recognitions dim and faint,
And somewhat of a sad perplexity,
The picture of the mind revives again:
While here I stand, not only with the sense
Of present pleasure, but with pleasing thoughts

That in this moment there is life and food
For future years. And so I dare to hope,
Though changed, no doubt, from what I was when first
I came among these hills; when like a roe
I bounded o'er the mountains, by the sides
Of the deep rivers, and the lonely streams,
Wherever nature led: more like a man
Flying from something that he dreads, than one
Who sought the thing he loved. For nature then
(The coarser pleasures of my boyish days,
And their glad animal movements all gone by)
To me was all in all.—I cannot paint
What then I was. The sounding cataract
Haunted me like a passion: the tall rock,
The mountain, and the deep and gloomy wood,
Their colours and their forms, were then to me
An appetite; a feeling and a love,
That had no need of a remoter charm,
By thought supplied, nor any interest
Unborrowed from the eye.—That time is past,
And all its aching joys are now no more,
And all its dizzy raptures. Not for this
Faint I, nor mourn nor murmur, other gifts
Have followed; for such loss, I would believe,
Abundant recompence. For I have learned
To look on nature, not as in the hour
Of thoughtless youth; but hearing oftentimes
The still, sad music of humanity,
Nor harsh nor grating, though of ample power
To chasten and subdue. And I have felt
A presence that disturbs me with the joy
Of elevated thoughts; a sense sublime
Of something far more deeply interfused,
Whose dwelling is the light of setting suns,
And the round ocean and the living air,
And the blue sky, and in the mind of man;
A motion and a spirit, that impels
All thinking things, all objects of all thought,

And rolls through all things. Therefore am I still
A lover of the meadows and the woods,
And mountains; and of all that we behold
From this green earth; of all the mighty world
Of eye, and ear,—both what they half create,
And what perceive; well pleased to recognise
In nature and the language of the sense,
The anchor of my purest thoughts, the nurse,
The guide, the guardian of my heart, and soul
Of all my moral being.
Nor perchance,
If I were not thus taught, should I the more
Suffer my genial spirits to decay:
For thou art with me here upon the banks
Of this fair river; thou my dearest Friend,
My dear, dear Friend; and in thy voice I catch
The language of my former heart, and read
My former pleasures in the shooting lights
Of thy wild eyes. Oh! yet a little while
May I behold in thee what I was once,
My dear, dear Sister! and this prayer I make,
Knowing that Nature never did betray
The heart that loved her; 'tis her privilege,
Through all the years of this our life, to lead
From joy to joy: for she can so inform
The mind that is within us, so impress
With quietness and beauty, and so feed
With lofty thoughts, that neither evil tongues,
Rash judgments, nor the sneers of selfish men,
Nor greetings where no kindness is, nor all
The dreary intercourse of daily life,
Shall e'er prevail against us, or disturb
Our cheerful faith, that all which we behold
Is full of blessings. Therefore let the moon
Shine on thee in thy solitary walk;
And let the misty mountain-winds be free
To blow against thee: and, in after years,
When these wild ecstasies shall be matured

Into a sobre pleasure; when thy mind
Shall be a mansion for all lovely forms,
Thy memory be as a dwelling-place
For all sweet sounds and harmonies; oh! then,
If solitude, or fear, or pain, or grief,
Should be thy portion, with what healing thoughts
Of tender joy wilt thou remember me,
And these my exhortations! Nor, perchance—
If I should be where I no more can hear
Thy voice, nor catch from thy wild eyes these gleams
Of past existence—wilt thou then forget
That on the banks of this delightful stream
We stood together; and that I, so long
A worshipper of Nature, hither came
Unwearied in that service: rather say
With warmer love—oh! with far deeper zeal
Of holier love. Nor wilt thou then forget,
That after many wanderings, many years
Of absence, these steep woods and lofty cliffs,
And this green pastoral landscape, were to me
More dear, both for themselves and for thy sake!

Lines Written in Early Spring

William Wordsworth (1798)

I heard a thousand blended notes,
While in a grove I sate reclined,
In that sweet mood when pleasant thoughts
Bring sad thoughts to the mind.
To her fair works did Nature link
The human soul that through me ran;
And much it grieved my heart to think
What man has made of man.
Through primrose tufts, in that green bower,
The periwinkle trailed its wreaths;
And 'tis my faith that every flower
Enjoys the air it breathes.
The birds around me hopped and played,
Their thoughts I cannot measure:—

But the least motion which they made
It seemed a thrill of pleasure.
The budding twigs spread out their fan,
To catch the breezy air;
And I must think, do all I can,
That there was pleasure there.
If this belief from heaven be sent,
If such be Nature's holy plan,
Have I not reason to lament
What man has made of man?

Anecdote for Fathers

William Wordsworth (1798)

I have a boy of five years old;
His face is fair and fresh to see;
His limbs are cast in beauty's mould,
And dearly he loves me.
One morn we strolled on our dry walk,
Our quiet home all full in view,
And held such intermitted talk
As we are wont to do.
My thoughts on former pleasures ran;
I thought of Kilve's delightful shore,
Our pleasant home when spring began,
A long, long year before.
A day it was when I could bear
Some fond regrets to entertain;
With so much happiness to spare,
I could not feel a pain.
The green earth echoed to the feet
Of lambs that bounded through the glade,
From shade to sunshine, and as fleet
From sunshine back to shade.
Birds warbled round me—and each trace
Of inward sadness had its charm;
Kilve, thought I, was a favoured place,
And so is Liswyn farm.
My boy beside me tripped, so slim

And graceful in his rustic dress!
And, as we talked, I questioned him,
In very idleness.
"Now tell me, had you rather be,"
I said, and took him by the arm,
"On Kilve's smooth shore, by the green sea,
Or here at Liswyn farm?"
In careless mood he looked at me,
While still I held him by the arm,
And said, "At Kilve I'd rather be
Than here at Liswyn farm."
"Now, little Edward, say why so:
My little Edward, tell me why."—
"I cannot tell, I do not know."—
"Why, this is strange," said I;
"For, here are woods, hills smooth and warm:
There surely must some reason be
Why you would change sweet Liswyn farm
For Kilve by the green sea."
At this, my boy hung down his head,
He blushed with shame, nor made reply;
And three times to the child I said,
"Why, Edward, tell me why?"
His head he raised—there was in sight,
It caught his eye, he saw it plain—
Upon the house-top, glittering bright,
A broad and gilded vane.
Then did the boy his tongue unlock,
And eased his mind with this reply:
"At Kilve there was no weather-cock;
And that's the reason why."
O dearest, dearest boy! my heart
For better lore would seldom yearn,
Could I but teach the hundredth part
Of what from thee I learn.

Influence of Natural Objects
Wordsworth (1799)

Influence of Natural Objects,

In calling forth and strengthening
The imagination in boyhood and early youth
Wisdom and Spirit of the universe!
Thou Soul, that art the Eternity of thought!
And giv'st to forms and images a breath
And everlasting motion! not in vain,
By day or star-light, thus from my first dawn
Of childhood didst thou intertwine for me
The passions that build up our human soul;
Not with the mean and vulgar works of Man;
But with high objects, with enduring things,
With life and nature; purifying thus
The elements of feeling and of thought,
And sanctifying by such discipline
Both pain and fear,—until we recognise
A grandeur in the beatings of the heart.
Nor was this fellowship vouchsafed to me
With stinted kindness. In November days,
When vapours rolling down the valleys made
A lonely scene more lonesome; among woods
At noon; and 'mid the calm of summer nights,
When, by the margin of the trembling lake,
Beneath the gloomy hills, homeward I went
In solitude, such intercourse was mine:
Mine was it in the fields both day and night,
And by the waters, all the summer long.
And in the frosty season, when the sun
Was set, and, visible for many a mile,
The cottage-windows through the twilight blazed,
I heeded not the summons: happy time
It was indeed for all of us; for me
It was a time of rapture! Clear and loud
The village-clock tolled six—I wheeled about,
Proud and exulting like an untired horse
That cares not for his home.—All shod with steel
We hissed along the polished ice, in games
Confederate, imitative of the chase
And woodland pleasures,—the resounding horn,

The pack loud-chiming, and the hunted hare.
So through the darkness and the cold we flew,
And not a voice was idle: with the din
Smitten, the precipices rang aloud;
The leafless trees and every icy crag
Tinkled like iron; while far-distant hills
Into the tumult sent an alien sound
Of melancholy, not unnoticed while the stars,
Eastward, were sparkling clear, and in the west
The orange sky of evening died away.
Not seldom from the uproar I retired
Into a silent bay, or sportively
Glanced sideway, leaving the tumultuous throng,
To cut across the reflex of a star;
Image, that, flying still before me, gleamed
Upon the glassy plain: and oftentimes,
When we had given our bodies to the wind,
And all the shadowy banks on either side
Came sweeping through the darkness, spinning still
The rapid line of motion, then at once
Have I, reclining back upon my heels,
Stopped short; yet still the solitary cliffs
Wheeled by me—even as if the earth had rolled
With visible motion her diurnal round!
Behind me did they stretch in solemn train,
Feebler and feebler, and I stood and watched
Till all was tranquil as a summer sea.

Lucy Gray

William Wordsworth (1799)

Or, Solitude
Oft I had heard of Lucy Gray:
And, when I crossed the wild,
I chanced to see at break of day
The solitary child.
No mate, no comrade Lucy knew;
She dwelt on a wide moor,
—The sweetest thing that ever grew

Beside a human door!
You yet may spy the fawn at play,
The hare upon the green;
But the sweet face of Lucy Gray
Will never more be seen.
"To-night will be a stormy night—
You to the town must go;
And take a lantern, Child, to light
Your mother through the snow."
"That, Father! will I gladly do:
'Tis scarcely afternoon—
The minster-clock has just struck two,
And yonder is the moon!"
At this the Father raised his hook,
And snapped a faggot-band;
He plied his work;—and Lucy took
The lantern in her hand.
Not blither is the mountain roe:
With many a wanton stroke
Her feet disperse the powdery snow,
That rises up like smoke.
The storm came on before its time:
She wandered up and down;
And many a hill did Lucy climb:
But never reached the town.
The wretched parents all that night
Went shouting far and wide;
But there was neither sound nor sight
To serve them for a guide.
At day-break on a hill they stood
That overlooked the moor;
And thence they saw the bridge of wood,
A furlong from their door.
They wept—and, turning homeward, cried,
"In heaven we all shall meet;"
—When in the snow the mother spied
The print of Lucy's feet.
Then downwards from the steep hill's edge

They tracked the footmarks small;
And through the broken hawthorn hedge,
And by the long stone-wall;
And then an open field they crossed:
The marks were still the same;
They tracked them on, nor ever lost;
And to the bridge they came.
They followed from the snowy bank
Those footmarks, one by one,
Into the middle of the plank;
And further there were none!
—Yet some maintain that to this day
She is a living child;
That you may see sweet Lucy Gray
Upon the lonesome wild.
O'er rough and smooth she trips along,
And never looks behind;
And sings a solitary song
That whistles in the wind.

She Dwelt Among the Untrodden Ways

William Wordsworth (1799)

She dwelt among the untrodden ways
Beside the springs of Dove,
A Maid whom there were none to praise
And very few to love:
A violet by a mossy stone
Half hidden from the eye!
—Fair as a star, when only one
Is shining in the sky.
She lived unknown, and few could know
When Lucy ceased to be;
But she is in her grave, and, oh,
The difference to me!

Nutting

William Wordsworth (1799)

..............It seems a day

(I speak of one from many singled out)
One of those heavenly days that cannot die;
When, in the eagerness of boyish hope,
I left our cottage-threshold, sallying forth
With a huge wallet o'er my shoulders slung,
A nutting-crook in hand; and turned my steps
Tow'rd some far-distant wood, a Figure quaint,
Tricked out in proud disguise of cast-off weeds
Which for that service had been husbanded,
By exhortation of my frugal Dame—
Motley accoutrement, of power to smile
At thorns, and brakes, and brambles,—and, in truth,
More ragged than need was! O'er pathless rocks,
Through beds of matted fern, and tangled thickets,
Forcing my way, I came to one dear nook
Unvisited, where not a broken bough
Drooped with its withered leaves, ungracious sign
Of devastation; but the hazels rose
Tall and erect, with tempting clusters hung,
A virgin scene!—A little while I stood,
Breathing with such suppression of the heart
As joy delights in; and, with wise restraint
Voluptuous, fearless of a rival, eyed
The banquet;—or beneath the trees I sate
Among the flowers, and with the flowers I played;
A temper known to those, who, after long
And weary expectation, have been blest
With sudden happiness beyond all hope.
Perhaps it was a bower beneath whose leaves
The violets of five seasons re-appear
And fade, unseen by any human eye;
Where fairy water-breaks do murmur on
For ever; and I saw the sparkling foam,
And—with my cheek on one of those green stones
That, fleeced with moss, under the shady trees,
Lay round me, scattered like a flock of sheep—
I heard the murmur and the murmuring sound,
In that sweet mood when pleasure loves to pay

Tribute to ease; and, of its joy secure,
The heart luxuriates with indifferent things,
Wasting its kindliness on stocks and stones,
And on the vacant air. Then up I rose,
And dragged to earth both branch and bough, with crash
And merciless ravage: and the shady nook
Of hazels, and the green and mossy bower,
Deformed and sullied, patiently gave up
Their quiet being: and, unless I now
Confound my present feelings with the past;
Ere from the mutilated bower I turned
Exulting, rich beyond the wealth of kings,
I felt a sense of pain when I beheld
The silent trees, and saw the intruding sky—
Then, dearest Maiden, move along these shades
In gentleness of heart; with gentle hand
Touch—for there is a spirit in the woods.

Song for the Wandering Jew

William Wordsworth (1800)

Though the torrents from their fountains
Roar down many a craggy steep,
Yet they find among the mountains
Resting-places calm and deep.
Clouds that love through air to hasten,
Ere the storm its fury stills,
Helmet-like themselves will fasten
On the heads of towering hills.
What, if through the frozen centre
Of the Alps the Chamois bound,
Yet he has a home to enter
In some nook of chosen ground:
And the Sea-horse, though the ocean
Yield him no domestic cave,
Slumbers without sense of motion,
Couched upon the rocking wave.
If on windy days the Raven

Gambol like a dancing skiff,
Not the less she loves her haven
In the bosom of the cliff.
The fleet Ostrich, till day closes,
Vagrant over desert sands,
Brooding on her eggs reposes
When chill night that care demands.
Day and night my toils redouble,
Never nearer to the goal;
Night and day, I feel the trouble
Of the Wanderer in my soul.

My Heart Leaps Up

William Wordsworth (1802)

My heart leaps up when I behold
A rainbow in the sky:
So was it when my life began;
So is it now I am a man;
So be it when I shall grow old,
Or let me die!
The Child is father of the Man;
I could wish my days to be
Bound each to each by natural piety.

The Solitary Reaper

William Wordsworth (1803)

Behold her, single in the field,
Yon solitary Highland Lass!
Reaping and singing by herself;
Stop here, or gently pass!
Alone she cuts and binds the grain,
And sings a melancholy strain;
O listen! for the Vale profound
Is overflowing with the sound.
No Nightingale did ever chaunt
More welcome notes to weary bands

Of travellers in some shady haunt,
Among Arabian sands:
A voice so thrilling ne'er was heard
In spring-time from the Cuckoo-bird,
Breaking the silence of the seas
Among the farthest Hebrides.
Will no one tell me what she sings?—
Perhaps the plaintive numbers flow
For old, unhappy, far-off things,
And battles long ago:
Or is it some more humble lay,
Familiar matter of to-day?
Some natural sorrow, loss, or pain,
That has been, and may be again?
Whate'er the theme, the Maiden sang
As if her song could have no ending;
I saw her singing at her work,
And o'er the sickle bending;—
I listened, motionless and still;
And, as I mounted up the hill
The music in my heart I bore,
Long after it was heard no more.

I Wandered Lonely as a Cloud

William Wordsworth (1804)

I wandered lonely as a cloud
That floats on high o'er vales and hills,
When all at once I saw a crowd,
A host, of golden daffodils;
Beside the lake, beneath the trees,
Fluttering and dancing in the breeze.
Continuous as the stars that shine
And twinkle on the milky way,
They stretched in never-ending line
Along the margin of a bay:
Ten thousand saw I at a glance,
Tossing their heads in sprightly dance.

The waves beside them danced; but they
Out-did the sparkling waves in glee:
A poet could not but be gay,
In such a jocund company:
I gazed—and gazed—but little thought
What wealth the show to me had brought:
For oft, when on my couch I lie
In vacant or in pensive mood,
They flash upon that inward eye
Which is the bliss of solitude;
And then my heart with pleasure fills,
And dances with the daffodils.

To a Skylark

William Wordsworth (1805)

Up with me! up with me into the clouds!
For thy song, Lark, is strong;
Up with me, up with me into the clouds!
Singing, singing,
With clouds and sky about thee ringing,
Lift me, guide me till I find
That spot which seems so to thy mind!
I have walked through wildernesses dreary
And to-day my heart is weary;
Had I now the wings of a Faery,
Up to thee would I fly.
There is madness about thee, and joy divine
In that song of thine;
Lift me, guide me high and high
To thy banqueting-place in the sky.
Joyous as morning
Thou art laughing and scorning;
Thou hast a nest for thy love and thy rest,
And, though little troubled with sloth,
Drunken Lark! thou would'st be loth
To be such a traveller as I.
Happy, happy Liver,

With a soul as strong as a mountain river
Pouring out praise to the Almighty Giver,
Joy and jollity be with us both!
Alas! my journey, rugged and uneven,
Through prickly moors or dusty ways must wind;
But hearing thee, or others of thy kind,
As full of gladness and as free of heaven,
I, with my fate contented, will plod on,
And hope for higher raptures, when life's day is done.

The World Is Too Much With Us

William Wordsworth (1806)

The world is too much with us; late and soon,
Getting and spending, we lay waste our powers:
Little we see in Nature that is ours;
We have given our hearts away, a sordid boon!
The Sea that bares her bosom to the moon;
The winds that will be howling at all hours,
And are up-gathered now like sleeping flowers;
For this, for everything, we are out of tune;
It moves us not.—Great God! I'd rather be
A Pagan suckled in a creed outworn;
So might I, standing on this pleasant lea,
Have glimpses that would make me less forlorn;
Have sight of Proteus rising from the sea;
Or hear old Triton blow his wreathed horn.

Ode: Intimations of Immortality

William Wordsworth (1807)

Intimations of Immortality From Recollections of Early Childhood

I

There was a time when meadow, grove, and stream,
The earth, and every common sight,
To me did seem
Apparelled in celestial light,

The glory and the freshness of a dream.
It is not now as it hath been of yore;—
Turn wheresoe'er I may,
By night or day,
The things which I have seen
I now can see no more.

II

The Rainbow comes and goes,
And lovely is the Rose,
The Moon doth with delight
Look round her when the heavens are bare,
Waters on a starry night
Are beautiful and fair;
The sunshine is a glorious birth;
But yet I know, where'er I go,
That there hath past away a glory from the earth.

III

Now, while the birds thus sing a joyous song,
And while the young lambs bound
As to the tabor's sound,
To me alone there came a thought of grief:
A timely utterance gave that thought relief,
And I again am strong:
The cataracts blow their trumpets from the steep;
No more shall grief of mine the season wrong;
I hear the Echoes through the mountains throng,
The Winds come to me from the fields of sleep,
And all the earth is gay;
Land and sea
Give themselves up to jollity,
And with the heart of May
Doth every Beast keep holiday;—
Thou Child of Joy,
Shout round me, let me hear thy shouts, thou happy
Shepherd-boy!

IV

Ye blessed Creatures, I have heard the call
Ye to each other make; I see

The heavens laugh with you in your jubilee;
My heart is at your festival,
My head hath its coronal,
The fulness of your bliss, I feel—I feel it all.
Oh evil day! if I were sullen
While Earth herself is adorning,
This sweet May-morning,
And the Children are culling
On every side,
In a thousand valleys far and wide,
Fresh flowers; while the sun shines warm,
And the Babe leaps up on his Mother's arm:—
I hear, I hear, with joy I hear!
—But there's a Tree, of many, one,
A single Field which I have looked upon,
Both of them speak of something that is gone:
The Pansy at my feet
Doth the same tale repeat:
Whither is fled the visionary gleam?
Where is it now, the glory and the dream?

V

Our birth is but a sleep and a forgetting:
The Soul that rises with us, our life's Star,
Hath had elsewhere its setting,
And cometh from afar:
Not in entire forgetfulness,
And not in utter nakedness,
But trailing clouds of glory do we come
From God, who is our home:
Heaven lies about us in our infancy!
Shades of the prison-house begin to close
Upon the growing Boy,
But He beholds the light, and whence it flows,
He sees it in his joy;
The Youth, who daily farther from the east
Must travel, still is Nature's Priest,
And by the vision splendid
Is on his way attended;

At length the Man perceives it die away,
And fade into the light of common day.

VI

Earth fills her lap with pleasures of her own;
Yearnings she hath in her own natural kind,
And, even with something of a Mother's mind,
And no unworthy aim,
The homely Nurse doth all she can
To make her Foster-child, her Inmate Man,
Forget the glories he hath known,
And that imperial palace whence he came.

VII

Behold the Child among his new-born blisses,
A six years' Darling of a pigmy size!
See, where 'mid work of his own hand he lies,
Fretted by sallies of his mother's kisses,
With light upon him from his father's eyes!
See, at his feet, some little plan or chart,
Some fragment from his dream of human life,
Shaped by himself with newly-learned art;
A wedding or a festival,
A mourning or a funeral;
And this hath now his heart,
And unto this he frames his song:
Then will he fit his tongue
To dialogues of business, love, or strife;
But it will not be long
Ere this be thrown aside
And with new joy and pride
The little Actor cons another part;
Filling from time to time his "humorous stage"
With all the Persons, down to palsied Age,
That Life brings with her in her equipage;
As if his whole vocation
Were endless imitation.

VIII

Thou, whose exterior semblance doth belie
Thy Soul's immensity;

Thou best Philosopher, who yet dost keep
Thy heritage, thou Eye among the blind,
That, deaf and silent, read'st the eternal deep,
Haunted for ever by the eternal mind,—
Mighty Prophet! Seer blest!
On whom those truths do rest,
Which we are toiling all our lives to find,
In darkness lost, the darkness of the grave;
Thou, over whom thy Immortality
Broods like the Day, a Master o'er a Slave,
A Presence which is not to be put by;
Thou little Child, yet glorious in the might
Of heaven-born freedom on thy being's height,
Why with such earnest pains dost thou provoke
The years to bring the inevitable yoke,
Thus blindly with thy blessedness at strife?
Full soon thy Soul shall have her earthly freight,
And custom lie upon thee with a weight
Heavy as frost, and deep almost as life!

IX

O joy! that in our embers
Is something that doth live,
That nature yet remembers
What was so fugitive!
The thought of our past years in me doth breed
Perpetual benediction: not indeed
For that which is most worthy to be blest—
Delight and liberty, the simple creed
Of Childhood, whether busy or at rest,
With new-fledged hope still fluttering in his breast:—
Not for these I raise
The song of thanks and praise;
But for those obstinate questionings
Of sense and outward things,
Fallings from us, vanishings;
Blank misgivings of a Creature
Moving about in worlds not realised,
High instincts before which our mortal Nature

Did tremble like a guilty Thing surprised:
But for those first affections,
Those shadowy recollections,
Which, be they what they may,
Are yet the fountain light of all our day,
Are yet a master light of all our seeing;
Uphold us, cherish, and have power to make
Our noisy years seem moments in the being
Of the eternal Silence: truths that wake,
To perish never;
Which neither listlessness, nor mad endeavour,
Nor Man nor Boy,
Nor all that is at enmity with joy,
Can utterly abolish or destroy!
Hence in a season of calm weather
Though inland far we be,
Our Souls have sight of that immortal sea
Which brought us hither,
Can in a moment travel thither,
And see the Children sport upon the shore,
And hear the mighty waters rolling evermore.

X

Then sing, ye Birds, sing, sing a joyous song!
And let the young Lambs bound
As to the tabor's sound!
We in thought will join your throng,
Ye that pipe and ye that play,
Ye that through your hearts to-day
Feel the gladness of the May!
What though the radiance which was once so bright
Be now for ever taken from my sight,
Though nothing can bring back the hour
Of splendour in the grass, of glory in the flower;
We will grieve not, rather find
Strength in what remains behind;
In the primal sympathy
Which having been must ever be;
In the soothing thoughts that spring

Out of human suffering;
In the faith that looks through death,
In years that bring the philosophic mind.

XI

And O, ye Fountains, Meadows, Hills, and Groves,
Forebode not any severing of our loves!
Yet in my heart of hearts I feel your might;
I only have relinquished one delight
To live beneath your more habitual sway.
I love the Brooks which down their channels fret,
Even more than when I tripped lightly as they;
The innocent brightness of a new-born Day
Is lovely yet;
The Clouds that gather round the setting sun
Do take a sobre colouring from an eye
That hath kept watch o'er man's mortality;
Another race hath been, and other palms are won.
Thanks to the human heart by which we live,
Thanks to its tenderness, its joys, and fears,
To me the meanest flower that blows can give
Thoughts that do often lie too deep for tears.

Chapter 10

Summary and Analysis of Popular Poems of William Wordsworth

Summary and Analysis of "A slumber did my spirit seal"

In the first of the poem's two stanzas, the speaker declares that a "slumber" has kept him from realizing reality. In essence, he has been in a dream-like state, devoid of any common fears ("human fears"). To the speaker, "she" (his unnamed female love) seemed like she would never age:

A slumber did my spirit seal;
I had no human fears:
She seemed a thing that could not feel
The touch of earthly years.
In the second and final stanza,
however, we learn that she has died.
She lies still and can no longer see or hear.
She has become a part of the day-to-day
course of the earth:
No motion has she now, no force:
She neither hears nor sees,
Rolled round in earth's diurnal course
With rocks and stones and trees.

Analysis

"A slumber did my spirit seal" is one of Wordsworth's "Lucy Poems," which focus primarily on the death of a young woman named Lucy (though she remains unnamed in this poem). Many scholars and literary historians have offered theories as to who Lucy was, but her true identity remains a mystery. The poem is comprised of only two four-line stanzas, and yet a great deal happens in this narrow space. We see the speaker's realization not only that this young woman has died, but also that bad things can happen in a beautiful world.

In the first stanza the speaker is innocently unaware that age can touch the woman, but he is quickly taught a harsh lesson when she dies between stanzas one and two. The choice to hide the death between the stanzas is interesting, as it seems to imply that the speaker is unable to verbalize the pain that goes along with the sudden loss. On the other hand, the poem may be less about the speaker's innocence than about his belief in the young woman's power. Indeed, he seems to have built her up in his mind into a goddess, untouched by age and mortality. This desire to keep her perpetually young is a testament to the speaker's feelings for the young woman.

In the second stanza Wordsworth offers an eerie description of the woman's current situation. She is blind and deaf—wholly incapable of taking in the world around her. This is a particularly painful idea in a Wordsworth poem, because he is generally so focused on experiencing the senses. The speaker also mentions that she is now without motion or force. This, of course, is true of all dead people, but by stating the obvious the speaker helps the reader to imagine the way the young woman once was: full of life and vigour.

In the last two lines the speaker describes the young woman trapped beneath the surface of the earth. In fact, she has become a part of the earth, rolling with it as it turns day to day. The very last line of the poem is especially interesting, because the speaker lists both rocks and stones, which are essentially the same. It may be that he intends to reference both gravestones and common rocks. Alternatively, the speaker may intend to emphasize the "dead" things of the earth over living things like trees (which are mentioned only once).

"A slumber did my spirit seal" is a ballad, though a very short one. The stanzas follow an abab rhyme scheme, and the first and third lines are in iambic tetrameter, while the second and forth lines are in iambic trimeter.

Summary and Analysis of "Composed upon Westminster Bridge"

In lines 1 through 8, which together compose a single sentence, the speaker describes what he sees as he stands on Westminster Bridge looking out at the city. He begins by saying that there is nothing "more fair" on Earth than the sight he sees, and that anyone who could pass the spot without stopping to look has a "dull" soul. The poem takes place in the "beauty of the morning," which lies like a blanket over the silent city. He then lists what he sees in the city and mentions that the city seems to have no pollution and lies "Open unto the fields, and to the sky."

Earth has not anything to show more fair:
Dull would he be of soul who could pass by
A sight so touching in its majesty:
This City now doth, like a garment, wear
The beauty of the morning; silent, bare,
Ships, towers, domes, theatres, and temples lie
Open unto the fields, and to the sky;
All bright and glittering in the smokeless air.

In lines 9 through 14, the speaker tells the reader that the sun has never shone more beautifully, even on nature ("valley, rock, or hill"), and that he has never seen or felt such deep calm. He goes on to describe the way that the river (which he personifies) glides along at the slow pace it chooses. The poem ends with an exclamation, saying that "the houses seem asleep" and the heart of the city is still.

Never did sun more beautifully steep
In his first splendour, valley, rock, or hill;
Ne'er saw I, never felt, a calm so deep!
The river glideth at his own sweet will:
Dear God! the very houses seem asleep;
And all that mighty heart is lying still!

Analysis

"Composed upon Westminster Bridge, September 3, 1802" is an Italian sonnet, written in iambic pentameter with ten syllables per line. The rhyme scheme of the poem is abbaabbacdcdcd. The poem was actually written about an experience that took place on July 31, 1802 during a trip to France with Wordsworth's sister, Dorothy Wordsworth.

The poem begins with a rather shocking statement, especially for a Romantic poet: "Earth has not anything to show more fair."

This statement is surprising because Wordsworth is not speaking of nature, but of the city. He goes on to list the beautiful man-made entities therein, such as "Ships, towers, domes, theatres and temples." In fact, nature's influence isn't described until the 7th line, when the speaker relates that the city is "open to the fields, and to the sky."

While the city itself may not be a part of nature, it is certainly not in conflict with nature. This becomes even more clear in the next line, when the reader learns that the air is "smokeless" (free from pollution). Wordsworth continues to surprise his reader by saying that the sun has never shone more beautifully, even on natural things. He then personifies the scene, giving life to the sun, the river, the houses, and finally to the whole city, which has a symbolic heart. The reader imagines that the city's heart beats rapidly during the day, while everything and everyone in it is bustling about, but now, in the early morning hours, the city's heart is "lying still." By using personification in his poem, Wordsworth brings a kind of spirit to the city, which is usually seen as a simple construction of rock and metal.

Summary and Analysis of "I wandered Lonely as a Cloud"

In the first stanza the speaker describes a time when he meandered over the valleys and hills, "lonely as a cloud." Finally, he came across a crowd of daffodils stretching out over almost everything he could see, "fluttering and dancing in the breeze":

I wandered lonely as a cloud
That floats on high o'er vales and hills,
When all at once I saw a crowd,
A host, of golden daffodils;

Beside the lake, beneath the trees,
Fluttering and dancing in the breeze.

In the second stanza the speaker goes into more detail about the daffodils. They reminded him of the Milky Way, because there were so many flowers packed together that they seemed to be neverending. The speaker guesses that there were ten thousand daffodils, which were "Tossing their heads in sprightly dance":

Continuous as the stars that shine
And twinkle on the milky way,
They stretched in never-ending line
Along the margin of a bay:
Ten thousand saw I at a glance,
Tossing their heads in sprightly dance.

In the third stanza the speaker compares the waves of the lake to the waves of daffodils and decides that even though the lake is "sparkling," the daffodils win because they have more "glee." He then comments that he, like any other poet, could not help but be happy "in such a jocund company." He looked at the scene for a long time, but while he was there he was unable to understand what he had gained from the experience:

The waves beside them danced; but they
Out-did the sparkling waves in glee:
A poet could not but be gay,
In such a jocund company:
I gazed—and gazed—but little thought

What wealth the show to me had brought: In the fourth and final stanza the poet describes what he gained from the experience. Afterwards, when he was lonely or feeling "pensive," he could remember the daffodils, seeing them with his "inward eye," and be content:

For oft, when on my couch I lie
In vacant or in pensive mood,
They flash upon that inward eye
Which is the bliss of solitude;
And then my heart with pleasure fills,
And dances with the daffodils.

Analysis

"I wandered lonely as a cloud" takes place in the Lake District of Northern England. The area is famous for its hundreds of lakes, gorgeous expanses of springtime daffodils, and for being home to the "Lakeland Poets": William Wordsworth, Samuel Coleridge, and Robert Southey.

This poem, obviously inspired by Wordsworth's stomping grounds, is well-loved because of its simple yet beautiful rhythms and rhymes, and its rather sentimental topic. The poem consists of four six-line stanzas, each of which follow an ababcc rhyme scheme and are written in iambic tetrameter, giving the poem a subtle back-and-forth motion that recalls swaying daffodils. By comparing himself to a cloud in the first line of the poem, the speaker signifies his close identification with the nature that surrounds him. He also demonstrates this connection by personifying the daffodils several times, even calling them a "crowd" as if they are a group of people. The idea of remembering the beauty of nature even when not in its presence appears in several of Wordsworth's later poems, including "Tintern Abbey," "Ode; Intimations of Immortality," and "The Solitary Reaper." Even though the speaker is unable to appreciate the memory he is creating as he stands in the field, he later realizes the worth that it takes on in sad and lonely moments.

Summary and Analysis of "It is a beauteous evening"

The speaker begins by describing the scene. It is a calm and beautiful evening, and the sun is setting peacefully as the sky hangs over the sea:

It is a beauteous evening, calm and free,
The holy time is quiet as a Nun
Breathless with adoration; the broad sun
Is sinking down in its tranquility;

The gentleness of heaven broods o'er the Sea: At line six the speaker begins to address someone who turns out to be a young girl. He tells her to listen, that "the mighty Being is awake" and making a "sound like thunder" that lasts forever:

Listen! the mighty Being is awake,

And doth with his eternal motion make
A sound like thunder—everlastingly.

The speaker then tells the child (actually his daughter, Caroline) who is walking beside him that even though she isn't affected by the solemn ideas he has when he comes face to face with nature, she is not any less divine. In fact, she "liest in Abraham's bosom all year," because God is with her even when she is not aware of Him:

Dear Child! dear Girl! that walkest with me here,
If thou appear untouched by solemn thought,
Thy nature is not therefore less divine:
Thou liest in Abraham's bosom all the year;
And worship'st at the Temple's inner shrine,
God being with thee when we know it not.

Analysis

"It is a beauteous evening" does exactly what its title implies it will—it describes a beautiful evening scene—and yet this sonnet goes far beyond aesthetic pleasures, paralleling a simple walk along the beach with the religious power that Wordsworth feels in nature. The poem gains even more power when the reader learns that the child Wordsworth walks with is his daughter Caroline, whom he has not seen in ten years because he has been separated from her and her mother by the war in France. The child's innocence is inspirational: even though she is not actively considering the power of the nature that surrounds them, she is a part of it nevertheless. And because, for Wordsworth, the very fact of being in nature is enough to inspire a powerful religious experience, he envisions his pure daughter standing alongside God, as if she has been accepted into heaven well before the hour of her death.

Summary and Analysis of "Lines Composed a Few Miles above Tintern Abbey"

Full Title: "Lines Composed a Few Miles above Tintern Abbey; On Revisiting the Banks of the Wye During a Tour, July 13, 1798"

"Lines Composed a Few Miles above Tintern Abbey" was

written in July of 1798 and published as the last poem of Lyrical Ballads, also in 1798. At the age of twenty-three (in August of 1793), Wordsworth had visited the desolate abbey alone. In 1798 he returned to the same place with his beloved sister, Dorothy Wordsworth, who was a year younger. Dorothy is referred to as "Friend" throughout the poem.

Often the poem is simply called "Tintern Abbey." The abbreviated title is effective for clarity's sake, but it is also misleading, as the poem does not actually take place in the abbey. Wordsworth begins his poem by telling the reader that it has been five years since he has been to this place a few miles from the abbey. He describes the "Steep and lofty cliffs," the "wild secluded scene," the "quiet of the sky," the "dark sycamore" he sits under, the trees of the orchard, and the "pastoral farms" with "wreaths of smoke" billowing from their chimneys.

In the second stanza Wordsworth tells his readers that his first visit to this place gave him "sensations sweet" when he was in the "lonely rooms" of the city. He intimates that these "feelings... / Of unremembered pleasure" may have helped him to be a better person, perhaps simply by putting him in a better mood than he would have been in otherwise:

As have no slight or trivial influence
On that best portion of a good man's life,
His little, nameless, unremembered, acts
Of kindness and of love. Nor less, I trust,
To them I may have owed another gift,
Of aspect more sublime; that blessed mood,
In which the burthen of the mystery,
In which the heavy and the weary weight
Of all this unintelligible world,
Is lightened

Wordsworth goes on to suggest his spiritual relationship with nature, which he believes will be a part of him until he dies:

Until, the breath of this corporeal frame,
And even the motion of our human blood
Almost suspended, we are laid sleep

In body, and become a living soul:
While with an eye made quiet by the power
Of harmony, and the deep power of joy,
We see into the life of things.

In the third stanza, he begins to consider what it would mean if his belief in his connection to nature were misguided, but stops short. Seeming not to care whether the connection is valid or not, he describes the many benefits that his memories nature give him. At the end of the stanza he addresses the Wye River: "How oft, in spirit, have I returned to thee / O sylvan Wye! Thou wanderer through the woods, / How often has my spirit returned to thee!"

In the fourth stanza, Wordsworth begins by explaining the pleasure he feels at being back in the place that has given him so much joy over the years. He is also glad because he knows that this new memory will give him future happiness: "in this moment there is life and food / for future years." He goes on to explain how differently he experienced nature five years ago, when he first came to explore the area. During his first visit he was full of energy:

like a roe
I bounded o'er the mountains, by the sides
Of the deep rivers, and the lonely streams,
Wherever nature led: more like a man
Flying from something that he dreads, than one
Who sought the thing he loved. For nature then
(The coarser pleasures of my boyish days,
And their glad animal movements all gone by)
To me was all in all.—I cannot paint
What then I was. The sounding cataract
Haunted me like a passion: the tall rock,
The mountain, and the deep and gloomy wood,
Their colours and their forms, were then to me
An appetite; a feeling and a love,
That had no need of a remoter charm,
By thought supplied, nor any interest
Unborrowed from the eye.

Wordsworth quickly sets his current self apart from the

way he was five years ago, saying, "That time is past." At first, however, he seems almost melancholy about the change: "And all its aching joys are now no more, / And all its dizzy raptures." Over the past five years, he has developed a new approach to nature:

For I have learned
To look on nature, not as in the hour
Of thoughtless youth, but hearing oftentimes
The still, sad music of humanity.

As a more sophisticated and wiser person with a better understanding of the sad disconnection of humanity, Wordsworth feels a deeper and more intelligent relationship with nature:

And I have felt
A presence that disturbs me with the joy
Of elevated thoughts; a sense sublime
Of something far more deeply interfused...

Wordsworth is "still / A lover of the meadows and the woods," but has lost some of his gleeful exuberance. Instead, he views nature as the "anchor of [his] purest thoughts, the nurse, / The guide, the guardian of my heart, and soul / of all my moral being."

In the fifth and last stanza, Wordsworth addresses his sister Dorothy, calling her both "Sister" and "dear Friend." Through her eyes, Wordsworth can see the wild vitality he had when he first visited this place, and this image of himself gives him new life. It is apparent at this point in the poem that Wordsworth has been speaking to his sister throughout. Dorothy serves the same role as nature, reminding Wordsworth of what he once was:

...in thy voice I catch
The language of my former heart, and read
My former pleasure in the shooting lights
Of thy wild eyes. Oh! yet a little while
May I behold in thee what I was once,
My dear, dear Sister!

Wordsworth then shares his deepest hope: that in the future, the power of nature and the memories of himself will stay with Dorothy. He is implying that he will die before she does (even though she is only a year younger), and hopes that in her memory he will be kept alive:

If solitude, or fear, or pain, or grief,
Should be thy portion, with what healing thoughts
Of tender joy wilt thou remember me,
And these my exhortations!

Even as Wordsworth thinks about dying, he is given new strength and vitality at the thought that his sister will remember him. He describes the setting vigorously:

Nor, perchance,
If I should be, where I no more can hear
Thy voice, nor catch from thy wild eyes these gleams
Of past existence, wilt thou then forget
That on the banks of this delightful stream
We stood together; and that I, so long
A worshipper of Nature, hither came...

At the end of the poem, Wordsworth combines their current setting with his sister's future memory of the moment. He is satisfied knowing that she will also carry the place, the moment, and the memory with her:

Nor wilt thou then forget,
That after many wanderings, many years
Of absence, these steep woods and lofty cliffs,
And this green pastoral landscape, were to me
More dear, both for themselves, and for thy sake.

Analysis

Published in 1798 in Lyrical Ballads, this poem is widely considered to be one of Wordsworth's masterpieces. It is a complex poem, addressing memory, mortality, faith in nature, and familial love. The poem's structure is similarly complex, making use of the freedom of blank verse (no rhyming) as well as the measured rhythm of iambic pentameter (with a few notable exceptions). The flow of the writing has been described as that of waves, accelerating only to stop in the middle of a line (caesura). The repetition of sounds and words adds to the ebb and flow of the language, appropriately speaking to the ebb and flow of the poet's memories. Divided into five stanzas of different lengths, the poem begins in the present moment, describing the natural setting. Wordsworth emphasizes the act of returning by making extensive use of repetition: "Five years have passed; five summers, with the length / Of five long winters! and again I hear / These waters..." He also uses the phrase "once again" twice, both times in the middle of a line, breaking the flow of the text. It is in this manner that the reader is introduced to the natural beauty of the Wye River area.

In the second stanza, Wordsworth departs from the present moment to describe how his memories of the scene inspired and sustained him over the past five years. Life away from nature is described as being "in lonely rooms, and mid the din / Of towns and cities." Meanwhile, nature is described with almost religious fervor: Wordsworth uses words such as "sublime," "blessed," and "serene." Wordsworth refers to a "blessed mood" twice, emphasizing his spiritual relationship with nature. Interestingly, while Wordsworth uses many words related to spirituality and religion in this poem, he never refers to God or Christianity. It seems that nature is playing that role in this poem, especially at the end of the second stanza, when Wordsworth describes a sort of transcendent moment:

Until, the breath of this corporeal frame,
And even the motion of our human blood
Almost suspended, we are laid asleep
In body, and become a living soul:
While with an eye made quiet by the power
Of harmony, and the deep power of joy,
We see into the life of things.

Nature, it seems, offers humankind ("we") a kind of insight ("We see into the life of things") in the face of mortality ("we are laid asleep"). Wordsworth lays emphasis on the last line by making it only eight syllables (four iambs) long, as opposed to ten.

In the third stanza, Wordsworth returns to the present and acknowledges that his faith might be in "vain," but reiterates how important his memories of this landscape have been to him, addressing the river directly: "O sylvan Wye!" As in many of his other poems, Wordsworth personifies natural forms or nature as a whole by addressing them directly (apostrophe).

Wordsworth seems to value this period of his life, and remembers it with a somewhat nostalgic air, although he admits that in this simpler time ("The coarser pleasures of my boyish days"), he was not so sophisticated as he is now. In the present, he is weighed down by more serious thoughts. He alludes to a loss of faith and a sense of disheartenment. This transition is widely believed to refer to Wordsworth's changing attitude towards the French Revolution. Having visited France at the height of the Revolution, Wordsworth was inspired by the ideals of the Republican movement. Their emphasis on the value of the individual, imagination, and liberty inspired him and filled him with a sense of optimism. By 1798, however, Wordsworth was already losing faith in the movement, as it had by then degenerated into widespread violence. Meanwhile, as France and Britain entered the conflict, Wordsworth was prevented from seeing his family in France and lost his faith in humanity's capacity for harmony. Wordsworth turns to nature to find the peace he cannot find in civilization.

Wordsworth goes on to describe a spirit or a being connected with nature that elevates his understanding of the world:

And I have felt a presence that disturbs me with the joy
Of elevated thoughts; a sense sublime
Of something far more deeply interfused,
Whose dwelling is the light of setting suns,
And the round ocean, and the living air,
And the blue sky, and in the mind of man,
A motion and a spirit, that impels
All thinking things, all objects of thought,
And rolls through all things.

This "presence" could refer to God or some spiritual consciousness, or it could simply refer to the unified presence of the natural world. In the interconnectedness of nature,

Wordsworth finds the sublime harmony that he cannot find in humankind, and for this reason he approaches nature with an almost religious fervor:

Therefore am I still
A lover of the meadows and the woods,
And mountains; and of all that we behold
From this green earth; of all the mighty world
Of eye and ear, both what they half-create,
And what perceive; well pleased to recognize
In nature and the language of the sense,
The anchor of my purest thoughts...

In this key passage, Wordsworth outlines his understanding of consciousness. Like other Romantic poets, Wordsworth imagines that consciousness is built out of subjective, sensory experience. What he hears and sees ("of all that we behold... / of all the mighty world/ Of eye and ear") creates his perceptions and his consciousness ("both what they half-create, / And what perceive"). The "language of the sense"—his sensory experiences—are the building blocks of this consciousness ("The anchor of my purest thoughts"). Thus, he relies on his experience of nature for both consciousness and "all [his] moral being."

In the last stanza, Wordsworth returns to the present to address his sister Dorothy, and explains that like his memory of this natural place, her presence offers a kind of continuity in his life. Although he experiences anxiety about his own mortality, the idea that Dorothy will remember him and remember this moment after his death comforts him. Dorothy offers continuity because Wordsworth sees himself in her (Dorothy was also a poet and the two spent a great deal of time together), literally seeing his "former pleasures in the shooting lights / Of thy wild eyes." Wordsworth sees that Dorothy experiences the Wye with the same enthusiasm as he did five years earlier. Moving into a discussion of the future, he hopes that Dorothy's memories of this landscape will sustain her in sad times the way they sustained him, and offers up a "prayer" that this will be the case:

And this prayer I make,

Knowing that Nature never did betray
The heart that loved her; 'tis her privilege,
Through all the years of this our life, to lead
From joy to joy...

Again, Wordsworth addresses nature with a sort of spiritual faith without actually citing God or religion. Instead, he focuses entirely on nature and on Dorothy.

In the last lines of the poem, Wordsworth creates a sort of pact between Dorothy, the natural environment, and himself, as if trying to establish and capture the memory of this precise moment forever:

Nor wilt though then forget,
That after many wanderings, many years
Of absence, these steep woods and lofty cliffs,
And this green pastoral landscape, were to me
More dear, both for themselves, and for thy sake.

With these words, Wordsworth creates a beautiful illustration of the mechanics of memory. Not only does he want to remember this moment in this beautiful landscape, but he also wants Dorothy to remember how much he loved it, and how much more he loved it because he knew that she would remember it too. Thus, nature is not only an object of beauty and the subject of memories, but also the catalyst for a beautiful, harmonious relationship between two people, and their memories of that relationship. This falls in line with Wordsworth's belief that nature is a source of inspiration and harmony that can elevate human existence to the level of the sublime in a way that civilization cannot.

Although the poem is often referred to simply as "Tintern Abbey," this is misleading because the poem is actually located "a few miles" away! At the time the poem was written, Tintern Abbey was already just the ruins of a gothic cathedral—a stone shell with no roof, carpeted with grass. Although it is a romantic image, it is not the subject of the poem.

Summary and Analysis of "Lines Written in Early Spring"

In this poem Wordsworth describes a bittersweet moment.

The speaker reclines in a beautiful grove surrounded by the "blended notes" of nature, and yet, even as he enjoys the scene, it inspires a melancholy mood and the speaker begins to have dark thoughts about humanity:

I heard a thousand blended notes,
While in a grove I sate reclined,
In that sweet mood when pleasant thoughts
Bring sad thoughts to the mind.

Nature has connected itself to the speaker's soul, leading him to sadly consider "What man has made of man." Even as he does this, however, he takes in the beautiful scene that surrounds him:

To her fair works did Nature link
The human soul that through me ran;
And much it grieved my heart to think
What man has made of man.
Through primrose tufts, in that green bower,
The periwinkle trailed its wreaths;
And 'tis my faith that every flower
Enjoys the air it breathes.
The birds around me hopped and played,
Their thoughts I cannot measure: —
But the least motion which they made,
It seemed a thrill of pleasure.

At the end of the poem the speaker looks more closely at the seemingly jubilant birds, plants, and other creatures of nature, trying to decide whether or not they are really full of pleasure. He decides that they are. In the last stanza, he asks whether, if it is true that nature is full of pleasure, he then has a good reason to be sad about "what man has made of man":

The budding twigs spread out their fan,
To catch the breezy air;
And I must think, do all I can,
That there was pleasure there.
If this belief from heaven be sent,
If such be Nature's holy plan,
Have I not reason to lament
What man has made of man?

Analysis

"Lines Written in Early Spring" has a rather simple form: it is composed of only six four-line stanzas, and is written in iambs with an abab rhyme scheme for each stanza. The simplicity of the poem is representative of the bulk of the rest of Wordsworth's works (and of most Romantic poetry). The simple words and style of the Romantic Movement came from a complete rejection of the flowery, lofty style that was popular in previous years.

The connection with nature in this poem is very apparent. Wordsworth strengthens the bond by placing the speaker in the middle of nature, all alone except for the plants and animals around him. He also personifies nature, giving her the ability to make decisions, to link herself to his soul, and to experience pleasure. Nature, in this poem, does everything right; it is man who has failed by rejecting nature.

Another interesting aspect of this poem is the fact that the perfection of nature saddens the speaker. Melancholy sets in almost immediately because of the striking contrast between nature and humanity. The speaker seems to feel that it is his responsibility to ponder the mistakes of humanity. This is especially evident in the question posed in the last stanza.

The speaker suggests that man can simultaneously be a part of nature and rational, in control of himself, and in control of his surroundings. The speaker is a thoughtful being, a philosopher of sorts, and is certainly reasonable, and yet he is at peace with nature in a way that would likely strike many of his contemporaries as odd.

Summary and Analysis of "London, 1802"

In the beginning of "London, 1802" William Wordsworth cries out to the dead poet, John Milton, telling him that he should be alive, because England needs him now. He goes on to describe England as a swampy marshland of "stagnant waters" where everything that was once a natural gift (such as religion, chivalry, and art, symbolized respectively by the altar, the sword, and the pen) has been lost to the scourge of modernity:

Milton! thou shouldst be living at this hour;
England hath need of thee: she is a fen
Of stagnant waters: altar, sword, and pen,
Fireside, the heroic wealth of hall and bower,
Have forfeited their ancient English dower
Of inward happiness.

The speaker continues by telling Milton that the English are selfish and asking him to raise them up. He asks Milton to bring the English ("us") "manners, virtue, freedom, power":

We are selfish men;
Oh! raise us up, return to us again;
And give us manners, virtue, freedom, power.

The speaker then tells Milton that his "soul was like a Star," because he was different even from his contemporaries in terms of the virtues listed above. The speaker tells Milton that his voice was like the sea and the sky, a part of nature and therefore natural: "majestic, free." The speaker also compliments Milton's ability to embody "cheerful godliness" even while doing the "lowliest duties":

Thy soul was like a Star, and dwelt apart;
Thou hadst a voice whose sound was like the sea:
Pure as the naked heavens, majestic, free,
So didst thou travel on life's common way,
In cheerful godliness; and yet thy heart
The lowliest duties on herself did lay.

Analysis

"London, 1802" is a sonnet with a rhyme scheme of abbaabbacddece. The poem is written in the second person and addresses the late poet John Milton, who lived from 1608-1674 and is most famous for having written Paradise Lost.

The poem has two main purposes, one of which is to pay homage to Milton by saying that he can save the entirety of England with his noblity and virtue. The other purpose of the poem is to draw attention to what Wordsworth feels are the problems with English society.

According to Wordsworth, England was once a great place of happiness, religion, chivalry, art, and literature, but at the present moment those virtues have been lost. Wordsworth can only describe modern England as a swampland, where people are selfish and must be taught about things like "manners, virtue, freedom, power."

Notice that Wordsworth compliments Milton by comparing him to things found in nature, such as the stars, the sea, and "the heavens." For Wordsworth, being likened to nature is the highest compliment possible.

Summary and Analysis of "My Heart Leaps up when I behold"

In this very short poem consisting of only 9 lines, the speaker begins by declaring that he is moved by nature, and especially by nature's beauty: "My heart leaps up when I behold / A Rainbow in the sky." He goes on to say that he has always felt the impact of nature, even when he was an infant: "So was it when my life began; / So is it now I am a man." The speaker is so certain of his connection with nature that he says it will be constant until he becomes an old man, or else he would rather die: "So be it when I shall grow old, / Or let me die!" In the next line he declares that children are superior to men because of their proximity to nature: "The Child is father of the Man." For this reason, he wishes to bind himself to his childhood self: "And I could wish my days to be / Bound each to each by natural piety."

Analysis

Written on March 26, 1802 and published in 1807 as an epigraph to "Ode: Intimations of Immortality," this poem addresses the same themes found in "Tintern Abbey" and "Ode; Intimations of Immortality," albeit in a much more concise way. The speaker explains his connection to nature, stating that it has been strong throughout his life. He even goes so far as to say that if he ever loses his connection he would prefer to die.

The seventh line of the poem is the key line: "The Child is father of the Man." This line is often quoted because of its ability to express a complicated idea in so few words. The speaker believes (as explained in more detail in "Tintern Abbey") that children are closer to heaven and God, and through God, nature, because they have recently come from the arms of God. The speaker understands the importance of staying connected to one's own childhood, stating: "I could wish my days to be / Bound each to each by natural piety."

Wordsworth chooses the word "piety" to express the bond he wishes to attain (and maintain) with his childhood self, because it best emphasizes the importance of the bond. His readers would have been accustomed to the idea of piety in the religious sense, and would thus have been able to translate the meaning behind the word to an understanding of the power of the bond Wordsworth hopes to attain.

The format of "My heart leaps up when I behold" gives the poem a somewhat staccato feeling and forces the reader to pause at important points in the poem. For instance, the two short lines of the poem are both quite significant. First, "A rainbow in the sky" harkens back to God's promise to Noah signifying their bond, and foreshadows the speaker's wish to be "Bound...by natural piety." The sixth line, "Or let me die!" shows the strength of the speaker's convictions.

Summary and Analysis of "Ode; Intimations of Immortality"

Full Title: "Ode; Intimations of Immortality from Recollections of Early Childhood"

The speaker begins by declaring that there was a time when nature seemed mystical to him, like a dream, "Apparelled in celestial light." But now all of that is gone. No matter what he does, "The things which I have seen I now can see no more."

In the second stanza the speaker says that even though he can still see the rainbow, the rose, the moon, and the sun, and even though they are still beautiful, something is different...something has been lost: "But yet I know, where'er I go, / That there hath past away a glory from the earth." The speaker is saddened by the birds singing and the lambs jumping in the third stanza. Soon, however, he resolves not to be depressed, because it will only put a damper on the beauty of the season. He declares that all of the earth is happy, and exhorts the shepherd boy to shout.

In the fourth stanza the speaker continues to be a part of the joy of the season, saying that it would be wrong to be "sullen / While Earth herself in adorning, / And the Children are culling / On every side, / In a thousand valleys far and wide." However, when he sees a tree, a field, and later a pansy at his feet, they again give him a strong feeling that something is amiss. He asks, "Whither is fled the visionary gleam? / Where is it now, the glory and the dream?"

The fifth stanza contains arguably the most famous line of the poem: "Our birth is but a sleep and a forgetting." He goes on to say that as infants we have some memory of heaven, but as we grow we lose that connection: "Heaven lies about us in our infancy!" As children this connection with heaven causes us to experience nature's glory more clearly. Once we are grown, the connection is lost. In the sixth stanza, the speaker says that as soon as we get to earth, everything conspires to help us forget the place we came from: heaven. "Forget the glories he hath known, and that imperial palace whence he came."

In the seventh stanza the speaker sees (or imagines) a six-year-old boy, and foresees the rest of his life. He says that the child will learn from his experiences, but that he will spend most of his effort on imitation: "And with new joy and pride / The little Actor cons another part." It seems to the speaker that his whole life will essentially be "endless imitation." In the eighth stanza the speaker speaks directly to the child, calling him a philosopher. The speaker cannot understand why the child, who is so close to heaven in his youth, would rush to grow into an adult. He asks him, "Why with such earnest pains dost thou provoke / The years to bring the inevitable yoke, / Thus blindly with thy blessedness at strife?" In the ninth stanza (which is the longest at 38 lines) the speaker experiences a flood of joy when he realizes that through memory he will always be able to connect to his childhood, and through his childhood to nature.

Hence is a season of calm weather
Though inland far we be,
Our souls have sight of that immortal sea
Which brought us hither,
Can in a moment travel thither,
And see the Children sport upon the shore,
And hear the might water rolling evermore.

In the tenth stanza the speaker harkens back to the beginning of the poem, asking the same creatures that earlier made him sad with their sounds to sing out: "Then sing, ye Birds, sing, sing a joyous song!" Even though he admits that he has lost some of the glory of nature as he has grown out of childhood, he is comforted by the knowledge that he can rely on his memory. In the final stanza the speaker says that nature is still the stem of everything is his life, bringing him insight, fueling his memories and his belief that his soul is immortal: "To me the meanest flower that blows can give / Thoughts that do often lie too deep for tears."

Analysis

"Ode; Intimations of Immortality" is a long and rather complicated poem about Wordsworth's connection to nature and his struggle to understand humanity's failure to recognize the value of the natural world. The poem is elegiac in that it is about the regret of loss. Wordsworth is saddened by the fact that time has stripped away much of nature's glory, depriving him of the wild spontaneity he exhibited as a child. As seen in "The world is too much with us," Wordsworth believes that the loss stems from being too caught up in material possessions. As we grow up, we spend more and more time trying to figure out how to attain wealth, all the while becoming more and more distanced from nature. The poem is characterized by a strange sense of duality. Even though the world around the speaker is beautiful, peaceful, and serene, he is sad and angry because of what he (and humanity) has lost. Because nature is a kind of religion to Wordsworth, he knows that it is wrong to be depressed in nature's midst and pulls himself out of his depression for as long as he can.

In the seventh stanza especially, Wordsworth examines the transitory state of childhood. He is pained to see a child's close proximity to nature being replaced by a foolish acting game in which the child pretends to be an adult before he actually is. Instead, Wordsworth wants the child to hold onto the glory of nature that only a person in the flush of youth can appreciate. In the ninth, tenth and eleventh stanzas Wordsworth manages to reconcile the emotions and questions he has explored throughout the poem. He realizes that even though he has lost his awareness of the glory of nature, he had it once, and can still remember it. The memory of nature's glory will have to be enough to sustain him, and he ultimately decides that it is. Anything that we have, for however short a time, can never be taken away completely, because it will forever be held in our memory.

Summary and Analysis of "The Solitary Reaper"

In the first stanza the speaker comes across a beautiful girl working alone in the fields of Scotland (the Highland). She is "Reaping and singing by herself." He tells the reader not to interrupt her, and then mentions that the valley is full of song.

Behold her, single in the field,
Yon solitary Highland Lass!
Reaping and singing by herself;
Stop here, or gently pass!
Alone she cuts and binds the grain,
And sings a melancholy strain;
O listen! for the Vale profound
Is overflowing with the sound.

The second stanza is a list of things that cannot equal the beauty of the girl's singing:

No Nightingale did ever chaunt
More welcome notes to weary bands
Of travellers in some shady haunt,
Among Arabian sands:
A voice so thrilling ne'er was heard
In spring-time from the Cuckoo-bird,
Breaking the silence of the seas

Among the farthest Hebrides.

In the third stanza the reader learns that the speaker cannot understand the words being sung. He can only guess at what she might be singing about:

Will no one tell me what she sings?—
Perhaps the plaintive numbers flow
For old, unhappy, far-off things,
And battles long ago:
Or is it some more humble lay,
Familiar matter of to-day?
Some natural sorrow, loss, or pain,
That has been, and may be again?

In the fourth and final stanza the speaker tells the reader that even though he did not know what she was singing about, the music stayed in his heart as he continued up the hill:

Whate'er the theme, the Maiden sang
As if her song could have no ending;
I saw her singing at her work,
And o'er the sickle bending;—
I listened, motionless and still;
And, as I mounted up the hill
The music in my heart I bore,
Long after it was heard no more.

Analysis

"The Solitary Reaper" was written on November 5, 1805 and published in 1807. The poem is broken into four eight-line stanzas (32 lines total). Most of the poem is in iambic tetrameter. The rhyme scheme for the stanzas is either abcbddee or ababccdd. (In the first and last stanzas the first and third lines don't rhyme, while in the other two stanzas they do.)

This poem is unique in Wordsworth's oeuvre because while most of his work is based closely on his own experiences, "The Solitary Reaper" is based on the experience of someone else: Thomas Wilkinson, as described in his Tours to the British Mountains. The passage that inspired Wordsworth is the following: "Passed a female who was reaping alone: she sung in Erse [the Gaelic language of Scotland] as she bended over her sickle; the sweetest human voice I ever heard: her strains were tenderly melancholy, and felt delicious, long after they were heard no more" (as qtd. in The Norton Anthology English Literature).

Part of what makes this poem so intriguing is the fact that the speaker does not understand the words being sung by the beautiful young lady. In the third stanza, he is forced to imagine what she might be singing about. He supposes that she may be singing about history and things that happened long ago, or some sadness that has happened in her own time and will happen again. As the speaker moves on, he carries the music of the young lady with him in his heart. This is a prevalent theme in much of Wordsworth's poetry. For instance, the same idea is used in "I wandered lonely as a cloud" when the speaker takes the memory of the field of daffodils with him to cheer him up on bad days.

Summary and Analysis of "The Tables Turned"

The speaker begins by telling his friend to stop reading books; he'll become fat from being sedentary. The speaker then asks why he chooses to be so serious while outside there is a beautiful evening scene:

Up! up! my Friend, and quit your books;
Or surely you'll grow double:
Up! up! my friend, and clear your looks,
Why all this toil and trouble?
The sun above the mountain's head,
A freshening lustre mellow
Through all the long green fields has spread,
His first sweet evening yellow.

The speaker continues, telling his friend that books are dull and tedious. Rather than reading, he should venture outside to where the linnet (a small finch) and the throstle (a song bird) are singing beautiful music containing more wisdom than any book. The two lines that follow (15 and 16) are probably the most important in the poem: "Come forth into the light of things, / Let Nature be your teacher." The speaker is telling his friend that Nature has more to teach than books, and that he should go outside rather than seek refuge in dry pages:

Books! 'tis a dull and endless strife:
Come, hear the woodland linnet,
How sweet his music! on my life,
There's more of wisdom in it.
And hark! how blithe the throstle sings!
He, too, is no mean preacher:
Come forth into the light of things,
Let Nature be your teacher.

In the next two stanzas the speaker tells his friend that Mother Nature is full of wealth, and that she is ready to bestow her fruits on our minds and hearts. He also says that in nature wisdom comes from being happy and healthy, and that a person can learn more about humanity and about good and evil from a tree than from a sage:

She has a world of ready wealth,
Our minds and hearts to bless—
Spontaneous wisdom breathed by health,
Truth breathed by cheerfulness.
One impulse from a vernal wood
May teach you more of man,
Of moral evil and of good,
Than all the sages can.

The speaker suggests that even though nature brings humanity sweet traditions of intelligence, we tend to ruin that knowledge by dissecting it. Instead, we should reject traditional science and art and simply come into nature ready to learn with "a heart / That watches and receives":

Sweet is the lore which Nature brings;
Our meddling intellect
Mis-shapes the beauteous forms of things:—
We murder to dissect.
Enough of Science and of Art;
Close up those barren leaves;
Come forth, and bring with you a heart
That watches and receives.

Analysis

"The Tables Turned" consists of eight four-line stanzas in interlocking rhymes (abab). It is in ballad form, written in iambs with four beats in the first and third lines of each stanza, and three beats in the second and fourth lines.

It certainly seems strange to find a poet telling his friend (and through his friend his readers) to stop reading, and yet much of what Wordsworth is saying in "The Tables Turned" fits perfectly with the Romantic Movement, which emphasizes the importance of being a part of nature. For Wordsworth there is much more to be learned by watching, listening to, and simply taking in one's surroundings than by studying books. At the same time, there is a strong element of irony at play here.

First of all, Wordsworth is making these statements in a poem, which will become (as he knew it would) a part of a book meant to be read. Even though he believes that nature is a great teacher, he is not ready to throw away books altogether.

It is important to note the poem's title: "The Tables Turned." The title leads us to believe that Wordsworth is reacting to the status quo, or to the way that people usually think, which in this case is that books are the best way to learn. In order to make the strongest statement possible, Wordsworth goes to the opposite extreme, even though his true feelings probably lie somewhere in the middle.

Summary and Analysis of "The world is too much with us"

The speaker begins this poem by saying that the world is too full of humans who are losing their connection to divinity and, even more importantly, to nature. Humans, the speaker says, have given their hearts away, and the gift is a morally degraded one:

The world is too much with us; late and soon,
Getting and spending, we lay waste our powers;
Little we see in Nature that is ours;
We have given our hearts away, a sordid boon!

In the second quartet the speaker tells the reader that everything in nature, including the sea and the winds, is gathered up in a powerful connection with which humanity is "out of tune." In other words, humans are not experiencing nature as they should:

This Sea that bares her bosom to the moon,
The winds that will be howling at all hours,
And are up-gathered now like sleeping flowers,
For this, for everything, we are out of tune;
It moves us not.

The speaker ends the poem by saying that he would rather be a pagan attached to a worn-out system of beliefs than be out of tune with nature. At least if he were a pagan he might be able to see things that would make him less unhappy, like the sea gods Proteus and Triton:

Great God! I'd rather be
A Pagan suckled in a creed outworn;
So might I, standing on this pleasant lea,
Have glimpses that would make me less forlorn;
Have sight of Proteus rising from the sea;
Or hear old Triton blow his wreathed horn.

Analysis

"The world is too much with us" is a sonnet with an abbaabbacdcdcd rhyme scheme. The poem is written from a place of angst and frustration. All around him, Wordsworth sees people who are obsessed with money and with manmade objects. These people are losing their powers of divinity, and can no longer identify with the natural world.

This idea is encapsulated in the famous lines: "Getting and spending, we lay waste our powers; / Little we see in Nature that is ours." Wordsworth believes that we have given our hearts (the centre of ourselves) away in exchange for money and material wealth. He is disgusted at this especially because nature is so readily available; it almost calls to humanity. In the end, Wordsworth decides that he would rather be a pagan in a complete state of disillusionment than be out of touch with nature.

The final image of the poem is of Wordsworth standing on a lea (or a tract of open land) overlooking the ocean where he sees Proteus and Triton. He is happy, but this happiness is not what the reader is meant to feel. In actuality, the reader should feel saddened by the scene, because Wordsworth has given up on humanity, choosing instead to slip out of reality.

Summary and Analysis of "Three years she grew"

The poem begins with the personified Nature noticing Lucy at three years old. Nature thinks she is the most beautiful thing on earth, and promises to take her to make "A Lady of her own":

Three years she grew in sun and shower,
Then Nature said, "A lovelier flower
On earth was never sown;
This Child I to myself will take;
She shall be mine, and I will make
A Lady of my own.

Nature then expounds on what it means to be Nature's lady for several stanzas. Nature promises to make Lucy into a part of nature itself. She will be a part of the rocks, the earth, the heaven, the glades, the mountain springs, the clouds, the trees, and the storms. In addition, Lucy will fully enjoy nature and understand it. It will be as if they are in constant communication:

Myself will to my darling be
Both law and impulse: and with me
The Girl, in rock and plain,
In earth and heaven, in glade and bower,
Shall feel an overseeing power
To kindle or restrain.
She shall be sportive as the fawn
That wild with glee across the lawn,
Or up the mountain springs;
And her's shall be the breathing balm,
And her's the silence and the calm
Of mute insensate things.
The floating clouds their state shall lend
To her; for her the willow bend;
Nor shall she fail to see

Even in the motions of the Storm
Grace that shall mould the Maiden's form
By silent sympathy.
The stars of midnight shall be dear
To her; and she shall lean her ear
In many a secret place
Where rivulets dance their wayward round,
And beauty born of murmuring sound
Shall pass into her face.
And vital feelings of delight
Shall rear her form to stately height,
Her virgin bosom swell;
Such thoughts to Lucy I will give
While she and I together live
Here in this happy dell.

In the last stanza Nature declares that her work is done: she has fulfilled her promise to Lucy, letting her grow into a mature woman (as promised in the sixth stanza). The speaker declares, "How soon my Lucy's race was run!" When she dies, she leaves the speaker a calm scene to enjoy along with the beautiful memory of her:

Thus Nature spake—The work was done—
How soon my Lucy's race was run!
She died, and left to me
This heath, this calm, and quiet scene;
The memory of what has been,
And never more will be.

Analysis

"Three years she grew" is made up of seven six-line stanzas that each have an aabccb rhyme scheme. This poem is one of a set usually called the "Lucy Poems." The identity of Lucy has never been discovered.

Nature takes on an interesting role in this poem—she is beautiful and giving, and yet ultimately dictates the circumstances of Lucy's death. The poem becomes a beautiful elegy written to a woman who has died and who Wordsworth admired not only for her beauty, but also for her connection to nature, which Wordsworth felt was the highest possible achievement. Also worthy of note is the fact that the speaker does not speak until the final stanza. For the first six stanzas he simply describes the declarations and promises of Nature. It is only in the end that the reader finally learns what happened to Lucy (she died as soon as she reached maturity) and why the speaker is writing the poem (out of grief).

Summary and Analysis of "We Are Seven"

The speaker begins this poem by asking what a simple child who is full of life could know about death. He then meets "a little cottage Girl" who is eight years old and has thick curly hair. She is rustic and woodsy, but very beautiful, and she makes the speaker happy. He asks her how many siblings she has, to which she replies that there are seven including her:

—A simple child,
That lightly draws its breath,
And feels its life in every limb,
What should it know of death?
I met a little cottage girl:
She was eight years old, she said;
Her hair was thick with many a curl
That clustered round her head.
She had a rustic, woodland air,
And she was wildly clad:
Her eyes were fair, and very fair;
—Her beauty made me glad.
"Sisters and brothers, little maid,
How many may you be?"
"How many? Seven in all," she said,
And wondering looked at me.

The speaker then asks the child where her brothers and sisters are. She replies "Seven are we," and tells him that two are in a town called Conway, two are at sea, and two lie in the church-yard. She and her mother live near the graves:

"And where are they? I pray you tell."
She answered, "Seven are we;
And two of us at Conway dwell,

And two are gone to sea.
"Two of us in the churchyard lie,
My sister and my brother;
And, in the churchyard cottage, I
Dwell near them with my mother."

The speaker is confused and asks her how they can be seven, if two are in Conway and two gone to sea. To this, the little girl simply replies, "Seven boys and girls are we; / Two of us in the churchyard lie, / Beneath the churchyard tree." The speaker says that if two are dead, then there are only five left, but the little girl tells him that their green graves are nearby, and that she often goes to sew or eat supper there while singing to her deceased siblings:

"You say that two at Conway dwell,
And two are gone to sea,
Yet ye are seven! I pray you tell,
Sweet maid, how this may be."
Then did the little maid reply,
"Seven boys and girls are we;
Two of us in the churchyard lie,
Beneath the churchyard tree."
"You run about, my little maid,
Your limbs they are alive;
If two are in the churchyard laid,
Then ye are only five."
"Their graves are green, they may be seen,"
The little maid replied,
"Twelve steps or more from my mother's door,
And they are side by side.
"My stockings there I often knit,
My kerchief there I hem;
And there upon the ground I sit,
And sing a song to them.
"And often after sunset, sir,
When it is light and fair,
I take my little porringer,
And eat my supper there.

The little girl then explains that first her sister Jane died from sickness. She and her brother John would play around her grave until he also died. Now he lies next to Jane:

"The first that died was sister Jane;
In bed she moaning lay,
Till God released her of her pain;
And then she went away.
"So in the churchyard she was laid;
And, when the grass was dry,
Together round her grave we played,
My brother John and I.
"And when the ground was white with snow
And I could run and slide,
My brother John was forced to go,
And he lies by her side."

The man again asks how many siblings she has now that two are dead. She replies quickly, "O Master! we are seven." The man tries to convince her saying, "But they are dead," but he realizes that his words are wasted. The poem ends with the little girl saying, "Nay, we are seven!"

"How many are you, then," said I,
"If they two are in heaven?"
Quick was the little maid's reply,
"O master! we are seven."
"But they are dead; those two are dead!
Their spirits are in heaven!"
'Twas throwing words away; for still
The little maid would have her will,
And said, "Nay, we are seven!"

Analysis

"We Are Seven" was written in 1798, when Wordsworth was only 18 years old. The poem is composed of sixteen four-line stanzas, and ends with one five-line stanza. Each stanza has an abab rhyming pattern. Wordsworth has noted that he wrote the last line of this poem first, and that his good friend Samuel Coleridge wrote the first few stanzas.

The poem is an interesting conversation between a man and a young girl. It is especially intriguing because the conversation could have been less than five lines, and yet it is 69 lines long. The reason for this is that the man cannot accept that the young girl still feels she is one of seven siblings even after two of her siblings have died, and even though she now lives at home alone with her mother.

The speaker begins the poem with the question of what a child should know of death. Near the beginning it seems as if the little girl understands very little. She seems almost to be in denial about the deaths of her siblings, especially because she continues to spend time with them and sing to them. By the end of the poem, however, the reader is left with the feeling that perhaps the little girl understands more about life and death than the man to whom she is speaking. She refuses to become incapacitated by grief, or to cast the deceased out of her life. Instead she accepts that things change, and continues living as happily as she can.

Chapter 11

Critical Essays

Wordsworth and Blake: The Plight of Mankind

William Wordsworth and William Blake were both distraught by the plight of man in the early nineteenth century. Their separate but somewhat unified visions of man's problems are displayed in their poems "Lines Written in Early Spring," (lines 5-24) and "London," respectively. They both make use of several poetic devices in very different manners to convey nearly the same meaning. Each poet uses the mood of his poem to show how deep in strife man truly is, though the tone of each poem vastly contrasts with the other. Both Blake and Wordsworth also link man to another entity, and each also use meter and rhyme scheme to show the same. Stylistically, the poems are extremely dissimilar, and the contents of each are tremendously unalike, but ultimately, they both point out the same issues with which man is dealing.

Wordsworth's "Lines" sets the tone immediately by setting the reader in a pleasant situation and using peaceful imagery. The reader is brought to a grove in which the writer is observing Nature; the birds "hopped and played" , which "seemed a thrill of pleasure" , and "The budding twigs spread out their fan/To catch the breezy air" . He works at illustrating the joy and serenity around him while only hinting at the much darker plight of man without spelling it out, without even coming close to breaking the tone he has so carefully constructed. In fact, because he purposely avoids saying exactly what it is that "man has made of man" , he allows the reader to imagine the entire quandary on his own, and in contrast to the peaceable surroundings at the grove, the reader is very likely to imagine the worst. Blake, on the other hand, uses harsh and tragic imagery to convey just how harsh and tragic the world was. While Wordsworth's tactic was to use soft imagery to show how troubled man was, Blake utilizes severe imagery to show the same. He writes that the "hapless Soldier's sigh/Runs in blood down Palace walls" , and makes use twice of infants crying (6,15). He uses words that press upon the reader images of being ruled, of being oppressed. The minds of the working class men are shackled, and the streets and the river themselves are "chartered," or sanctioned by the ruling class.

He juxtaposes the words 'marriage' and 'hearse' in the last line, as the final two words of the poem, to show that everything that once stood for life and happiness now means death and sadness. While Wordsworth subtly hints at the problems man has imposed upon himself, Blake forces them upon the reader so that the point cannot be missed.

One of the most vivid images Blake brings into play is that of the "black'ning church" . It is crucial that one takes into account the meanings of this line. The word 'black'ning' functions as both transitive and intransitive. The church is both becoming more blackened and working as a blackening agent to the people, such as the chimney sweeper in the preceding line. The church, or those who run the church, are not doing their jobs in the world that Blake is depicting. The church is associated with the elitist ruling class, and the church itself is becoming filthy, covered with the soot of oppression while dishing it out, perpetuating the ruling class tyranny.

Wordsworth also brings God into his poem and comments upon His role in the world he is describing. In "Lines," man is tied to Nature, and Nature to God. Every element in Wordworth's poem is enjoying the simple act of being. When he writes in the last stanza, "If this belief from heaven be sent/ If such be Nature's holy plan/Have I not reason to lament/What man has made of man?" , he is saying clearly that though we are intended to live as Nature lives, man is not doing so, hence his sadness. We are not following the plan. In both poems,

God is being disobeyed, and it is in part this disobedience that is causing so much discord, though perhaps it is said more explicitly by Blake than Wordsworth.

In writing about Nature enjoying the act of being, Wordsworth is doing more than just showing that we are not following God's plan. He is also showing the link between man and Nature through personification. He writes that "...every flower/Enjoys the air it breathes" , and that the branches "...spread out their fan/To catch the breezy air". Earlier, in saying that Nature is linked to "The human soul that through me ran" , he is later showing how there is a little human soul in every movement and action of Nature, such as in the acts of the flower enjoying breathing and the twigs finding pleasure in the breeze. He is writing about how things should be, and simply stating that they are not.

Blake, on the other hand, writes bluntly about what is, and does not bother with how things should be. He does this by linking the working man to the institution of the elitist oppressing upper class. Blake strategically capitalizes only particular words in his poem. Every word he capitalizes is either a member of the rural class. He is showing subtly that man and the institution are in direct opposition to one another, and by capitalizing them, he is giving them both the power to dominate. Both poets link man with another entity in order to show a problem in the system.

Blake and Wordsworth also use their language to help express the crisis of man. Blake uses complex wording to reflect the complexity of the problems. He is trying to depict a world in which the rapidly industrializing economy is corrupting and poisoning everything with which it comes into contact. He uses lines such as "mind-forged manacles" , which is a complicated and terrible thought conveyed in a mere two words, and "Every black'ning Church appalls" , which is also a complicated line, being that it can have more than one meaning. He urges the reader to stop and think about what he is saying, and not to take it lightly. His metaphors are stark and violent, and his lines move quickly and seem almost rushed. This parallels how he feels about man's plight. It is difficult, violent, and is continuing to grow at a rapid pace. Wordsworth, however, uses simple language to show that the problem we have is simple at its base. He uses very a very basic vocabulary to portray very basic imagery; in fact he uses only one word in the entire poem that is more than two syllables.

The reader does not need more than this in order to see that a problem exists, particularly since Wordsworth wants the reader to envision the problem in his own way. More complex words might invite a more complex image, which the poet does not want. He merely wants to show that man is not in accordance with his roots, which is a simple idea that can be expressed in a simple manner. The roots themselves are simple, being that man should enjoy life for what it is, and not make anything else of mankind.

The meter and rhyme scheme of both poems are also very simple, both being written in iambic pentameter nearly the entire way through, and each sharing an ABAB rhyme scheme. These alternate rhyming lines in "London" serve to perpetuate the monotony and repetitive predictability of the circle of suffering in the city. However, the meter in the poem is not consistent throughout, beginning with iambic pentameter and then veering towards less conventional trochaic pentameter at line 9, but returning to iambic pentameter for the final line.

This is to assist in showing that everything is not as it should be; the world is in discord. Though Blake makes tremendous effort to show 'how things are,' he makes an effort here to show that this is not how they should be. Things just don't make sense as they are. Wordsworth uses the same sort of strategy in "Lines" as does Blake. Each verse is written in iambic pentameter, with the same simple rhyme scheme as "London." However, the final and fourth line of every stanza is written in iambic tetrameter, being a foot short of the rest of the verse. This leaves the reader feeling somewhat dissatisfied, feeling as is something is missing, that there should be something more. Wordsworth does this for the same reason that Blake does it; to subtly let the reader know that something really isn't right. It leaves the reader with a sensation of discontent, perhaps even near frustration, and causes further thought upon the poem, which is what both poets had planned.

It can be seen through these often subtle and sometimes blatant poetic devices that both Blake and Wordsworth are trying to convey to the reader that there is an underlying problem facing mankind. Though they go about it in contrasting ways, the means with which they portray their particular ideas are the same. Through imagery, tone, and meter, among other tactics, each shows in his own way that there is something very wrong with man in this particular time setting.

Chapter 12

Figures of Revision in Wordsworth's Critical Arguments

This essay deals with three key arguments in Wordsworth's poetics: the theorisation of tautology; the definition of the poet; and the relationship between thoughts and feelings. The peculiar discursive manoeuvres of these three arguments may be called figurative revisions. Although the literal notion of revision has its own place, the more comprehensive conceptualisation of revision presented here cannot rely solely on it: understandably, the notion of revision, therefore, has reference not only to that literal activity of making retrospective changes in a text, but even more so to that turning around associated with it.

It is in this turning around, this looking again, that revision—or re-vision1—constitutes a form of textual self-consciousness that is examined here. No less is revision a form of reflexivity.

But this conceptual broadening also requires a reassessment of the relationship between the literal and figurative already radicalised by Derrida's conceptualisation of writing not as a mere scriptive activity but as a spatio-temporal structure. Tracing the "metaphoric transitions" in Freud's theorisation of the psyche in a "Note on the Mystic Pad" Derrida asserts that "the 'objectivist' or 'worldly' consideration of writing teaches us nothing if reference is not made to a psychical space of writing".

Thus no more is the figurative a supplement of the literal; in fact, it is the figurative, according to Derrida, which constitutes the conditions of possibility for a conceptualisation of the literal. Moreover, this methodological initiative gives us incentive to treat the seemingly incidental as being essentially central. Consider how Derrida traces out the process by which scriptural metaphors enter into and take over Freud's model of memory.

As always, a problem of this nature begs the question: what procedure do we adopt to assess such an elusive issue? We may try to answer such a question by examining the manner in which the problematic begins to be articulated for us in critical discourse.

Even the most abbreviated survey suggests how we encounter it disguised, for instance, as Frances Ferguson's notion of "reading" that "proleptic and retrogressive movement in Wordsworth's poetry" (xiv); as Clifford Siskin's "interpretation"; as Isobel Armstrong's "repetition"; as Cynthia Chase's "disfigurement". (Or even as Howard Bloom's "revisionary ratios" which stipulate that all writing is indeed rewriting.) Nowhere is it more pronounced than in Armstrong's suggestion that in critical moments Wordsworth's poetry appears to "reread" itself like a text. To sum it up in Raymond Carney's words, "we need to begin to talk about writing as a process with a significance in and of itself, composition as an activity of consciousness and not merely as a means of producing ultimate meanings".

The obvious lack of coordination between these various pronouncements issues its own methodological challenges. But these may need to be taken up elsewhere. For the time being, however, these critical gestures serve to situate the issue for us: Wordsworth's discourse gives evidence of the unintended textualisation of self-division. At the same time, these articulations of the problematic of revision become the pretext for our particular interventions in Wordsworth scholarship.

Although the examples given here refer only to the occurrences of figurative revisions in Wordsworth's poetic discourse, the present inquiry takes it even further to demonstrate how such revisions, in fact, occur in another form in Wordsworth's critical discourse. These examples of

Wordsworth's critical discourse, we further argue, become self-enacting revisions when they trace out their own procedures. Taken together with Wordsworth's habits of composition (characterised by the incessant revisions of The Prelude, for instance), these discursive manoeuvres cannot be ignored: perhaps, these more figurative forms of revision foreground the possibility of an actual romantic praxis.4 That is why they are also prefigurative.

In methodological matters we will, therefore, be guided not only by Derrida's notion of the inseparability of the literal and the figurative mentioned above, but also by Hayden White's insights into the prefigurative possibilities of discourse. The very nature of the issue makes this both a necessity and a possibility. As Hayden White suggests, "troping is the soul of discourse" which effects its "adequation by a prefigurative move that is more tropical than logical"

This prefigurative move in Wordsworth's case, we argue, is apparent in such discursive gestures as, for instance, his valorisation of tautology. If troping is the soul of discourse, then the proximity of repetition and revision may not be dismissed as incidental. Following Derrida's methodology of tracing out the metaphoric transitions in Freud's discussion of memory mentioned earlier we affirm the essential centrality of the apparently incidental. Repetition thus becomes the possibility for revision. As we shall see, the figure of revision continues to insinuate itself throughout Wordsworth's discourse as a master trope.

But this is no ordinary trope, either; revision, we might say, is a trope of trope contingently produced by certain discursive movements. The difficulty in describing it derives in no small measure from this form of constitutedness: thus, while the examples of discourse in which the figure of revision lies embedded are themselves actual, the discursive manoeuvres which produce it are not. These are notional.

Wordsworth's spirited defence of tautology5 in "The Note to 'The Thorn,'" (1800) is an instructive example for our argument and sets the stage for a discussion of our subsequent examples:

There is a numerous class of readers who imagine that the same words cannot be repeated without tautology: this is a great error: virtual tautology is much oftener produced by using different words when the meaning is exactly the same... . There are also various other reasons why repetition and apparent tautology are frequently beauties of the highest kind. Among the chief of these reasons is the interest which the mind attaches to words, not only as symbols of the passion, but as things, active and efficient, which are of themselves part of the passion.

It is Wordsworth's particular form of problematisation that invites speculation about repetition as a condition of possibility for revision as a master trope: tautology is consolidated by the very processes aimed at eliminating it. Thus the very strategies aimed at eliminating tautology (for instance, using different words when the meaning is the same) leads even more to "virtual tautology."

Tautology is thus far more fundamental than it initially appears; it is connected with the functioning of meaning in language. If different words can be used when the meaning is the same, then it suggests that meaning exceeds the expressive powers of words. Meaning cannot be completely exhausted by words and continues beyond them. In fact, tautology it seems occurs when language runs up against its own representational limitations. But interestingly, tautology marks not only the representational limitations of language, but the very possibility of transcending them.

This is a crucial point. Because it is here that the argument begins to turn into a self-performing trope. Notice Wordsworth's ambivalence towards "repetition and apparent tautology" which are seen initially as the externalities of language, its form, as distinct from its content, "the meaning." But the implicit privileging of a presumed content of language over its form notwithstanding, Wordsworth asserts ultimately that "there are also various other reasons why repetition and apparent tautology are frequent beauties of the highest kind." Far from being a mindless repetition of words, tautology is an expression of this complexity and depth of human feelings.6

The distinct stages of Wordsworth's argument here form a dialectical pattern: first, tautology is presented as an inevitability connected with the functioning of meaning in language; second, it is seen as an externality; third, it is reassimilated into a final synthesis as an essential part of the very content to which it was considered external. The same manoeuvre is discernible in Wordsworth's assertion that not only are words "symbols of the passion," but also "themselves part of the passion." Words are not just representations of our feelings but also constitutive of them.

In this synthesis of form and content Wordsworth's argument executes that turning movement we call a figurative revision. With neither form or content left as an absolute origin any perceived discrepancies may have been resolved pre-emptively. This is essentially a reflexive moment in which the discourse comes to terms with itself. Thus Wordsworth's argument for repetition not only promotes the possibility of revision but also enacts it discursively.

The thrust of our argument is in the direction of the notion of trope as a form of self-enacting stylistics. Hayden White delineates the process by which the different meanings (from classical Greek, Koiné, classical and late Latin) sedimented in the early English word trope, capture the force of the concept that modern English intends by the word sty1e, a concept that is especially apt for the consideration of that form of verbal composition which, in order to distinguish it from logical demonstration on the one side and from pure fiction on the other, we call by the name of discourse.

Taking this as an endorsement for the tropological possibilities of Wordsworth's discourse that we have been developing, we can further demonstrate the preponderance of the figures of revision in his other arguments. The self-performing nature of such revisions is nowhere more apparent than in Wordsworth's definition of a poet:

What is a Poet? To whom does he address himself? And what language is to be expected from him?—He is a man speaking to men: a man it is true, endowed with more lively sensibility, more enthusiasm and tenderness, who has a greater knowledge of human nature, and a more comprehensive soul, than are supposed to be common among mankind. ("The Preface" 138)

This is an argument for difference of degree as distinct from a difference of kind: the poet possesses "more" of the same sensibilities as the "common man." What is interesting about this argument is the manner in which it sustains itself through a tropological effect enacted by means of a progressive repetition, if you will. Consider, for instance, the almost interminable chain of comparatives: "more enthusiasm and tenderness"; "greater knowledge of human nature"; "a more comprehensive soul"; "rejoices more than other men in the spirit of life"; "a disposition to be affected more than other men by absent things as if they were present"; "a greater readiness and power in expressing what he thinks and feels." The multiplicity of disparate elements notwithstanding, in the end what we have is the repetition of that sense of "moreness." This is only one aspect of the self-performing revision.

However, what we seek to disclose ultimately is that form of revision which arises as a direct consequence of the inherent difficulties in Wordsworth's formulations. In this case as we note, Wordsworth's strategy consists of deploying the principle of difference of degree as a way out of the difficulty: "Among the qualities there enumerated as principally conducing to form a Poet, is implied nothing differing in kind from other men, but only in degree" ("The Preface" 142).

But this, too, smacks of hierarchy that Wordsworth might have liked to avoid. The democratisation Wordsworth sought was fraught with difficulties even at a discursive level. Revisions are symptomatic of the many pitfalls of Wordsworth's particular form of reasoning; and the attempt to forestall the aporetic crises to which they give rise. (Whether these attempts succeed is another matter).

The argument for difference of degree is another aspect of the argument for difference in similarity. The latter surfaces in the course of Wordsworth's associationist arguments as he asserts that the mind recognises a major contrast between the language of the common people and the metre which is superimposed upon it. But each—that is, the language of the common people and the super-imposed metre—evokes in its turn its own kind of associations: Wordsworth's language is meant to evoke the language of the common people on which it is modelled; while metre is intended to evoke the memory of "pleasure which has been previously received from works of rhyme or metre of the same or similar construction." Together, "all these imperceptibly make up a complex feeling of delight" ("The Preface" 151); and it is this complex feeling of delight that results in the heightening of the language of the common people. Thus difference can be accommodated to similarity.

We should keep in mind that this accommodation of difference to similarity is also consistent with the general programme of "The Preface" which seeks to highlight "the pleasure which the mind derives from the perception of similitude in dissimilitude" . "This principle," as Wordsworth maintains, "is the great spring of the activity of our minds, and their chief feeder." So seminal is this principle—of similitude in dissimilitude and dissimilitude in similitude—that Wordsworth connects it with the "sexual appetites"; "the life of our ordinary conversation"; and our "tastes and our moral feelings."

The attendant difficulties of the argument for difference of degree, however, continue to dog his steps: this occurs, for instance, when Wordsworth moves on to describe the poet in terms of his ability to make the absent present. If the poet, as Wordsworth maintains, is separated from his audience in possessing a deeper perception of things (although not a different language), then he is even more different in possessing the power to make the absent present. But these are contradictory demands.

It is in order to reconcile them that Wordsworth suggests that the role of the poet is that of "a translator, who does not scruple to substitute excellencies of another kind for those which are unattainable by him; and endeavours occasionally to surpass his original, in order to make some amends for the general inferiority to which he feels that he must submit" ("The

Preface" 139). Is nature, then, inferior to art? The poet, Wordsworth suggests, "considers man and nature as essentially adapted to each other, and the mind of man as naturally the mirror of the fairest and most interesting properties of nature" ("The Preface" 140). In defining the role of the poet as that of a translator Wordsworth abandons the mimetic in favour of the transformative as the principal criterion of Romantic art that the poet must endeavour to fulfil. In fact, this oscillation between the mimetic and transformative in "The Preface" indicates Wordsworth's attempt to balance each criterion against the other and resolve the contradictions which would otherwise lead to absurd conclusions.

How can the poet represent the absent without falsifying it? And how can the poet represent the real without being unpleasant? The notion of revision we are proposing serves as a description of the implicit strategies of containment adopted by Wordsworth's discourse. The formulation of critical issues apart, the discourse in "The Preface" is implicated in averting its own crises of self-dissolution.

Consider how Wordsworth anticipates the problem of representation when he says that although the poet "describes and imitates passions, his employment is in some degree mechanical, compared with the freedom and power of real and substantial action and suffering" ("The Preface" 138). The poet's imagined passions are no substitute for the emotions arising out of real situations—and the poet's passions are always imagined passions because the poet's task is to conjure up emotions not immediately present; in other words, to re-present the absent, or more significantly, to revise the absent original. Wordsworth maintains a distinction between reality and its representation.

It is because of this distinction that Wordsworth is able to suggest that the poet must endeavour not only to "bring his feelings near to those of the persons whose feelings he describes," but must also when necessary, "let himself slip into an entire delusion, and even confound and identify his own feelings with theirs"—but not without modifying "the language which is thus suggested to him by a consideration that he describes for a particular purpose, that of giving pleasure." Thus, although the poet's imitation of emotions should conform to the highest standards of fidelity, the language he uses must on the other hand be modified where necessary. The so-called "principle of selection" which enables the poet to filter out "what would otherwise be painful or disgusting in the passion" constitutes in essence a form of revision which is integral to the sort of poetic theory Wordsworth is endorsing.

In an earlier statement Wordsworth observes parenthetically that although he has adopted the language of the common people he has, nevertheless, purified it "from what appear to be its real defects, from all lasting and rational causes of dislike or disgust" ("The Preface" 125). There seems to be a fundamental contradiction here: Wordsworth believes that he must incorporate the language of the common people in his poetry and yet he finds that in its natural state this language has elements that are unsuitable for his poetry.

Throughout "The Preface" Wordsworth's customary practice has been to resolve contradictions by playing them down and then reassimilating them by means of a revisionary manoeuvre. As in this case, Wordsworth begins by affirming his faith in the language of the rural masses as a model worthy of emulation. The language of the rural masses was chosen "because such men hourly communicate with the best objects from which the best part of language is originally derived" ("The Preface" 125).

But even as Wordsworth is making this argument he realises that eventually it cannot stand up to scrutiny; and towards the end of a series of long statements maintaining his faith in the virtues of "humble and rustic life" Wordsworth cannot refrain from expressing his doubts albeit parenthetically. Why should a language allegedly suited for poetry require purification? As Wordsworth tells us, "such a language arising out of repeated experience and regular feelings, is a more permanent, and a far more philosophical language" than the one substituted for it by poets. In other words, such a language is unpremeditated and sincere. But this formulation comes at the cost of a critical blindness on Wordsworth's part: when emulated in poetry this language cannot remain unpremeditated.

What Wordsworth calls "purification" itself constitutes a form of revision: the language of the common people has been "purified indeed from what appear to be its real defects, from all lasting and rational causes of dislike or disgust." Wordsworth's argument would suggest that nature in its pristine state still needs modification in order to be integrated into the subject's consciousness. The manifest ambivalence of Wordsworth's discourse highlighted thus far arises as a consequence of revisions, the strategies of containment which assume a number of forms, some of them self-performing. But perhaps the self-performing aspect of such revisions is nowhere more evident than in his discussion on the relation between thoughts and feelings:

> For our continued influxes of feeling are modified and directed by our thoughts, which are indeed the representatives of all our past feelings; and, as by contemplating the relation of these general representatives to each other, we discover what is really important to men, so by the repetition and continuance of this act, our feelings will be connected with important subjects.

At first, thoughts appear to be prior to feelings; but the distinction between thoughts and feelings is collapsed as we learn that thoughts are actually "representatives of all our past feelings" transformed by protracted introspection—the Wordsworthian "contemplation." Thoughts "direct"—that is, correct—feelings in such a manner that we could say that feelings are re-vised by the higher faculty of thought. But this revision is pre-eminently a self-revision, the self-revision of feeling, for in the beginning, if we follow Wordsworth's logic, before thoughts have become feelings there are only feelings. For these first feelings which are prior to thoughts—the ur-thoughts—to become thoughts there must be some kind of self-transformation brought on by contemplation as there are no prior thoughts to direct them. Contemplation—or as we often call it, reflection—is a process in which consciousness examines itself and its own contents; it becomes aware of itself as consciousness. This opens up a further possibility for our discussion of revision: revision-as-reflection.

Self-reflexiveness, Wordsworth seems to suggest, is an originary act. Feelings can come into being only if they become aware of their status as feelings—that is, by a self-reflexiveness that is also the property of consciousness. Wordsworth's hierarchisation of thoughts and feelings appears to be only provisional—and it is in its provisionality that this hierarchisation proves to be self-deconstructive: at first feelings are directed by thoughts, which are themselves past feelings modified by contemplation.

In this inconsistent problematisation of origins Wordsworth's revisionary manoeuvre is to assimilate thoughts to feelings. But this still leaves "feelings" as an absolute origin. As we reach back, we find feelings to be prior to thoughts when we thought it to be otherwise. What, then, differentiates thoughts and feelings is revision: feelings (self-)revised are thoughts. And so the process continues, as Wordsworth himself points out, "by the repetition and continuance of this act." Continuity and revision go hand in hand—only through repeated acts of revision can continuity be maintained. Revision ensures the continuity of Continuity.

The preceding analysis of thoughts modifying feelings paves the way for an understanding of the role of meditation and the notion of revision-as-reflection. We move towards these through Wordsworth's awareness that his poetry is set against that of his contemporaries—whose "triviality and meanness" he roundly derides. The distinctive feature of his poetry as he tells us is that it has a "worthy purpose". Purpose is thus the differentiating feature of Wordsworth's poetry; but unfortunately, this differentiating feature contradicts another cardinal principle of Wordsworth's poetry: spontaneity. The contrary demands of purpose and spontaneity must now be balanced:

> Not that I always began to write with a distinct purpose formally conceived; but habits of meditation have, I trust, so prompted and regulated my feelings, that my descriptions of such objects as strongly excite those feelings, will be found to

carry along with them a purpose. If this opinion be erroneous, I can have little right to the name of a Poet. For all good poetry is the spontaneous overflow of powerful feelings. As a poet Wordsworth has trained himself to be introspective: although the feelings he experiences—even in the absence of real events and objects of nature that occasion them—are spontaneous they are nevertheless modified—that is, "regulated"—by introspection. Without such regulation the spontaneous overflow of powerful feelings would degenerate into mere sentimentality, and, purposelessness. The Wordsworthian notion of spontaneity is thus not an unqualified one and is subordinated to Romantic meditation.

Although all good poetry as Wordsworth tells us is the spontaneous overflow of powerful feelings, these feelings have been transformed through meditation into the artistic substance of poetry. But crucially such a transformation constitutes a form of revision. After all, no good poetry, as Wordsworth says, was ever produced "but by a man who, being possessed of more than unusual organic sensibility, had also thought long and deeply" ("The Preface" 127). Sensibility itself is not enough to qualify one for the office of a poet; to be a poet one must possess the ability to transform one's sensibility into the artistic substance of poetry through contemplation. It is this formulation of Romantic meditation that opens up the possibility of conceptualising it as revision-as-reflection.

The now-famous passage in "The Preface" can be taken as a comment on the nature of Romantic meditation which is at once revisionary and transformative:

> I have said that poetry is the spontaneous overflow of powerful feelings: it takes its origin from emotion recollected in tranquillity: the emotion is contemplated till, by a species of re-action, the tranquillity gradually disappears, and an emotion, kindred to that which was before the subject of contemplation, is gradually produced, and does itself actually exist in the mind.

Recollection presupposes a temporal separation that itself imposes a form of revision, or re-vision, that is, a looking again, or looking back at the real events which gave rise to the emotions now being contemplated in tranquillity. But recollection simultaneously puts us in a reflective or contemplative mood. In this sense recollection and contemplation go together. We do not just remember past events, we also meditate upon them and examine their constitution. In recollecting them we also transform them. Recollection is thus also an examination of the contents of consciousness in the sense of reflection. Together recollection and contemplation form a complex process—that "species of re-action" which, to reiterate an earlier point made in this discussion, make for the possibility of revision-as-reflection.

In analysing the discursive manoeuvres of the key arguments of "The Preface" we have encountered the various figures of revision. These essentially imply a sense of doubling. The same sense of doubling also informs the literal act of reconfiguring a text through retrospective insertions and extensions. But the crux of the matter is that such an act, however literal, cannot take place without figurative self-transformations of consciousness. In taking the text from one configuration to another consciousness—or what has been called consciousness-as-writing cannot but revise itself in the process. Thus the embededness of the figurative in the literal.

The conceptual framework for such a theory of revision that we have been implicitly sketching out rests on our understanding of Wordsworth's own formulation of repetition delineated above—an approximation of which can be found in Wordsworth's poetic practices: repetition marks a peculiar motion illustrated fittingly by such descriptions as "My horse trudg'd on, and we drew nigh"; or, "My horse mov'd on; hoof after hoof". Trudging on constitutes progression through repetitiveness, bringing precept and praxis together. Evidently, repetition does not carry the pejorative connotations of stasis; rather it signifies advancement for Wordsworth, albeit by degrees. As Søren Kierkegaard says, "Indeed, if there were no repetition, what then would life be? Who would wish to be a tablet upon which time writes every instant a new inscription? or to be a mere memorial of the past?" .

The purpose here has not been to trip Wordsworth over

as he goes about the business of constructing the arguments crucial to his poetics; but to show the discursive struggles inherent in such a project. We have also demonstrated how the possibilities for a broader formulation of revision, one that embraces the literal and figurative at once, is already available to us in Wordsworth's "Prefaces." Both its discursive manoeuvres (explored here through some of Hayden White's insights into the tropological qualities of discourse) and its formulations offer such possibilities. We have also argued that the possibility for such a conceptualisation of revision lies through an essential crisis that shows how tentative the boundaries between the literal and the figurative are. The object in this enterprise has been to understand the "psychical space of writing"—or, as in this case, revision—by enlisting Wordsworth on our side.

Chapter 13

The Religious Influence of the Romantic Poets

For the present purposes, our interest in the romantic poets is less for the sake of their own convictions than for ascertaining the nature of their influence on English society. In their critique of modern society the Lake poets, in common with so many nineteenth century critics, tended to idealize the medieval period.

The new industrialism they believed carried with it a dehumanization, a loss of many values that the Middle Ages had honored by preserving the religious heritage of Europe. The ramshackle, crowded, and noisome tenements in the modern industrial towns compared badly with what they imagined to be the felicities of the stone cottages of previous centuries. Pride in work well done had given way to shoddy goods sold at the highest possible prices.

Paradoxically, then, the Lake romantics in opening up to nineteenth-century readers a segment of reality closed by the ideological narrowness of the Enlightenment, at the same time denied their readers the perspective to be afforded by a historical viewpoint less colored by sentimentality and wishful thinking. But withal the tendency to obscure certain aspects of reality, the romantics retained, as their contemporaries the utilitarians did not, the conviction that society could not progress beyond the spiritual level of the populace. "There is no other means whereby nations can be reformed," Southey wrote, "than by that which alone individuals can be regenerated" [Quoted in Roberts, Paternalism, 60].

These poets influenced their society in ways that are literally immeasurable because they were repeated in thousands of anonymous individual hearts. The memoirs of the intellectuals who tell of this influence must be multiplied many times to gain an understanding of the work that was done. When John Stuart Mill descended into a state of severe depression that he feared would never release him, a victim of the dehumanizing Benthamite philosophy in which his father had trained him, Wordsworth lifted him out of it with poetry that acted, as Mill put it, like "medicine" to his soul. At the same time Coleridge delivered him from an atomistic philosophy to a recognition of the organic nature of society.

Wordsworth also played a marked role on the Oxford, or Tractarian, movement, and therefore on the religious history of much of the century, through his influence on John Keble. Keble's enormously popular book of devotional poetry, The Christian Year (1827), was inspired largely by Wordsworth's influence, and so was his Lectures on Poetry. When Keble published the latter volume in 1844 it was with a dedication to Wordsworth. To william wordsworth true philosopher and inspired poet who by the special gift and calling of almighty god whether he sang of man or of nature failed not to lift up men's hearts to holy things nor ever ceased to champion the cause of the poor and simple and so in perilous times was raised up to be a chief mlnister 3 not only of sweetest poetry

But also of high and sacred truth..

The two close friends Wordsworth and Coleridge represent a one-two punch on the English mind for much of the nineteenth century.

Wordsworth, as we saw in Mill's testimony, provided a kind of soul-healing in people coming out of a the bleak night of a dehumanized rationalism and needed to be taught that it was legitimate to have and show feelings, while Coleridge's rooting of theology in its historical context anchored it in the realities of collective human experience, much as the Bible did. [I take this analysis from Prickett, 148f.] "Yet in spite of his acknowledged influence on Keble and Newman, it is still all too easy to overlook the enormous influence Wordsworth had on the development of English theology in these years. To some extent this is a matter of kinds of influence. The contrast with Coleridge is instructive. The Coleridge who was important to nineteenth-century thought was Coleridge the metaphysician and theologian, not Coleridge the poet — even though it would be true to say that Coleridge could only have been the massive theological influence he was because he remained first and foremost a poet. Wordsworth's influence, in contrast, is not theoretical at all. His achievement was that he transformed the whole climate of feeling in the first half of the nineteenth century in England.

He was not a source of ideas, but he had a very great effect on the emotional structure which produced and nourished those ideas. His influence is pervasive and diffuse rather than concentrated and specific, but the testimony of such temperamental opposites as Mill and Keble is strong evidence of his power over the emotional development of a whole generation. What Wordsworth offered sensitive minds in the 1820s and '30s (in a way that not even Coleridge could) was the affirmation that man was more than a mere biological mechanism: he was a creature of profound and subtle feelings. 'Feelings' became for many Wordsworthians a touchstone of their humanity — a proof of Being.

It is easy for the modern reader, outside this emotional climate, to misunderstand the impact of a poem like Simon Lee, which is a poem about feeling. Wordsworth not merely asserted the value of feeling humanity he showed it as an artist, as a poet. His readers could feel the value of feeling. In a vulgarised strain a similar spirit had entered the novel— responsible, alas!, for some of Dickens's weepiest writing, which dates from this period."]

Another Christian poet, the only outstanding one of the Anglican Evangelical party, was William Cowper, whose poems were recited and sung for many decades, indeed up to the present. The young Edward Fitzgerald, future translater of Omar Khayyam, wrote to Thackeray that some of Cowper's poems are more affecting than anything in the language. "...they make me cry"

Chapter 14

The Poetics of Place and Time in Wordsworth's "Tintern Abbey"

Tintern Abbey is, today, a ruin, as it was when Wordsworth visited it in 1793 and again in 1798. The abbey no longer serves its original function as a place of worship, but it still stands as a reminder, a monument to that original function—we therefore call it a ruin. The process of falling-into-ruin has both a temporal and a spatial dimension. A ruin has fallen away both from the moment and the form of its original determination. Wordsworth's poem, "Tintern Abbey, "is, today, a ruin—a textual trace whose meaning is constituted by temporal and spatial references that have fallen away.

It has been set adrift from its proper historical and geographical site, subjected to a series of displacements—an errance. Each reading that we give it, each new critical treatment, displaces it further from itself.

In some ways, of course, one can say that about many poems. What makes "Tintern Abbey" fascinating is that the original site of determination within the poem already contains a lack, a lacuna that stands as the prefiguration of falling-into-ruin. This Promethean sign, as it were, has then determined the trajectory of this textual ruin's errance. The aim of my paper today is to outline this textual absence, and to describe the ways in which it has conditioned a particular trajectory of scholarship on the poem.

I will begin, not at the beginning, but in 1986, with Marjorie Levinson's book entitled "Wordsworth's Great Period Poems." This text itself occupies a very interesting position in the history of Romantic criticism. Writing at a time when historicism had just emerged as a major methodology in the study of literature, Levinson sets it against Yale'criticism: Bloom, Abrams and de Man.

Levinson's textual agenda is complicated, for it attempts actually to mediate between the two schools rather than simply describe or oppose them. We are unable to consider it fully here, but this mediation will make itself apparent as we turn to one of the chapters—"Insight and Oversight: Reading 'Tintern Abbey.'" Rather than summarise the argument of this chapter, which some of you are already familiar with, I will try to bring out the hermeneutic model at work in it, and some of the critical assumptions that provide the grounding logic.

Levinson points out that movements of dissolution recur within the poem, moments of dispersion that always seem to follow the apparition of seemingly stable points of reference: "an object does not materialize in the poem before it is effaced or smudged; a thought does not find its full articulation before it is qualified or deconstructed; a point of view is not established before it dissolves into a series of impressions". Taken together with the very conspicuous absence of any description or substantive reference to the Abbey itself in the poem that bears it in its title, Levinson identifies the key poetic gesture in the poem as one of escape or erasure. Faced with such a lack of textual co-operation, the critical piece retreats to "the writing dimension -the order of authorial and contextual urgencies".

Levinson's reading centers on the first stanza of the poem, which is read in terms of metaphoric transformations, yielding a structure that is then used as "a synecdoche for Wordsworth's overall poetic project". This structure, according to Levinson, is characterised by the systematic replacement of physical components of the prospect as it presented itself to Wordsworth as observer, with the sensations and feelings which they produce. The critical task at hand would be to undo this substitution, this erasure, in order to read. The text therefore becomes for Levinson a palimpsest. One reads a palimpsest, of course, by erasing text after text, and that is what Levinson attempts to do—to strip away layers of concealment, mystification and aestheticisation to reveal the poem's true meaning:

In order to make sense of Wordsworth's advertised exclusion, one would have to infer some problem—in the poet's mind, in the prospect, or in both—that the poem at once solves and conceals .

The final goal, then, is what Northrop Frye calls the "occasion" of lyric poetry—an original event that is the cause of poetry, and whose passing away is the aim of poetry.

The texts of a palimpsest are written one atop another, and its reading involves the successive erasure of these textual layers. Each new layer that is written on a palimpsest is blind to the previous one; its inscription depends on the erasure of the existing text, but no semantic leakage occurs from one layer to another. By giving us the metaphor of the palimpsest alongside the rhetorical device of synecdoche, Levinson installs doubly a particular hermeneutic logic—once a poetic gesture is described, its subsequent reiterations bear to the original only a relationship of sameness. Repetition itself yields no difference; each instance can be recuperated without residue to the original event.

This is perhaps what explains the most obvious oversight of this critical text itself. The disruptive effect of repetition on the origin, of the recurrence of the same within a structure of difference is a key trope in Wordsworth's poem—in particular, but not exclusively, as it manifests itself as memory. Turning a blind eye to this trope obscures a certain rhetorical trajectory within the poem, creating the false or reduced dichotomy between subjectivity and objectivity, and installing a phantasmagorical dialectic whose sublation constitutes a refusal of historical knowledge.

The best way to elucidate this point would be to turn to the poem itself.

Five years have past; five summers, with the length
Of five long winters! and again I hear
These waters, rolling from their mountain-springs
With a soft inland murmur.

The poem begins with what is already a comment on the ontological position of the original event. Its first words are not the "infinite I AM"of the lyric subject, but rather the setting down of temporal parameters. The occurrence of an original event is held up alongside the time and place of the poetic Jetztzeit. This gesture of setting aside a piece of time, with a past event that flashes up in the present to be apprehended—in short, historical knowledge—is anterior to the lyric subject's act of speaking itself.

The first person pronoun "I" is, here and in each of its subsequent occurrences in the first stanza, bound by the temporal adverbial "again." Within this initial matrix, we already have an explicit situation of lyric subjectivity in relation to history. One would almost be tempted to say that historical knowledge precedes and is therefore logically prior to the authorial voice here, except that the historical itself problematises the origin as event and refuses a simple linear vector of dependence along the axis of temporality.

Each instance of the "I" in the first stanza thus carries an extended referential force. Each acts as an indexical to the speaking subject of the present utterance, but this subject is presented specifically as a double, a simulacrum of an original "I." The multiple acts of deixis in this first stanza similarly inscribe not stable points of reference but traces—cliffs, trees, springs that are both objects-at-hand and objects-past-seen. These ghostly objects are not the products of a destabilising gaze that attempts to transfigure them; rather, their fractured ontology is determined by a fissure within the lyric subject itself. The accumulation of deictic references in these lines therefore signifies an accretion of uncanny simulacra, whose dual natures are held in co-existence.

The holding-in-suspension of this duality does not reify them; instead, it results in a oscillation between the poles of presence and absence, one that is constantly faced with the threat of collapse into an undifferentiated sameness. The movement of the stanza towards this "one green hue," in which historical difference and geographical structures would "lose themselves, "is what Levinson picks up on and calls "organically sublative evolution". At the point of imminent collapse, however, the poem makes an interesting turn, one whose abruptness calls into question the adequacy of "evolution"as a description in this case:

... Once again I see
These hedge-rows, hardly hedge-rows, little lines
Of sportive wood run wild: these pastoral farms,
Green to the very door; and wreaths of smoke
Sent up, in silence, from among the trees,
With some uncertain notice, as might seem,
Of vagrant dwellers in the homeless woods,
Or of some hermit's cave, where by his fire
The hermit sits alone.

The movement from present material trace to original but absent event is here transposed into explicitly literary terms. From the visible wreaths of smoke, we move by specular, or speculative, association to vagrant dwellers. Rhetorical momentum then takes us to the figure of the hermit in his cave. This trajectory can be thus re-described: we move from the visible signifier of "wreaths of smoke,"to conjectured origin embodied as "vagrant dwellers,"to the hermit as mythic archetype. The solipsistic hermit who sits alone in his cave embodies the collapse that surrounds the first stanza as a threat; it is the aftermath of the sublation of sign and origin to yield a transcendent vision.

Where do we go from the hermit, then? How does poetry proceed after this figure of absolute silence and self-containment? Let us take a look:

These beauteous forms,
Through a long absence, have not been to me
As is a landscape to a blind man's eye:
But oft, in lonely rooms, and 'mid the din
Of towns and cities, I have owed to them
In hours of weariness, sensations sweet.

The lyric gaze deflects itself; it turns from the present landscape, with its ghostly history, to the space of time that separates this sighting from the original one. We have, therefore, a break in the flow of logic here, one that mirrors the break inpoetry, signified by the end of one stanza and the start of another. Levinson calls this second stanza the "antistrophe," a turn that enables the poetic subject to perform "a rejection of present place and occasion" to make room for "reflective revision" that will finally allow the subject to attain self-knowledge. This assumes, however, the possibility of a seamless recuperation of part to whole, and of a reconstitutable continuity in the poetic text. It does not take into account, then, the possible signifying function of what lies between strophes. The white space that separates the first stanza from the second represents the limits of poetry.

Within the hermit's cave, once we have attain this sublated position that radically excludes spatial and temporal contiguities, poetry is no longer possible. From this position which obliterates historical and geographical difference and replaces it with the figure of the hermit, the poetic gaze has to turn away. The multiple "I"s of this second stanza now refer to a subjectivity that is dispersed along the axis of temporality, occupying the infinite positions that stretch over the space of time separating original event and enunciatory context.

Each "oft" in this second section installs an instance of the lyric subject as it tries to recollect the original event in the five years that pass. Each, in its own lonely room, is a product of the cognitive act of recollection, a subject not prior to but contemporaneous with its cognitive performance. We have, in short, a decisive and abrupt fragmentation of the subject.

Through this plethora of subject positions, all held up in co-existence, runs another contrapuntal imperative -a suspension that threatens yet again to collapse them into non-differentiation. Again, this threat is transposed into an inward-moving momentum:

Until, the breath of this corporeal frame
And even the motion of our human blood
Almost suspended, we are laid asleep
In body, and become a living soul:
While with an eye made quiet by the power
Of harmony, and the deep power of joy,
We see into the life of things.

As the lyric subject contemplates its multiple fragments along the temporal axis, it holds them in a suspension that elevates them towards a transcendental unity. As before, though, we get a break in the poetry immediately following this point. This moment is represented as a negative ideal, an abyss that poetry is lured towards but which ultimately has to be refused.

Oscillation, suspension, movement towards stasis and unity, followed by blankness and dispersion—this progression is therefore more than a local device; it forms the structure of the poem. Levinson does not fail to note this:

These movements which Hartman designates as turns and counterturns might also be conceived as approaches to and withdrawals from the object of address. By this Pindaric allusion, so to speak, Wordsworth suggests the ultimately elusive, ineffable nature ofhis subject, and the necessity of an approach-avoidance relation to it .

Wordsworth's subject thus far in the poem, however, is nothing less than his own subjectivity. The true other to the lyric voice are the multiple "I"s that have been installed. The approaches and withdrawals, moments of unity and dispersion, therefore destabilise lyric subjectivity itse lf. Within a poem that presents the lyric subject reading himself, we therefore have a structure that renders problematic both the subject matter of the poem and the subjectivity that subtends it.

We move ahead a little now, to the final stanza of the poem, which contains the intriguing address to the figure of the sister:

For thou art with me here upon the banks
Of this fair river; thou my dearest Friend
My dear, dear Friend, and in thy voice I catch
The language of my former heart, and read
My former pleasures in the shooting lights
Of thy wild eyes.

This figure makes is part of the set of circumstances that metonymically surround the lyric speaker. It stands, however, both in a relationship of similarity as well as contiguity to the lyric speaker. The apo strophe thus yields a figure that is present as voice and text, to be heard and read, as well as to hear and read. It is, in short, a full-fledged double of the lyric "I." In this concluding stanza, then, the split between the present lyric "I" and its various manifestations are situated within a dialogic structure.

The addressee is a containing figure, a receptacle in which resides the lyric "I"s fragmented otherness, shards of subjectivity that manifest themselves as the"shooting lights"of the figure's wild eyes. It is at this point, after the trope of address, that the lyric "I" manages for the first time to articulate a presence that does not threaten to sublate into transcendence or fall into fragmentation:

Oh! yet a little while
May I behold in thee what I was once,
My dear, dear Sister! and this prayer I make,

Deixis in the poem—the act of picking out certain unique entities in a given context by the use of terms like "this,"here,"and "now—has thus far been singularly unsuccessful. Seemingly stable or unique objects have repeatedly been exposed as simulacra, fragments of an unavailable whole. In these lines, however, we witness felicitous deixis—the phrase "this prayer"picks out nothing more or less than itself; its reference is neither before nor behind articulation, but contemporaneous with it.

This is the concluding restitution of the poem—the possibility of knowledge and enunciation is available only in this limited sense, as a particular function of articulation and textuality. The lyric subject contains a breach within itself, a lacuna that condemns its attempts at self-knowledge to inevitable failure, for this breach is reproduced in each poetic utterance. It is only by splitting itself off into an equal other, which acts as a mirroring gaze, that it can find a configuration within which the lyric voice and its utterances can persist. This addressee becomes a rhetorical investment, charged with the recollection and reproduction of the poetic subject at a later point in time. It is thus that the poetic text provides for its own survival beyond inevitable death, its own after-life, as it were.

The question, then, is: how do we read such a text today? The problem with Levinson's reading is that it assumes that the poetry originates in illusion and blindness to its own mode of production. This radical skepticism denies the possibility that the poem can itself comment on its origination, and cannot account for such moments in the poem. In the case of "Tintern Abbey, "this insight manifests itself as the critique of unified subjectivity and the lyric voice. The dissolution and dispersion of spatial and historical categories are effects of this fragmentation within the subject. Reconstruction of context, without attentiveness to this relationship, will therefore always yield an incomplete text that cannot be completed by further elaborations along the same lines.

How do we describe the alternative, then? To provide us the terms, I will turn to a later text by Levinson, called "Back to the Future: Wordsworth's New Historicism."Published in The South Atlantic Quarterly in 1989, it is a condensed version of a longer chapter in a collection entitled Rethinking Historicism: Critical Readings in Romantic History. In it, Levinson attempts to describe a historicist reading that is not simply a virtuoso performance of ventriloquism, in which the past becomes a dummy that expresses the truths of our age while our own lips remain unmoving.

As a model of a historicismthat is more genuine, Levinson turns to Benjamin's "The Task of the Translator,"and his mode of translation as a prototype for the sort of criticism that would be able to "restore to the dead their own, living language" . What I want to consider, as a closing gesture, is how Benjamin's text comments on the texts that we have considered so far, and particularly on the notion of history.

Benjamin speaks of translatability as an essential feature of certain works. Linguistic creations can call for their own translation; a particular lack or lac una in the original can manifest itself in its translatability.

The translation belongs to the after-life of the original, and allows it to return at a later point in its history, beyond its own death. Criticism, too, is capable of operating in this particular mode, such that it becomes a part of the continued life of literary works. To do so, the critic has to identify, within the original, the point of lack, the lacuna that manifests itself as a call for critical reading. Benjamin describes this mode thus:

Unlike a work of literature, translation does not find itself in the centre of the language forest but on the outside facing the wooded ridge; it calls into it without entering, aiming at that single spot where the echo is able to give, in its own language, the reverberation of the work in the alien one .

The final product of this mode, then, is an echo, a reverberation that originates from the original work but only after the activation provided by criticism.

In our particular case, with Wordsworth's "Tintern Abbey,"the poem is explicit in naming this necessary lack that will enable its subsequent survival. The Abbey that is so conspicuously missing continues to call for critical reading even today. Too much of this criticism, however, concerns its elf with filling in this lack; the proper place of this lacuna within the poem and its criticism should be as an enabling absence, one that forms the conditions of the possibility of poetry and criticism. Rather than attempt to reconstitute an original whole text, criticism should be conscious of its own place in the history of the text, which, as Paul de Man has argued, is a history of infinite breakages and errance. The poem itself has evacuated the position of origin, by setting into motion the seeminglyoriginal event in a trajectory of infinite regression. The poetic utterance is therefore already adrift, fallen away from this origin.

As our reading of the poem has shown us, movement towards reconciliation with the origin is always synonymous with approaching an abyss, a silence which would obliterate both poetry and criticism. For criticism, this attainment of this moment would be, in Benjamin's terms, the slamming shut of the gates of language to enclose the critic with utter silence. Criticism itselfmust navigate the same treacherous itinerary between the Scylla of irrecuperable fragmentation and the Charybdis of petrified silence.

This is what Benjamin means when he says that original and translation must match each other, although they need not belike one another. The original site of production—Wordsworth's original event, or Benjamin's die reine Sprache—is always already lost; criticism must content itself with being the articulation of fragment to fragment, in order to constitute yet more fragments. We produce, therefore, a textual history that is constantly in errance; to speak in Benjamin's terms, we pile wreckage upon wreckage and hurl them at the feet of the angel of history.

Chapter 15

"Tintern Abbey" and the "Spiritual Presence of Absent Things"

"Tintern Abbey" has been characterized as a poem of absences, with critics such as Jerome McGann citing its "disappearance of particulars," its "strategy of displacement" , and Marjorie Levinson taking issue with its "acts of exclusion" . Their point has been to convince us that the poem is irresponsible, that it obscures socio-economic and political truths that even guidebook writer William Gilpin, in his 1770 description of the Wye Valley (which Wordsworth consulted), did not ignore. I argue, however, that "Tintern Abbey" does indeed possess a moral conscience, though in a form that may be difficult for cultural materialists to comprehend.

When Levinson, for example, says that the poem's values "define a negative ideal: the escape from cultural values" (p.16), she apparently does not include religion as a "cultural value." Thus for her, the poem's many biblical allusions may have seemed insignificant. Indeed, that Wordsworth belonged to a generation "steeped in the Bible— able to use it, quote it and recognise even the most fleeting references or turns of phrase from the Authorised Version... a generation still emotionally in contact with the biblical framework of history" , does not require that he be, in 1798, a proper Anglican. In fact, depending on who was defining Wordsworth's religious proclivities, he was a pantheist , a proponent of "natural religion," or a "semi-atheist." Yet the biblical allusions in "Tintern Abbey" suggest that, whatever Wordsworth did _not_ believe in 1798, he _did_ "believe"; and his faith, embodied by his sister, Dorothy, and based on a culturally deep experience of the Bible and of Anglican liturgy, led him to offer spiritual immortality as the solution to the problems discussed in the poem.

As such, it is a solution we might prefer to believe only an older and more conventional William Wordsworth would dare offer. Yet in the context of "Tintern Abbey"— in the poem Wordsworth _did_ write, not the one he is criticized for not having written— his solution is a conceivably efficacious one aimed at a very narrowly defined set of problems.

Immortality is rooted in duality, in division. It is no accident that, three lines into "Tintern Abbey," Wordsworth begins to divide the landscape: on one hand is the Wye River, and on another is the sky, the two of them connected by the "steep and lofty cliffs" . The first stanza also prefigures the body/soul dichotomy that the second stanza will elaborate on in another way, offering an Edenic setting intended to echo that described in Genesis, the "birthplace" of duality. It was in Eden that man became a "living soul" when God "breathed into his nostrils the breath of life"

Prior to this act, man was merely an "empty" body crafted, as the word "Adame" suggests, from "earth." Like Adam, Wordsworth tells us, we are body first; though we have souls, nature must intervene to remind us of that fact, lulling us into a meditative state in which our "breath" and the "motion of our human blood / [are] [a]lmost suspended" (ll. 44-46). Nature's power to transform the body into "a living soul" is thus a metonymizing one, a short-hand description of God's own act. Seen in this light, pantheism is little more than displaced (or perhaps misprisioned) theism. But then, so is the act of writing poetry.

For the ambiguity of the second stanza allows us to understand that Wordsworth is also asserting a dichotomy between man and poet, the former dulled by the "weary weight / Of all this unintelligible world" (ll. 40-41), and the latter, the "living soul," able to "see into the life of things" (l. 50). To nature the poet owes "another gift" as well, his own creative ability. The possibility that Wordsworth lacks such power, that his belief in himself is in "vain," is one explanation of what distresses him at the beginning of the third stanza.

It is as a poet that Wordsworth best understood the act of creation. Yet the dichotomy he describes in "Tintern Abbey" is more obviously religious than metapoetic. Wordsworth, we recall, had a devout mother, attended church school as a boy and compulsory Chapel at Cambridge, and was intended for the clergy. Even if such experiences had not familiarized him with I Corinthians, its use as the Anglican-prescribed text at funerals could not have escaped him: "And so it is written, The first man Adam, was made a living soul, the last Adam was made a quickning spirit.

Howbeit, that was not first, which was spiritual; but that which is naturall.... The first man is of the earth, earthy: the second man is the Lord from heaven." . To his confirmation of the duality first recorded in Genesis, Paul adds the New Testament promise of immortality: the "second man" is both Christ and our own eternal "quickning spirit."

Of course, it is the "first man" who is afflicted by the various evils that a belief in the soul offers eventual relief from. And it is in "Tintern Abbey's" first stanza that Wordsworth offends recent New Historicists by having the audacity to allude to socio-economic problems ("wreathes of smoke," "vagrant dwellers") that he then fails to address. Yet if we look at the poem carefully, we see the possibility that in "Tintern Abbey," Wordsworth did not believe he _was_ alluding to such problems.

In stanza two, he refers to the landscape he has just described as "[t]hese forms of beauty." Do we really believe the poet was callous enough to assert that industrial pollution and homelessness were beautiful? I suggest, instead, that Wordsworth, in the context of this poem, regarded the smoke and the vagrants as elements of the landscape. He was not ignoring a moral responsibility: he had not yet even shown us what that responsibility was.

A majority of the problems that Wordsworth focuses on in "Tintern Abbey" are not likely to be high on any Marxist's "misery list." He does not mention unemployment, poverty, starvation, servitude or sickness, focusing instead— in what is essentially an autobiographical poem— on the problems he faced himself.

The bourgeois Wordsworth experiences misery in "lonely rooms" and "the din of towns and cities," in the unintelligibility of the world, its "weary hours" and "still, sad music," and in man's "sneers," "[r]ash judgments," and "evil tongues." It is only in connection with Dorothy that he broadens his list, adding "fear, or pain, or grief" in recognition, we assume, of his sister's more vulnerable position. When he is no longer with her, such things might be her "portion," he says with dramatic self-importance, employing a biblical word most often used to describe a dowry or inheritance.

In "The Politics of Tintern Abbey,'" Kenneth Johnston comments on Wordsworth's tendency to "generalize... about human evil from a narrow base of negative emotions" . In addition to the fact that the poet concerns himself with personal, not necessarily "human," evil in "Tintern Abbey," we should consider that his refusal to more thoroughly delineate sin might represent a romantic refusal to discuss what is essentially a religious issue in conventional terms.

It might also have resulted from his being raised in the shadow of _The Book of Common Prayer_ which, had his family followed suggested practice, required that the "Litanie" be said or sung three times a week. Among the various evils Anglicans were to pray for deliverance from are blindness of heart, pride, vainglory, hypocrisy, envy, hatred, malice, uncharitableness, and fornication; all other deadly sins; all deceits of the world, the flesh, and the devil; all sedition, conspiracy, and rebellion; all false doctrine, heresy, and schism; hardness of heart; and contempt for God's word (pp. 73-74). A steady diet of the "Litanie"— which also fails to list real social evils— could easily convince a writer that "less is more," that the broad strokes of sin might have a more powerful effect on readers.

It is not uncharacteristic of Wordsworth to identify others' "sins" more readily than he does his own. Yet in the poem's fourth stanza, his use of phrases such as "coarser pleasures" and "animal movements" makes it clear that the "appetite" he confesses to alludes not only to nature but to Annette Vallon, who, like both nature and the French Revolution, provoked the aching joys" and dizzy raptures" he associates with the time [that] is past"(l. 84).

For this reason, Wordsworth's description of himself as a deer bounding "o'er the mountains" recalls the Bible's general use of the roe as a symbol of virility, and that symbol's particular appearance in the Song of Solomon: here, the bride, singing of her anticipated sexual union, calls to her bridegroom to be "a roe... / upon the mountains" (8:14). We are to believe, of course, that Wordsworth's boyish days" have been lost without regret.

That he will not "faint" or "murmur" ("murmur" being what biblical personae did when they spoke in opposition to the word of God) in response to his loss seems to echo Paul's admonition to the Corinthians to put their "childish— i.e., earthly or physical— things" behind them (13:11). For what he has lost, Wordsworth would have us believe, his maturer understanding of the import and power of nature has been "[a]bundant recompense." Yet line 89, which begins this assertion ("For I have learned / To look on nature, not as in the hour / Of thoughtless youth"), contains a reference to Philippians that seems to be stoically contradictory: "For I have learned," says Paul, "in whatever state I am, therewith to be content" (4:11).

While Wordsworth would have us believe that he has willingly turned his back on "coarser pleasures," his use of the Pauline allusion allows us to question the real extent of his spiritual growth. Yet this is neither the first nor the last time that he undercuts his own declaration of faith.

Richard Bourke has commented on the poem's disabling reluctance", Kenneth Johnston on its "negative rhetorical constructions" . The faltering they refer to occurs in lines 50-51 ("If this / Be but a vain belief, yet, oh!") and 112-113 ("Nor, perchance, / If I were not thus taught"), and is known rhetorically as _aposiopesis_, an abrupt halt in a text which suggests that its speaker is too excited or too upset to continue.

In "Tintern Abbey," the source of Wordsworth's distress, it seems to me, is his recognition of his own spiritual inadequacy. For while he identifies himself as a "good man" in stanza two, he has no illusions about the extent of that goodness. He wants to believe, and his imitation of the New Testament's Pauline rhythms, such that

... neither evil tongues,
Rash judgments, not the sneers of selfish men,
Nor greetings where no kindness is, nor all
The dreary intercourse of daily life,
Shall e'er prevail against us

mimics Paul's promise to the Romans, reflects that fact: "neither death," the Saint tells us, "nor life, nor angels, nor principalities, nor powers, nor things present, nor things to come, nor height, nor depth, nor any other creature, shall be able to separate us from the love of God, which is in Jesus Christ our Lord" (Romans 8:38-39). "Thus taught," Wordsworth nonetheless requires the support of a faith more steadfast than his own. In "Tintern Abbey"— as in real life— it was to his sister, Dorothy, that the poet turned.

Wordsworth is aware of Dorothy's own dualism, seeing in her, "for yet a little while," "what [he] was once" (ll. 120-121). That he couches her similarity to him in scriptural terms, however, draws our attention to her purity as much as to her youthfulness, and casts him in the role of disciple: in John 14:19, Christ advises his followers that "Yet a little while, and the world seeth me no more; but ye see me: because I live, ye shall live also." Similarly, while Wordsworth's reference to his sister's "wild eyes" is both a fact and a symbol of her passionate nature, the "lights" in her eyes also recall the manifestation of grace, as it is commonly described in the New Testament.

Appropriately, in its "Calendar"of suggested readings for July 13, the date included in "Tintern Abbey's" title, _The Book of Common Prayer_ lists 1 Thessalonians: "Ye are all the children of light, and the children of the day," we read in 5:5. Likewise, the July 13 morning prayer calls for John 1: "And the light shineth in darkness.... The true light... lighteth every man that cometh into the world" (vv. 5 and 9). It is her possession of this "light" that distinguishes Dorothy from her brother and marks her as his spiritual teacher— his own personal Christ.

By acting as a friend, a companion, a helpmeet, and yes, a substitute for the two women Wordsworth has already lost (his mother and Annette), Dorothy is indeed her brother's salvation. In this domestic context, however, the poem's final words, for thy sake," have a curious biblical reverberation.

In Genesis 12 we are told the story of Abraham who, though a nomad, was given by God the gift of land, a gift that requires that he and his descendants settle down. During their journey to this land, Abraham fears that the Egyptians will kill him in order to have his beautiful wife. "For thy sake" , he says to Sarah, "say thou art my sister, that it may be well with me" (v. 13). And indeed, as his sister, Sarah is welcomed into the Pharaoh's house— and bed— and both she and Abraham treated well. Presumably, we should treat this echo not as a subtext for incest but as a reminder that Dorothy, however god-like, is also a human being.

The most obvious biblical reference in "Tintern Abbey" is to the Twenty-Third Psalm, alluded to in Wordsworth's declaration to his sister that, regardless of the condition of his own religious faith ("If I were not thus taught," l. 113), he knows he can depend on hers: "For thou art with me," he says, "here, upon the banks / Of this fair river".

The considerable burden that he places on Dorothy is lessened somewhat when we consider, again, that Wordsworth is also addressing God, who has led him beside the still waters" of the Wye and who will care for him even when he faces the shadow of death"— which is precisely where Wordsworth imagines being when he can no more hear / [Dorothy's] voice." It is by accident that "Tintern Abbey," included in _Lyrical Ballads_ as an after-thought, became the twenty-third poem in the 1798 edition.

Yet it is an intriguing accident, one that marks the poem as the culminating "psalm" of the collection and thus elevates it as "scriptural" authority offering immortality as the solution to the various ills _Lyrical Ballads_ detail. Fortunately for me, the ramifications of the broader application of such a solution are beyond the scope of this paper.

If death _does_ separate Wordsworth from Dorothy, he asks her to "remember me," words which once again establish their respective positions as disciple and deity. Remember me, O Lord, with the favour that thou bearest unto thy people," the Psalmist cries (106:4). Remember me and strengthen me" is also Samson's cry to God from prison, as he prepares to have his vengeance on the Philistines (Judges 16:28). Most significantly, of course, is the echo in Luke: one of the criminals condemned with Christ asks him to remember me when thou comest into thy kingdom." Jesus's response, as we know, was, Today shalt thou be with me in Paradise" (23:42). Thus Wordsworth's task, in the final stanza of "Tintern Abbey," seems to be to prepare us for Dorothy's eventual apotheosis.

When the poet asks his sister to remember him in the Wye Valley, not just as [a] worshipper of Nature," but rather" as one with warmer love," far deeper zeal," holier love," he is, to be sure, speaking of his filial affection. At the same time, the escalation in the intensity of his feelings marks them as expressions of religious adoration, as well as underscoring his desire to convince Dorothy that he has returned to Tintern Abbey a better man than he was five years before— his love is "warmer," "deeper," more god-like (and thus more like hers) than it was in 1793. It is no coincidence that Paul's definition of love, which— perhaps to Wordsworth's relief— suggests that it is more powerful than even faith and hope, has become a standard part of many marriage ceremonies: Love "envieth not," "vaunteth not itself," "thinketh no evil," "[b]eareth all things, believeth all things, hopeth all things, endureth all things" (1 Corinthians 13:4-7).

In these verses, Paul is speaking in particular of God's love, which He demonstrated by sending Christ to die for humankind's sin. The passage's transvaluation in "Tintern Abbey" cannot disguise its origin, any more than Wordsworth's address to Dorothy secularizes (or disguises) his underlying intent. Wordsworth commented that, just as

The Prelude and _The Excursion_ are the antechapel to and body of a Gothic church, so his other poems are "the little cells, oratories, and sepulchral recesses, ordinarily included in those edifices" . As one of those "cells," "Tintern Abbey" suggests that, via nature and Christ-like love, Wordsworth can transcend his doubt and his proclivity to sin and be sinned against, thus ensuring his own immortality.

Yet the allusions that support this conclusion may not have been chosen consciously. In a critique of Jerome McGann's use of the term "displacement," James Longenbach reminds us that according to Freud, displacement is not the denial of meaning but "the means by which the dreamwork subverts repression, allowing thoughts access to the dream in a form that the censor will not recognize" . In "Tintern Abbey" (the displaced dream), Wordsworth's religious allusions could thus have escaped his attention and _still_ underscore his belief. Of course, his panacea may offer little more than emotional relief, but it was, after all, the solution to his own problems, not the Wye Valley's vagrant dwellers', that he chose to describe in "Tintern Abbey."

Strange Affinities: A Partial Return to Wordsworthian Poetics After Modernism

Almost thirty years ago I made what I thought was a convincing argument contrasting Wordsworth's aesthetics of immanence with Coleridge's "symbolist" poetics. In doing this I hoped to show how many aspects of what then seemed postmodern had a very different lineage from the symbolist values that had shaped modernism. Now I have to recognize several problems with that argument, but, as is the way of thirty year retrospects, I remain convinced that at core I got something right—if not about sixties postmodernism than about a strand of contemporary poetics that I find given exemplary articulation in Lyn Hejinian and Leslie Scalapino's collaborative text Sight.

My major mistake was in treating Wordsworth as only a poet of immanence. I did so in order to evade criticisms of Wordsworth's egotistical sublime, and so also to evade the heritage of confessional writing against which my postmoderns were attempting to define themselves. But I got two things wrong. First, there is no evading the egotistical sublime in Wordsworth: being able to exult in the "I" and so to feel its expansiveness was for him a central aspect of immanence. As we see in the great crescendo at the centre of "Tintern Abbey," immanence for Wordsworth consisted in being able to feel paratactic syntax expand to include within lyric celebration the furthest reaches of the poet's exalted speech. Immanence meant that even this reach of spirit could be as grounded in natural process as the meanest thing that blows. Second, I was wrong, or at least terribly limited, about why it might matter to pursue immanence.

I was driven by the need to find conceptual structures that could simultaneously justify what poets pursued and be justified by what they accomplished. Now I think one has to handle concepts like poetic immanence somewhat differently. The crucial fact is not what the poets thought but how their thinking made possible certain ways that language could be charged with affective intensity and so take on exemplary affective resonance.

Now I hope that by addressing these mistakes I can provide a more accurate and more consequential picture of why Wordsworth matters for the study of twentieth-century poetry in general and especially for contemporary concerns with how twentieth-century poets could use language to establish and celebrate new ways of realizing immanent values. Wordsworth matters first because of the curse that the egotistical sublime was to become.

High Victorian poets could not be content unless their speakers could take on personal stances dignified by Wordsworthian high eloquence. But they could no longer marry that eloquence to processes of sensation or to modes of symbol making. So the affective basis for self-projection came increasingly to have little but the poet's imaginary identification with the role of poet as sustenance for lyric eloquence.

Here I will use a short poem by Matthew Arnold to

illustrate features of self-projection that become even more striking in overtly Wordsworthian poems like "The Scholar Gypsy." Then I will show how modernist rejections of romanticism might better be seen as repudiations of Victorian versions of the romantic subject that had lost the possibility of keeping the ego continuous with sensation.

My second mistake now has to enter this story. If we deal with immanence primarily as a structure of ideas we simply cannot get back beyond the modernist rejection of Victorian versions of the Wordsworthian ego (which also all too often after 1815 became the actual Wordsworthian ego). Arnold's versions of Wordsworth may have destroyed for the foreseeable future the possibility of a poetry based on explicit value schemes (in contrast to a poetry that composes values by how it inhabits particular ways of attending to and composing experience).

But if we treat the poetics of immanence as primarily an emphasis on particular ways of getting as much of mind as possible made continuous with the senses, we can see that the anti-symbolist moderns and their heirs had to reinvent, sans egotistical sublime, what Wordsworth sought as his means of resisting the corrupt modes of feeling basic to social life. Wordsworth is the godfather of at least one strand of contemporary radical poetics because of how he enables us to escape the lyric heritage that Victorian poetics imposed upon him.

Wordsworth can directly speak to contemporary imaginations because he so tightly weaves the ego into elaborate textures of sensation, then treats language as itself so affectively charged that it simply continues sensation by other means. Moreover, by stressing sensation as one locus of self-consciousness, Wordsworth also made it possible to imagine at the other end of the ego, in effect, how poetry might move beyond the individual subject to the direct modeling of interpersonal subjective states.

If the sensations can be rendered so as to be shared, and if language is woven into the sensations, then the affects built out of that weaving become available for anyone who can fully assume the role of speaker of that specific linguistic formulation. By showing how our affective intensities are grounded by the modes of attention we adapt, Wordsworth also gives poetry a powerful social agenda that need not be connected to any specific political one.

In order to develop this story, I will have to presuppose an audience willing at least to entertain my description of Wordsworth without demanding further elaboration. I want to put all my emphasis on the path leading from Victorian versions of the lyrical speaking ego to contemporary fascinations with the entirely embodied authorial sensibility.

Therefore, I will rest my case on three examples that I hope get to the structural core of how our intimate psychological energies can be differently distributed. Other poets, and other poems by my authors, obviously will distribute these investments somewhat differently, but I hope my examples provide the basic terms for characterizing these differences. For Arnold I concentrate on his "Isolation.

To Marguerite" because this poem concisely makes visible both the power and the problems involved in seeking Wordsworthian affective satisfactions for the lyrical ego without Wordsworthian grounds. In this poem Arnold tries to build a plausible lyrical self by substituting for a failed love a projected identification with a nature now reduced to analogues for the poet's own loneliness. Ultimately even that projected affinity collapses into self-defensive fantasy as poetry yields itself entirely to shoring up ego-defenses under the guise of lyrical sensitivity.

Then, once we see how slippery the lyrical ego can be, we are in a position to appreciate why modernists were so leery of "emotion" and so eager to replace that emphasis with the lyric exploration of "feeling," an exploration whose fundamental possibilities I think took shape in Wordsworth's Prelude. To exemplify what modernists tried to make of this turn from emotion to feeling I will turn to two short lyrics by William Carlos Williams. Finally, I will take as my representative contemporary text a brief section of Lyn Hejinian and Leslie Scalapino's Sight because this text implicitly argues that Williams severely limits the domain of feeling by subordinating its fluid aspects to the powerful objectifying will of the artist as composer-antagonist (see Williams 186). From the perspective of contemporary radical or investigative poetry, composition is not so much a lonely forming of nature as it is a means of exploring transitional sites intensifying complex interrelationships between sensation and imagination.

In effect Hejinian and Scalapino reexamine the nature of feelings and find there resources for a model of authorship quite different from Williams's. They present composition not as the lonely giving shape to formed structures of sensations but as a reflexive means of intensifying complex interrelationships between sensation and imagination. My argument then takes the form of a historical progression. For each model depends on its predecessor for its urgency and for its self-definition. Yet it is also quite possible for each of the models to be isolated as one possibly representative rendering of affects important for contemporary life.

We need a few fundamental rough definitions in order to create a working vocabulary for dealing with affective energies within lyrics. Affect is for me the most general category for talking about how we find ourselves caring about our involvement in particular situations. Affects can be defined as states of the body experienced as inseparable from the presence of imaginary projection.

This distinguishes them on the one side from sensations, which involve simple awareness of bodily states, and on the other from beliefs, which can be articulated without relation to bodily states at all. Sensations can trigger imaginary projections, but imagination is not central to their modes of appearing for us. Consider the difference between noticing a bird and noticing that the bird's way of pecking reminds one of a certain person or state of mind.

Then think of making some argument about the bird, for example that it is a finch, not a hummingbird. Here imaginings might be present, but the discipline involved requires framing and testing them, not exploring where they come from and how those energies might generate additional connections. Affects often involve reasoning, but we do not expect reasoning either to cause them or to direct them. Even when reasoning controls our actions, it might not control the affects. I may believe on rational grounds that I should not hit a person a lot bigger than I am, but I may well stay angry and resentfully plot another form of revenge, now the more elaborate because my anger is mixed with shame at my weakness.

Once we establish a general link between sensation and imagination at the core of affectivity, we can then distinguish two basic kinds of imaginary projection, and hence between two basis structures of affect, which I will call feelings and emotions. Each mode of imagining in turn involves a different approach to agency, differences that prove central in making the historical claims I will propose. With emotions the imagination is synthetic. It projects causes, attaches itself to objects, and projects courses of action or structures of desire in relation to those objects.

That is why emotions tend to take place in terms of plots and to be correlated with the work of cognitive inquiry. When I am angry with someone, I imagine performing an action in relation to the person. More important, this practical orientation positions me toward two kinds of possible knowings. I have the potential of understanding something about myself because of how I plot the anger, and I am likely to recognize certain features of the person that I might not were I not invested in what might fuel or diminish the anger. (But my investment can also lead me to distort the importance of those traits I do see because emotions want to be fed as much as they want to find resolution.)

Feelings can occur as aspects of emotions. But their fundamental structure is quite different. With feelings, the imagination is participatory, not synthetic. Feelings are much more a matter of the moment than are emotions. Rather than seek their cause we simply attend to the qualities of appearance that they make possible. Consequently feelings appear usually as if they simply were extensions of the sensation.

They are not parts of plots but of processes set in motion by the energies that metaphors bring into relation with the sensation. Even the simplest feelings, like hunger, are projections into sensation. Feelings come closer to the aesthetic when sensation tilts toward some kind of fascination and partial identification for which no plot seems plausible. Think of kinetic art, where simple magnetic charges affecting filament-like tentacles seem inseparable from minimal but fundamental desire.

Or we might note the transition between watching the bird I referred to earlier and recognizing with Elizabeth Bishop's "Sandpiper" how the bird's activities take on anthromorphic qualities.

These two directions of the imagination also enable us to make useful distinctions between moods and passions, the other two basic types of affect. Moods are not quite feelings but they establish conditions in which feeling tone becomes a pervasive force. Here feelings are no longer attached to objects. Instead they seem continuous with some overall state of the subject.

But the continuity is insistently not one for which we can provide a narrative, perhaps because moods seem pervasive and so have no clear beginning and ending, only extension and duration. Passions on the other hand are something close to super-emotions. They are affective states circulating around plots within which the status of the I is put substantially at stake. Love is a passion because it defines who I am or who I want to be. Similarly civic emotions like pride and consideration are usually passions, while emotions exhausted in particular situations clearly are not passions. Momentary anger for example can be distinguished from the passion of abiding hatred; lust from love.

Making these distinctions has its ultimate payoff in showing us how different emphases among the affects emphasize substantially different orientations toward subjective agency, and hence toward how values get constructed and pursued. And it is the differences in agency that will underlie the historical tale I want to tell about poetry.

On the most general level we can say that emotions and passions invite Lacanian analysis, since their objects are constructed for the imagination, and the stakes involved shape what kinds of identities we can postulate and pursue. Moreover this mode of imagining cannot be easily reconciled with those who want to treat emotions as allied with reason.

Emotions do establish salience and do help us make perceptions relevant to our actions and plans. But they do so always with an urgency and sense of significance bringing to bear representations that are not quite subject to reason, at least not without destroying the very affective charge that reason seeks as its supplement.

Feelings and moods on the other hand tend not to rely on projections about ourselves as having specific identities. They stress dependencies on what we respond to, and they provide investments that bypass epistemic culture's usual ways of establishing meaning and importance. If emotions invite Lacanian analysis, feelings invite Levinasian ones in which we are aware that we are not the source of consciousness but are in a response mode, open to an otherness that exercises influence upon us.

We can build upon these general differences to isolate three particular arenas in which these contrasts play themselves out by creating a complex variety of psychological orientations—all of which become resources for poetic experiments. For example we have to keep in mind the relevance of classical oppositions between the passive and the active dimensions of affective life. At one pole we treat the expressive action as fundamentally symptomatic, at best a passive response to forces from beyond the self and at worst a drastic displacement or evasion of what observers might conclude that one is actually feeling.

At the other pole expression becomes a triumphant articulation, getting clear on something that has been bothering a person or breaking through so that the agent manages to participate actively in complex sets of emotions. Affects can dominate agency and affects can enhance an agent's sense of power and commitment. Second, we can cast the active-passive distinction in spatial terms to characterize how borders of the subject are constantly being negotiated. Some affects create states of intense concentration: the self becomes the only active force in an indifferent environment. Other affects distribute energies and investments so that personality seems almost irrelevant: what matters is how one experiences appearances taking on fresh vitality leading one to dwell imaginatively beyond the self. Finally, it is often crucial to distinguish different kinds of borders or passages among agents.

Some affects are presented as entirely specific to the subject: in experiencing this way I recognize only my own distinctive commitments. But many others have a very different structure. Think of religious emotions, or the feelings we experience in crowds or audiences, or those around natural scenes that move us because what they offer seems available for everyone. Part of the power of art is its capacity to explore the degree to which we can participate intensely in emotions not by sympathizing with characters but by our direct awareness of the site of emotion as itself public, and perhaps more stable and enduring than any of the agents who experience it in given moments.

Making that sense of transpersonal affective site a basic source for artistic experiment seems to me one of the great accomplishments of modernist abstraction, although the emphasis has always existed in music.

I present this abstract picture as a tentative grammar for appreciating the range for experiment that our affective lives afford artists and writers. Once we know where to look, we can shift much of the energy we have been putting into interpretation, the postulating of meaning and purpose for actions, into the exploration of who texts ask us to become if we participate in their particular ways of fusing sensation and imagination. Now then I can turn to exploring how that participation might take place in three quite distinct poems, the sequence of which I hope has some metaphorical force as literary history.

Arnold's "Isolation. To Marguerite" is to me the quintessential Victorian poem, intensely moving in its self-evasions and depressingly challenging to Modernists eager to escape the processes of self-absorption it embodies:

We were apart; yet, day by day
I bade my heart more constant be.
I bade it keep the world away,
And grow a home for only thee;
Nor fear'd but thy love likewise grew,
Like mine, each day, more tried, more true.
The fault was grave! I might have known,
What far too soon, alas! I learn'd—
The heart can bind itself alone,
And faith may oft be unreturn'd.
Self-sway'd our feelings ebb and swell—
Thou lov'st no more—Farewell! Farewell!
Farewell!— and thou, thou lonely heart,
Which never yet without remorse
Even for a moment didst depart
From thy remote and spheréd course
To haunt the place where passions reign—
Back to thy solitude again!
Back! with the conscious thrill of shame
Which Luna felt, that summer night,
Flash through her pure immortal frame,
When she forsook the starry height
To hang over Endymion's sleep
Upon the pine-grown Latmian steep.
Yet she, chaste queen, had never proved
How vain a thing is mortal love,
Wandering in Heaven, far removed.
But thou hast long had place to prove
This truth—to prove, and make thine own:
"Thou hast been, shall be, art, alone."
Or, if not quite alone, yet they
Which touch thee are unmating things—
Ocean and clouds and night and day;
Lorn autumns and triumphant springs;
And life, and others' joy and pain,
And love, if love, of happier men.

Of happier men—for they, at least,
Have dream'd two human hearts might blend
In one, and were through faith released
From isolation without end
Prolong'd; nor knew, although not less
Alone than thou, their loneliness.

We cannot summarize this emotion by any one label—if we could, there would be no point in writing the poem. Self-pity is probably the best general description, but we have to see the self-pity as also purposive, as an attempt to come to terms with the pain of being rejected as a lover. From my theoretical position then this poem invites us to participate self-reflexively in a process of negotiating the pain of rejection by the seductive ennobling promised by self-pity.

Expressing such elaborate symptomatic self-absorption is no easy task. Yet Arnold accomplishes it magnificently, in the process establishing a paradigm for how the Victorian age used a theater of nobility as its means of managing the pains of the failures of nobility inseparable from that dream. But self-reflection is a dangerous instrument. Arnold may be Eliot's Hamlet, unable quite to get a grip on an emotion he is doomed to keep repeating precisely because his sense of self-worth depends on achieving closure.

So an analysis of the affects in this poem helps us appreciate from the inside how a Victorian ego tries to build up its sense of identity through affect, and how in the process it reveals serious problems with the imaginary projections of agency inherent in that process. This analysis also shows us why Modernism had to pursue very different affective priorities, priorities that in turn require contemporary recastings of that modernist heritage.

In my view Arnold's is a great poem because it does not hide the raw pain and desperation underlying the text's effort to achieve resignation in self-pity. Even the basic structuring devices seem shaped by that pain. The poem opens with a remembered "we" instantly displaced into a needy "I" who has to serve as his own interlocutor. The poem is the mind's dialogue with itself trying to convince itself that this is nature's law for man. There are also two quite different past tenses, one caught up in the life now only remembered, and one, entering in the second stanza, that presents the speaker haunted by subjunctive possibilities that he has to fight off. Confronting those pasts is a bleak present threatening to swallow the future within it: "Thou hast been, shall be, art, alone." Being true to himself is inseparable from utter loneliness.

Yet Arnold's poem cannot stop with that absolute condemnation. Why? One reason is structural. The poem's first three stanzas move from the initial memory of a relationship to the pure acceptance of solitude, now having learned not to "haunt the place where passions reign." The last three stanzas go in the opposite direction, as if Arnold could not be content with the personal resolution without also universalizing the significance of his emotional state. Where stanza three ends by encountering the apparent truth of his personal plight, stanza five ends with an abstract generalization about that solitude. And even then the poem remains restless.

It may have arrived at the truth but it has not yet contextualized that truth in a way that the ego can accommodate. So Arnold adds two compensatory complications. He can reach some connection with the unmating things that accompany his loneliness. And, more important, he can position himself by an elaborate contrast with those who though unmating still dream of two hearts blending into one.

His dazzling play on the boundaries of what can and cannot be shared in loneliness makes his disappointment seem to him ultimately ennobling. After all he learns from his suffering. In fact he not only learns abstract truths, he also masters a new position for himself in relation to nature. He in effect learns to occupy its core, the one truly disillusioned person willing to accept fully the loneliness to which we are all condemned.

My students find this final self-congratulatory move appalling. But, older and lonelier, I want to keep sympathy for Arnold while recognizing just how deeply self-deluding this bid for an ennobling lucidity is. In effect we have now to read the poem backwards, recognizing how much he works to secure a self-image and tracing the moves that in seeming to make this possible also make it almost reprehensible. We have to appreciate how a sense of pathos seems to haunt this particular self-expressive process.

So rather than see the situation entirely through the speaker's interpretations we will shift to how the speaker goes about constructing the self that for him seems capable of providing a satisfying resolution to his pain. For that we should turn to those moments when the expressive activity tries too hard or falters—quintessentially in the poem's repetitions and in the central fourth stanza which I passed over in discussing the structure.

Why the repetitions? The first one is pretty easy to handle. Our speaker wants simply to say "farewell" to love, but he cannot because something important would not be resolved by that gesture. The obvious candidate for non-resolution is the state of his ego.

The "might have known" is not a sufficient ego position from which to walk away. So he has to keep reworking the situation until it seems that it was not she who chose to leave so much as it was he who was helped to realise that he had given into illusion. She tested and brought to the fore his ability to live with a full grasp of loneliness as an absolute condition. So "farewell" opens a condition of dialogue with himself and enables him to relegate to a mistake his leaving his solitude for the life of passion. From this new perspective her act of breaking their bond becomes almost irrelevant. The important romance is with himself.

But there is not yet a self sufficient for him to cathect to in the way that he had cathected to her. To get to that lovable self he needs another, this time quite revealing repetition generating the fourth stanza. Here he moves beyond recognition to fantasy, so that he participates in the romance imagination at the core of passion, but only insofar as he becomes the focus for those romance energies. To accomplish this he recasts his shame at being rejected into shame at having given way to this very way of imagining in romance terms.

Yet we also realise that the shame he postulates is not all the shame that he feels. For his mistake was less in yielding to passion than in putting himself in a situation where he could be rejected, where his own strange sense that one can treat the heart as duty bound might not be sufficient grounds for securing another's passion.

I cannot tell whether Arnold intended this level of exposure for his speaker. I suspect he did not. But his third repetition offers perhaps the most brilliant and most touching moment in this occluded drama. For at the end of the fifth stanza the speaker reaches his ultimate nadir—the realization of loneliness in past, present, and future.

No wonder that this repetition seems somewhat different. Rather than simply echoing the previous expression this one seeks a slight escape: some companionship is possible. For this speaker, however, even that glimpse of weakness seems vulnerability, so we get a fourth repetition which uses the figure of happier men as his contrast to his own freedom from illusion. Partial concession makes possible absolute repudiation. And here absolute repudiation turns out to be both true for the speaker and false as an analysis of his situation.

At his most intense acceptance of loneliness, the speaker is in fact desperately crying out for some kind of pity, or at least some recognition of a nobility that depends on his pain over these flimsy and needy contrasts. The poem's expressive intensity enables the speaker to assert an independence entirely belied by the rhetorical manipulations showing how badly he needs not only the posture but someone to convince of the posture. The I produced by passion seems an I desperately seeking a reflection, while in the process undermining the possibility of getting mirrored back what it wants to have seen.

History enters our story when we realise that our own readings quite likely echo those for whom struggle against Victorian poetry was necessary for survival. As readers become familiar with the poem they have to experience the speaker's pathos along with his power.

They are allowed the gestures of nobility only with an accompanying consciousness of all of the dependencies and pains such gestures must try to ignore. From this perspective then it is not surprising that Arnold's speaker becomes Eliot's Prufrock, forced to confront the displacing force of his own need for passions which might produce desired imaginary identities.

Nor should it be surprising that one of Eliot's basic theoretical concerns was to make sharp distinctions between emotions and feelings, the former dependent on self-staging plots while the latter afford affects more closely woven into the rendering of sensations. In that concreteness one can hope for intensities and attachments much less bound to the illusory project of constructing individual egos.

For heuristic purposes, the best quick way to indicate what this cultural shift involves is to turn to the lyrics of William Carlos Williams. For much of the power of these poems consists in their knowing how to resist becoming vehicles of emotion, and hence of plots involving imaginary identifications. In Williams readers have to learn to accept what the moment gives, and to have the discipline to engage the moment without attempting to build upon it.

Correspondingly, Williams shows how and why modernist constructivism tries to keep the focus on how the art composes the event rather than on how selves interpret and transform affect into "meanings" and roles. The idealized imaginary individual self has to give way to the floating modes of consciousness that can be composed by an impersonal constructivist intelligence.

I will concentrate on two short poems, one stressing how the composition of feeling thrives in its refusal of emotional build-up and the other articulating Williams's very unArnoldian rendering of personal identity within the lyric. "The Young Housewife" opens with the speaker alone in his car passing a housewife who "moves about in negligee behind/ the wooden walls of her husband's house." The poem ends:

Then again she comes to the curb
to call the ice-man, fish-man, and stands

shy, uncorseted, tucking in
stray ends of hair, and I compare her
to a fallen leaf.
The noiseless wheels of my car
rush with a crackling sound over
dried leaves as I bow and pass smiling. (Williams 57)

On the most general level the poem's energies are gathered in a contrast between what leads him to compare the wife to a fallen leaf and the sound of dried leaves marking his departure and somehow contributing to his smile. But I don't think we are intended to dwell much on this general level. The poem's energies are focused on the possibility of establishing concrete affective relations that depend on not letting the scene become metaphoric. Instead we have to let the juxtaposition of details do all of the work, without our irritable reaching for dramatic or thematic models.

Mention of "her husband's house" somewhat melodramatically sets the stage. In the first stanza everything is arranged, almost ceremonious. The second stanza then shifts to quite particular feelings gathering around the ways that her body contrasts with that order. Each detail complicates the picture. Her shyness defines an attitude; her uncorseted fleshiness indicates a simple voluptuousness; and her stray ends of hair mark a minimal rebelliousness or at least freedom to be something other than her husband's possession. Yet her freedom is severely limited and not internalized at all, the freedom one might say of a fallen leaf, attractive in its pure contingency and marginality.

It is crucial in developing this picture not to let the details add up into some kind of traditional snap photograph rendered in words. The details can be made to cohere. But we honour them best by keeping a distance between them so that all seem stray hair momentarily taking a particular pattern. Each detail then peeks out at us like an aspect of the woman's spirit, unpossessed but also undirected and unable to reach out to passers-by or to return whatever desire the watching generates. And the watcher knows that the desire cannot be returned. Accepting that is part of the texture of feeling preparing for the speaker's final return to his own version of contingent and frustrated freedom. We have to ask why the speaker smiles as he goes away. But we also have to be satisfied with an explanation as partial as the speaker's knowledge of the woman he watches.

In some respects the smile is ironic, or at least ruefully accepting. Whatever elicits the metaphor of a fallen leaf turns out to be reduced to the actual dead leaves filling the street. Contingency reigns. But the smile also has a self-reflective dimension. The speaker finds satisfaction I think in recognizing the pure momentariness of his vision. His glimpse is not unlike her uncorseted presence, a slight escape from being possessed.

Yet one can trust that freedom, just as one trusts the smile, so long as nothing more is asked of it. Any effort to base meaning on the scene or to expand the self's role would destroy this minimal freedom and reimpose the order in which husbands own houses and others comply with the rules of ownership. Any effort to make an emotion of this feeling would destroy what freedom is possible and put in its place a problematic self having to play out a doomed Arnoldian project of self-construction.

Williams's "Danse Russe" offers a more pronounced version of this effort to redistribute affective energies so that self is much less burdened than Arnold's by the need to rely on elaborate imaginative constructions. The speaker hypothesizes dancing naked in front of a mirror while everyone else in the household sleeps, singing to himself: "I am lonely, lonely,/ I was born to be lonely,/ I am best so!" "Danse Russe" ends:

If I admire my arms, my face,
my shoulders, flanks, buttocks
against the yellow drawn shades,—
Who shall say I am not
the happy genius of my household?

I will confine myself to two observations about this marvelously intricate poem. One involves how the poem empties out the form of traditional emotions, the other how it focuses energy instead on something like the immediacy of feelings won by holding off the demands of the imaginary ego. Our speaker is clearly a solipsist, not unlike Eliot's Prufrock.

Yet he has found an intriguing way of living with that solipsism. When he turns to himself in the conventional lyric space of self-possession, the only self he cares about is the one that manages not to be beholden to some examining eye or possessing spouse. Williams stresses the "not" because he is more interested in freedom or unsponsoredness than he is in attributing any clear judgment or even identity to his activity. This morning ritual is in the service of anti-identity, of being able to play out a momentary self precisely because he is beholden to no judges. And, as Gertrude Stein might say, perhaps sheer commitment to one's impulse without fear of judgment is precisely what it means to be a genius. But it cannot suffice to base genius on negativity. Hence the importance of my second observation. Williams's lineation is called upon to play a fundamental role in the poem. It has to provide affective intensity for a series of gestures that have little significant symbolic or imaginary force.

These acts, qua acts, will not sustain a rhetoric of genius or even of lyric significance. But this lineation holds them over against pure banality just enough to let them emerge as capable of bearing attention and hence of becoming fascinating in their own right. What merely passes has the capacities to behave as if it composed a picture, to invite dwelling on different rhythms of attention, and to give the body a passing delight in its own ordinariness. Making all of that possible, without a plot or deep psychology or promise of consequence, may be just what genius has to do in our secular century and in the speaker's otherwise orderly domestic life.

Contemporary American radical poetics has obviously learned a good deal from Williams about resisting the culture's primary modes of symbolic and imaginary identification. Yet the various orientations within this poetic also have to establish substantial differences from his characteristic lyric gestures. From those perspectives Williams is far too scenic.

The sensations basic to his poems are organized by a

dramatic sense of the world, with insufficient attention paid to the affects organized within the activity of writing. We are asked to identify with phenomenological stances by embodied characters rather than with the authorial activity, even though the constructive force of that activity is quite pronounced.

We feel the effects of lineation, but as an intensifying of the scene rather than as a presentation of authorial engagement. Correspondingly, radical poetics is not quite satisfied with how authorship is represented in Williams. He turns out to be at least as impersonal as the poet Eliot fantasized, with the author somewhat aloof from the perspectival energies organized within the work. No wonder that Williams projects the poet as composer-antagonist, standing out as a vertical force in a horizontal landscape. A new poetry would have to explore authorial subject positions more committed to challenging boundaries between subject and object as well as between subjects.

The poet could not rest in the safety of the composer position but would have to risk the range of sensual attachments available for the medium of writing. In taking those risks it might be possible to stage writing as an activity with exemplary social force because it can envision a version of affect capable of organizing shareable resistance to dominant cultural habits for orienting affective engagement.

I cannot here survey various styles within the poetic position I am characterizing in such general terms. Instead I am going to focus on one particular example of work that foregrounds its own self-conscious responsiveness to the concerns about affect and authorship that I have been summarizing. On the topic of affects elicited by self-consciousness about writing there is no contemporary work more suggestive than Sight, a collaboration between Lyn Hejinian and Leslie Scalapino.

For the collaboration itself takes on all sorts of exemplary qualities. Most collaborations try to fuse authorial energies, and so in effect pursue a synthetic version of the Arnoldian ego. But by taking turns responding to one another's brief units of two or three paragraphs based on some aspect of sight,

Hejinian and Scalapino take turns insisting on the pressure of differences that arise as each disposition expresses itself and as each contribution reorganizes the imaginative field the writing has to enter.

All the major LANGUAGE writers share this concern for foregrounding the activity of writing over the illusionary worlds it manages to project. Writing seems the thing in itself behind the appearances being reflected on the surface of our cave. But substantial differences emerge when we examine how this focus on writerly presence can fold affect into sensation and give the compositional energies exemplary social force.

Poets like Charles Bernstein and Bob Perelman, for example, take what we might call a fundamentally ironic attitude toward all expressivist ideals. They do not dismiss affect, but they also are very careful not to let ideals of intensity or depth seduce them into postures that lose sight of the irreducible writtenness, literal or figurative, of all our affective identifications. So they emphasize writerly engagement with and against the modes of affect inscribed in the social registers of our language.

Instead of the mind's dialogue with itself, these poets stage writing as dialogue with those registers of language. Lyric energy resides in the efforts of intelligence to hear its situatedness and to develop a little freedom for itself and the community it addresses, usually in the form of ironic play ranging from fierce opposition to reluctant complicity.

Hejinian and Scalapino have other ambitions. While they share Bernstein's and Perelman's suspicions about the rhetorics of sensibility, their work has been more phenomenological, more attentive to writing as a direct engagement with the dynamics of sensation and the projection of intimate desire. With Sight I think they have discovered a marvelous vehicle for foregrounding these differences, primarily because the dialogue form gives the writing a literal stage on which to play out through textual time complexities pervading the personal and transpersonal aspects of expressive activity. To frame these differences I will begin with an extended passage from the

"Introduction" to Hejinian's collection of essays, The Language of Inquiry:

> This is not to say that poetry is about transitions but that "aboutness" (in poetry, but, I would argue, also in life) is transitional, transitory; indeed poetry (and perhaps life) calls conventional notions of "aboutness" into question.... The language of poetry is a language of inquiry, not the language of a genre.
>
> It is that language in which a writer (or a reader) both perceives and is conscious of the perception. Poetry, therefore, takes as its premise that language is a medium for experiencing experience.... It is at points of linkage... that one discovers the reality of being in time, of taking one's chance, of becoming another, all with the implicit understanding that this is happening (The Language of Inquiry 2-3)

There are here three concepts at the core of a poetics that Hejinian and Scalapino share, even though their particular projects usually pursue quite different emphases and tones. The most fundamental belief is this insistence on a pervasive critique of conventional ideas of aboutness—not only in relation to how fictions portray worlds but also to how persons engage one another.

Traditionally aboutness is conceived in terms of representations. Language pictures events and agents provide accounts of themselves. But if one emphasizes writing as the locus of affective events, then the feelings become literal states. Writing does not comment about what one is feeling but makes articulate the actual event of feeling as it takes place, or makes a place for itself.

Radical as this claim sounds, I think all the great modernists would sympathize with it, if not subscribe to it. Hejinian pushes the resistance to aboutness in fresh directions when she adds a second claim insisting that the event becomes a vehicle for the experience of experience. Here all descriptive and dramatic and ironic notions of writing yield entirely to phenomenological ones.

Writing does not so much present a world as present the sensation of sensation or the experience of experience. This shift substantially alters what we can say about affect in poetry. For where Williams still locates affect in the rendering of a scene, and where Bernstein and Perelman tend to locate affect in various kinds of resistance to the public textures of language, Hejinian projects affect as itself the most fundamental of phenomenological states. Indeed one cannot imitate or describe the affects basic to lyric because the affects are inseparable from the qualities of self-consciousness one brings to the events taking place within the writing.

Finally, Hejinian suggests that this particular kind of affect has a distinctive social and ethical force because as event, as happening, the writing so involves the self that what appears is to some degree or another different even from the intentions that got one going in the first place.

The logic of event is inseparable from the logic that bases the possibility of ethical thinking on an irreducible responsiveness to the otherness of the other. For then we have no basis for imposing our own preconceptions. We are left only with the options of feeling our own emptiness or attempting to attune ourselves to the very processes by which that otherness emerges and takes on its own directions.

Sight seems to me a superb realization of all these possibilities because the affective texture is entirely woven into the structure of call and response. There are no imaginary selves invoked to explain emotions, since the affects only emerge at the intersection of selves. And there are no affects that the text gestures toward while keeping its aloofness. Hejinian and Scalapino share Williams's concern to keep the affects from taking on some separate reality apart from the specific modalities of perception and expression. But now the reality they do compose is not in some world over against the author but in the author's own articulated processes of sensation.

Here the author is always already audience. Writing becomes a constant process of recognizing the presence of others, of positioning oneself simultaneously in relation to another person and to various topics that arise, and of working constantly at the boundary between understanding and misunderstanding or sympathy and turning away toward the recesses of private obsession. Moreover because this process controls an entire volume, the poets manage also to capture the importance of repetition as a concrete index of those feelings which seem fundamental or unresolved or obsessive to the individuals.

However the individual is not asked to explain or interpret those feelings, nor is the interlocutor invited to play therapist. Feelings are not expressed to be interpreted so much as to be pursued so that one finds where they lead and tests what transitions their articulation makes possible. In fact the text suggests that we most fully respond to others not when we try to find words for what has been said but when we treat the other's expression as a provocation enabling us to change directions and try other routes of engagement.

This enables us to avoid attributing the kinds of causes that turn feelings into emotions and dialogue into therapy. Stressing writing as the locus of affect keeps the entire affective field fluid so that we are constantly aware of how our own self-reflection depends on what the presence of the other opens up for us. Friendship becomes a structure based on a dance of difference and realignment.

I have space only for one example, so I can illustrate only a very limited range of the complex play of writerly effects and affects made present within the text as a whole. The relevant sequence begins when Hejinian takes up an anxiety about the aesthetic being a means of evading the fact of actual wrecks. She tries to convince herself that instead of being an evasion this focusing of consciousness serves as a means of evaluation. But the two poets do not easily rest with that formulation. Memories of pain and fears of death occupy the text, until Hejinian turns from their dream-laden abstraction to the following passage, the only one in this section rendered as verse:

One is happy in one's susceptibility to chance, accident, hazard So a descriptive sentence (being an account of what unfolds to sensibility) may be precarious and must be careful As something's happening. The sentence says so with felicity

— that's what one might get when writing in sight with happy exactitude In the realm of death, too Each thing, no matter how happy in its word, is ('only') floated In the realm of life, too A hummingbird in the morning flies right up to me at the door and stays in the air.

I am moved in part by the ways that this passage resists my efforts to cite it as somehow a privileged example for the text. Each gesture here toward lyric closure suddenly lapses into something like prose, with its resistant wordly flatness and its utter openness to contingency. Hejinian probably wants us to feel how fleeting and ineffective our capacity for aestheticizing is in relation to the world of fact and disaster. Yet at the same time she wants that concern with aestheticizing to pervade the entire reflection so that we find ourselves strangely empowered by this particular overall attitude toward our own contingency and impotence.

We sense the sensation of impotence and fear made articulate, so that we cannot rest simply in those all too standard states, but we have to explore the complexity of feeling which the self-consciousness brings.

Hejinian's refusal of elaborate metaphor keeps her close to Williams. But that proximity serves primarily to set off basic differences between his subtle play of dramatic affect and her concern for the sensation of sensation as itself affectively charged. In one respect she is even more respectful than Williams of the limitations fact imposes on imagination.

Not only is there no synthetic work of the interpretive imagination, there is not even the faith that particular feelings provide moments of attention satisfying the speaker's desires. All the details up to the emergence of the hummingbird lead consciousness back to death and to chance. But the mind's play upon, or, better, within, those sensations opens a quite different space for feeling. (Relations between inside and outside are fundamental motifs in the volume as a whole.)

We are asked to experience strange investments in the very process of recognizing the problems of chance, accident, and hazard. For "happening," "hap," and "happiness" become here closely allied. This effect is not mere linguistic accident, but neither is it a Heideggerean attempt to put authority in etymology. Hejinian wants to earn the connection by making the feeling for the one merge with the feeling for the other, as if the very conditions generating fear were inseparable from what makes for happiness.

More important, one cannot read the poem carefully without experiencing the sense of constant movement between the registers of "happening" and "happiness," as if recognizing this fluidity could provide a basis for pursuing the satisfaction the poem seeks. Then we can speak of happiness without any need to speculate about moving from facts to values. Satisfaction comes not in what we believe but in how we go about processing our sense of what those facts involve.

Once we stress the feeling for feelings in the passage, many of its details begin to resonate, again without in any way being metaphorically transfigured. Notice how the second sentence has to bring some kind of concreteness to the initially vague and intuitively silly opening statement. Why is one happy in such susceptibility? Wouldn't one be much happier if there were no such problems? The resulting "so" has a lot of work to do in establishing an answer.

But our grasp of the difficulties can lead directly to an appreciation of how the specific choices here respond to the pressure. The contrast between "may" and "must" echoes and reverses the syntax at the end of Stevens's "Of Modern Poetry": "It must/ Be the finding of a satisfaction, and may/ Be of a man skating, a woman dancing, a woman/ Combing." For Hejinian the specific permissions do not matter. Everything rides on the imperative to be "careful."

In my view this imperative both describes and enacts the overall texture of feeling that the poem sets against its fears concerning contingencies of all sorts. "Careful" refers to all those fears.

The poem bears the weight of cares that constantly resist aestheticization. Yet "careful" also refers self-reflexively to the poem's efforts to embody a mode of activity that can be responsive to such weight. And this doubling of meaning prepares a specific model of reflexive action soon to be further elaborated when the relation of "happening" to "happiness" becomes explicit. That doubling in turn is framed by a more complex invocation of the way feelings or framing can pervade the effort at self-description. For Hejinian relies on the Stevensian resources of the "as," in order to show just what care can bring about. At first this "as" seems consumed simply in its temporal function: when something significant is happening pay attention to it. But my paraphrase seems to miss the mark on many levels.

One might also say that the care is necessary because something is happening. But this reading also keeps the care simply as something parallel to the happening. I think we also have to see care as continuous with the happening, perhaps an adverb modifying the very conditions that allow the happening entrance to consciousness. "As" here thickens the sense of two orders at work—one descriptive and one involving the ways that the mind finds itself an invested participant in the very possibilities of description.

It is not a large leap then to the next line, where self-reflection becomes explicit and the sentences become visible actors on the scene. But here Hejinian produces another surprise. She is not willing to let the self-reference flow smoothly into the practical situation or have its realization constitute a moment of triumph. The sentence's power to abstract itself from the particulars returns consciousness to all the fears circulating around death. It too shares with these multiple meanings a frightening weightlessness.

The very doubling of meanings linking hap to happiness and fear to concern also keeps present something like an awareness of the unbearable lightness of being.

And so we get our hummingbird. On one level, or better on all levels, this is just a moment of happenstance. Certainly no guardian spirit sends the bird and its hovering is not a symbol of grace. Yet the bird does take on many of the properties of grace simply because its concreteness brings all the strands of the poem into momentary coexistence. And that coexistence is insistently concrete.

The bird's most important action is simply its manifesting

its power to stay in the air. This cannot provide a thematic resolution except for something clunky and moralistic. Yet the bird does bring back the motif of care and establishes a situation where we see that not only words float in the air. And not all things that stay in the air need remind us (only) of death.

The hummingbird offers a parallel to the poem's own effort to keep reflective distance while hovering very close to worlds exhausted by description. So its hovering participates in the same basic forces as the double meanings that prevent key terms like "happening" from being reduced to the world of pure contingencies. In fact this hovering so perfectly matches what the mind has been doing that it allows author and readers to engage in self-reflexiveness without postulating any kind of empirical subject.

The hovering itself constitutes a version of engagement that all subjects can take as their own, without the mediation of personal plots. Satisfying as it is, this moment too must immediately pass, here into Scalapino's reply with its intense questioning of the effort to let the hummingbird serve any kind of resolving function: even if she wasn't [past] where at dawn on gorges burning the tar — migratory labour on roads — as it being at dawn 'only' there 'accident' of birds [that are] being in space. — singing too only floating in the realm of life too — are they at [their] present and past (at the same time) — and separately which is the space [them] — the figures the same as space, no other phenomena — 'something's happening' is this too these blossoms purple-white-fringed blooming in the time away from them — and before — at the same time as 'one' is happy

The abstractness that had existed only in affect organized by the doubleness of meaning now takes on something like an existence of its own. In fact the feeling of space as an abstracted floating becomes so intense that it works its effects on the very form of the sentence.

This mode of consciousness seems to need these brackets because all claims about existence and identification have to be bracketed. Just as one hummingbird must become many, one moment of satisfaction must be placed in a larger context where even the realm of life begins to float. Even the hummingbird gets abstracted into the bird song that dissipates into the atmosphere.

However even this level of abstraction generates a countermovement. The text modulates back to an awareness that in this space too "something's happening." For one is prepared to return to appreciate how blossoming flowers themselves offer something like a parallel to verbal abstraction, anchoring its ways of organizing sensation while itself taking on force as an overall field of relations. But Hejinian is not content. Her response repudiates all this abstractness for this prosaic passage:

The hummingbird is busy with the mass of sensations, 'up' and 'down,' advancing and receding, among cascades of accidental purple morning glories hanging (where they weren't meant to be) from a tree.

Perhaps it is better to say what seems repudiation is really an effort to right a balance and to use abstractness as a frame for bringing the aesthetic back into the world, ironically where it too is not meant to be but where it melds perfectly with strange contingencies in nature.

On the basis of this new concreteness, now charged with affect, Hejinian's passage returns to abstraction, but this time with all the sensations of floating beautifully anchored—in nature and in the mind's appreciation of the kinds of composure self-awareness can bring: Still the air sustains the sensation of relevance — that this is ' meant to be' — but the hummingbird flying about in it seems to go to one side Then the tree acts as an 'anchoring point' so the garden has 'top' and 'bottom'

The hummingbird makes a 'correction' — backs
"I" am still, so this is a still — in motion, blooming, and
fringed, in continuation
While this vocabulary, which is still, for seeing — another
at the same time — we pass

Here anchoring is inseparable from adjusting to how fluid movement creates a range of stills, each allowing for correction and readjustment. Wordsworth haunts this passage, since it seems desperate for a resolution of the mind's needs in natural process. But Hejinian uses this dependency to keep the mind foregrounded and to re-appropriate nature into mind. What matters is not so much the scene as the sense of activity it rewards and returns as an emblem for what can be involved in the sensation of sensation.

Wordsworth's glorious "I am still" in "Tintern Abbey" is followed by a long list of predicates, all there establishing credentials for the self as poet and interpreter of nature. For Hejinian the "I" appears only momentarily, to be quickly subsumed into a care for how the self's stillness provides a concrete focus for the use of a vocabulary of photography. The "I" manages a point of rest that is compatible with constant change. Contingency need not provoke the same anxieties as it did in the earlier passages because it is inseparable from the formation of a vocabulary for seeing and appreciating what engages our care.

The fact that this scene must pass proves inseparable from an eagerness to go beyond it to other possible scenes and, most important, to other configurations of consciousness in which both the "we" and the fact of passing seem entirely acceptable conditions. And yet nothing has changed at all except how the writing comes to a different sense of its own sensations and grounds its thinking about that sense in its awareness of its own resources.

The steps are simple ones. But the world we come to inhabit is a long way from the one oppressing Arnold's efforts to give individual meanings to what has to pass.

Strange Affinities: A Partial Return to Wordsworthian Poetics After Modernism

Almost thirty years ago I made what I thought was a convincing argument contrasting Wordsworth's aesthetics of immanence with Coleridge's "symbolist" poetics.[1] In doing this I hoped to show how many aspects of what then seemed postmodern had a very different lineage from the symbolist values that had shaped modernism. Now I have to recognize several problems with that argument, but, as is the way of thirty year retrospects, I remain convinced that at core I got something right—if not about sixties postmodernism than about a strand of contemporary poetics that I find given exemplary articulation in Lyn Hejinian and Leslie Scalapino's collaborative text Sight.

My major mistake was in treating Wordsworth as only a poet of immanence. I did so in order to evade criticisms of Wordsworth's egotistical sublime, and so also to evade the heritage of confessional writing against which my postmoderns were attempting to define themselves. But I got two things wrong.

First, there is no evading the egotistical sublime in Wordsworth: being able to exult in the "I" and so to feel its expansiveness was for him a central aspect of immanence. As we see in the great crescendo at the centre of "Tintern Abbey," immanence for Wordsworth consisted in being able to feel paratactic syntax expand to include within lyric celebration the furthest reaches of the poet's exalted speech. Immanence meant that even this reach of spirit could be as grounded in natural process as the meanest thing that blows. Second, I was wrong, or at least terribly limited, about why it might matter to pursue immanence.

I was driven by the need to find conceptual structures that could simultaneously justify what poets pursued and be justified by what they accomplished. Now I think one has to handle concepts like poetic immanence somewhat differently. The crucial fact is not what the poets thought but how their thinking made possible certain ways that language could be charged with affective intensity and so take on exemplary affective resonance.

Now I hope that by addressing these mistakes I can provide a more accurate and more consequential picture of why Wordsworth matters for the study of twentieth-century poetry in general and especially for contemporary concerns with how twentieth-century poets could use language to establish and celebrate new ways of realizing immanent values. Wordsworth matters first because of the curse that the egotistical sublime was to become.

High Victorian poets could not be content unless their speakers could take on personal stances dignified by Wordsworthian high eloquence. But they could no longer marry that eloquence to processes of sensation or to modes of symbol making. So the affective basis for self-projection came increasingly to have little but the poet's imaginary identification with the role of poet as sustenance for lyric eloquence. Here I will use a short poem by Matthew Arnold to illustrate features of self-projection that become even more striking in overtly Wordsworthian poems like "The Scholar Gypsy." Then I will show how modernist rejections of romanticism might better be seen as repudiations of Victorian versions of the romantic subject that had lost the possibility of keeping the ego continuous with sensation.

My second mistake now has to enter this story. If we deal with immanence primarily as a structure of ideas we simply cannot get back beyond the modernist rejection of Victorian versions of the Wordsworthian ego (which also all too often after 1815 became the actual Wordsworthian ego). Arnold's versions of Wordsworth may have destroyed for the foreseeable future the possibility of a poetry based on explicit value schemes (in contrast to a poetry that composes values by how it inhabits particular ways of attending to and composing experience). But if we treat the poetics of immanence as primarily an emphasis on particular ways of getting as much of mind as possible made continuous with the senses, we can see that the anti-symbolist moderns and their heirs had to reinvent, sans egotistical sublime, what Wordsworth sought as his means of resisting the corrupt modes of feeling basic to social life. Wordsworth is the godfather of at least one strand of contemporary radical poetics because of how he enables us to escape the lyric heritage that Victorian poetics imposed upon him.

Wordsworth can directly speak to contemporary imaginations because he so tightly weaves the ego into elaborate textures of sensation, then treats language as itself so affectively charged that it simply continues sensation by other means. Moreover, by stressing sensation as one locus of self-consciousness, Wordsworth also made it possible to imagine at the other end of the ego, in effect, how poetry might move beyond the individual subject to the direct modeling of interpersonal subjective states.

If the sensations can be rendered so as to be shared, and if language is woven into the sensations, then the affects built out of that weaving become available for anyone who can fully assume the role of speaker of that specific linguistic formulation. By showing how our affective intensities are grounded by the modes of attention we adapt, Wordsworth also gives poetry a powerful social agenda that need not be connected to any specific political one.

In order to develop this story, I will have to presuppose an audience willing at least to entertain my description of Wordsworth without demanding further elaboration. I want to put all my emphasis on the path leading from Victorian versions of the lyrical speaking ego to contemporary fascinations with the entirely embodied authorial sensibility. Therefore, I will rest my case on three examples that I hope get to the structural core of how our intimate psychological energies can be differently distributed.

Other poets, and other poems by my authors, obviously will distribute these investments somewhat differently, but I hope my examples provide the basic terms for characterizing these differences. For Arnold I concentrate on his "Isolation. To Marguerite" because this poem concisely makes visible both the power and the problems involved in seeking Wordsworthian affective satisfactions for the lyrical ego without Wordsworthian grounds. In this poem Arnold tries to build a plausible lyrical self by substituting for a failed love a projected identification with a nature now reduced to analogues for the poet's own loneliness.

Ultimately even that projected affinity collapses into self-defensive fantasy as poetry yields itself entirely to shoring up ego-defenses under the guise of lyrical sensitivity. Then, once we see how slippery the lyrical ego can be, we are in a position to appreciate why modernists were so leery of "emotion" and so eager to replace that emphasis with the lyric exploration of "feeling," an exploration whose fundamental possibilities I think took shape in Wordsworth's Prelude. To exemplify what modernists tried to make of this turn from emotion to feeling I will turn to two short lyrics by William Carlos Williams.

Finally, I will take as my representative contemporary text a brief section of Lyn Hejinian and Leslie Scalapino's Sight because this text implicitly argues that Williams severely limits the domain of feeling by subordinating its fluid aspects to the powerful objectifying will of the artist as composer-antagonist (see Williams 186). From the perspective of contemporary radical or investigative poetry, composition is not so much a lonely forming of nature as it is a means of exploring transitional sites intensifying complex interrelationships between sensation and imagination.

In effect Hejinian and Scalapino reexamine the nature of feelings and find there resources for a model of authorship quite different from Williams's. They present composition not as the lonely giving shape to formed structures of sensations but as a reflexive means of intensifying complex interrelationships between sensation and imagination. My argument then takes the form of a historical progression. For each model depends on its predecessor for its urgency and for its self-definition. Yet it is also quite possible for each of the models to be isolated as one possibly representative rendering of affects important for contemporary life.

We need a few fundamental rough definitions in order to create a working vocabulary for dealing with affective energies within lyrics. Affect is for me the most general category for talking about how we find ourselves caring about our involvement in particular situations. Affects can be defined as states of the body experienced as inseparable from the presence of imaginary projection.

This distinguishes them on the one side from sensations, which involve simple awareness of bodily states, and on the other from beliefs, which can be articulated without relation to bodily states at all. Sensations can trigger imaginary projections, but imagination is not central to their modes of appearing for us. Consider the difference between noticing a bird and noticing that the bird's way of pecking reminds one of a certain person or state of mind. Then think of making some argument about the bird, for example that it is a finch, not a hummingbird. Here imaginings might be present, but the discipline involved requires framing and testing them, not exploring where they come from and how those energies might generate additional connections.

Affects often involve reasoning, but we do not expect reasoning either to cause them or to direct them. Even when reasoning controls our actions, it might not control the affects. I may believe on rational grounds that I should not hit a person a lot bigger than I am, but I may well stay angry and resentfully plot another form of revenge, now the more elaborate because my anger is mixed with shame at my weakness.

Once we establish a general link between sensation and imagination at the core of affectivity, we can then distinguish two basic kinds of imaginary projection, and hence between two basis structures of affect, which I will call feelings and emotions. Each mode of imagining in turn involves a different approach to agency, differences that prove central in making the historical claims I will propose. With emotions the imagination is synthetic.

It projects causes, attaches itself to objects, and projects courses of action or structures of desire in relation to those objects. That is why emotions tend to take place in terms of plots and to be correlated with the work of cognitive inquiry. When I am angry with someone, I imagine performing an action in relation to the person. More important, this practical orientation positions me toward two kinds of possible knowings. I have the potential of understanding something about myself because of how I plot the anger, and I am likely to recognize certain features of the person that I might not were I not invested in what might fuel or diminish the anger. (But my investment can also lead me to distort the importance of those traits I do see because emotions want to be fed as much as they want to find resolution.)

Feelings can occur as aspects of emotions. But their

fundamental structure is quite different. With feelings, the imagination is participatory, not synthetic. Feelings are much more a matter of the moment than are emotions. Rather than seek their cause we simply attend to the qualities of appearance that they make possible. Consequently feelings appear usually as if they simply were extensions of the sensation.

They are not parts of plots but of processes set in motion by the energies that metaphors bring into relation with the sensation. Even the simplest feelings, like hunger, are projections into sensation. Feelings come closer to the aesthetic when sensation tilts toward some kind of fascination and partial identification for which no plot seems plausible. Think of kinetic art, where simple magnetic charges affecting filament-like tentacles seem inseparable from minimal but fundamental desire. Or we might note the transition between watching the bird I referred to earlier and recognizing with Elizabeth Bishop's "Sandpiper" how the bird's activities take on anthromorphic qualities.

These two directions of the imagination also enable us to make useful distinctions between moods and passions, the other two basic types of affect. Moods are not quite feelings but they establish conditions in which feeling tone becomes a pervasive force. Here feelings are no longer attached to objects. Instead they seem continuous with some overall state of the subject. But the continuity is insistently not one for which we can provide a narrative, perhaps because moods seem pervasive and so have no clear beginning and ending, only extension and duration. Passions on the other hand are something close to super-emotions.

They are affective states circulating around plots within which the status of the I is put substantially at stake. Love is a passion because it defines who I am or who I want to be. Similarly civic emotions like pride and consideration are usually passions, while emotions exhausted in particular situations clearly are not passions. Momentary anger for example can be distinguished from the passion of abiding hatred; lust from love.

Making these distinctions has its ultimate payoff in

showing us how different emphases among the affects emphasize substantially different orientations toward subjective agency, and hence toward how values get constructed and pursued. And it is the differences in agency that will underlie the historical tale I want to tell about poetry. On the most general level we can say that emotions and passions invite Lacanian analysis, since their objects are constructed for the imagination, and the stakes involved shape what kinds of identities we can postulate and pursue.

Moreover this mode of imagining cannot be easily reconciled with those who want to treat emotions as allied with reason. Emotions do establish salience and do help us make perceptions relevant to our actions and plans. But they do so always with an urgency and sense of significance bringing to bear representations that are not quite subject to reason, at least not without destroying the very affective charge that reason seeks as its supplement.

Feelings and moods on the other hand tend not to rely on projections about ourselves as having specific identities. They stress dependencies on what we respond to, and they provide investments that bypass epistemic culture's usual ways of establishing meaning and importance. If emotions invite Lacanian analysis, feelings invite Levinasian ones in which we are aware that we are not the source of consciousness but are in a response mode, open to an otherness that exercises influence upon us.

We can build upon these general differences to isolate three particular arenas in which these contrasts play themselves out by creating a complex variety of psychological orientations—all of which become resources for poetic experiments. For example we have to keep in mind the relevance of classical oppositions between the passive and the active dimensions of affective life.

At one pole we treat the expressive action as fundamentally symptomatic, at best a passive response to forces from beyond the self and at worst a drastic displacement or evasion of what observers might conclude that one is actually feeling. At the other pole expression becomes a triumphant articulation, getting clear on something that has been bothering a person or breaking through so that the agent manages to participate actively in complex sets of emotions. Affects can dominate agency and affects can enhance an agent's sense of power and commitment. Second, we can cast the active-passive distinction in spatial terms to characterize how borders of the subject are constantly being negotiated.

Some affects create states of intense concentration: the self becomes the only active force in an indifferent environment. Other affects distribute energies and investments so that personality seems almost irrelevant: what matters is how one experiences appearances taking on fresh vitality leading one to dwell imaginatively beyond the self. Finally, it is often crucial to distinguish different kinds of borders or passages among agents. Some affects are presented as entirely specific to the subject: in experiencing this way I recognize only my own distinctive commitments. But many others have a very different structure.

Think of religious emotions, or the feelings we experience in crowds or audiences, or those around natural scenes that move us because what they offer seems available for everyone. Part of the power of art is its capacity to explore the degree to which we can participate intensely in emotions not by sympathizing with characters but by our direct awareness of the site of emotion as itself public, and perhaps more stable and enduring than any of the agents who experience it in given moments. Making that sense of transpersonal affective site a basic source for artistic experiment seems to me one of the great accomplishments of modernist abstraction, although the emphasis has always existed in music.

I present this abstract picture as a tentative grammar for appreciating the range for experiment that our affective lives afford artists and writers. Once we know where to look, we can shift much of the energy we have been putting into interpretation, the postulating of meaning and purpose for actions, into the exploration of who texts ask us to become if we participate in their particular ways of fusing sensation and imagination. Now then I can turn to exploring how that participation might take place in three quite distinct poems, the sequence of which I hope has some metaphorical force as literary history.

Arnold's "Isolation. To Marguerite" is to me the quintessential Victorian poem, intensely moving in its self-evasions and depressingly challenging to Modernists eager to escape the processes of self-absorption it embodies:

We were apart; yet, day by day
I bade my heart more constant be.
I bade it keep the world away,
And grow a home for only thee;
Nor fear'd but thy love likewise grew,
Like mine, each day, more tried, more true.
The fault was grave! I might have known,
What far too soon, alas! I learn'd—
The heart can bind itself alone,
And faith may oft be unreturn'd.
Self-sway'd our feelings ebb and swell—
Thou lov'st no more—Farewell! Farewell!
Farewell!— and thou, thou lonely heart,
Which never yet without remorse
Even for a moment didst depart
From thy remote and spheréd course
To haunt the place where passions reign—
Back to thy solitude again!
Back! with the conscious thrill of shame
Which Luna felt, that summer night,
Flash through her pure immortal frame,
When she forsook the starry height
To hang over Endymion's sleep
Upon the pine-grown Latmian steep.
Yet she, chaste queen, had never proved
How vain a thing is mortal love,
Wandering in Heaven, far removed.
But thou hast long had place to prove
This truth—to prove, and make thine own:
"Thou hast been, shall be, art, alone."
Or, if not quite alone, yet they

Which touch thee are unmating things—
Ocean and clouds and night and day;
Lorn autumns and triumphant springs;
And life, and others' joy and pain,
And love, if love, of happier men.
Of happier men—for they, at least,
Have dream'd two human hearts might blend
In one, and were through faith released
From isolation without end
Prolong'd; nor knew, although not less
Alone than thou, their loneliness.

We cannot summarize this emotion by any one label—if we could, there would be no point in writing the poem. Self-pity is probably the best general description, but we have to see the self-pity as also purposive, as an attempt to come to terms with the pain of being rejected as a lover. From my theoretical position then this poem invites us to participate self-reflexively in a process of negotiating the pain of rejection by the seductive ennobling promised by self-pity.

Expressing such elaborate symptomatic self-absorption is no easy task. Yet Arnold accomplishes it magnificently, in the process establishing a paradigm for how the Victorian age used a theater of nobility as its means of managing the pains of the failures of nobility inseparable from that dream. But self-reflection is a dangerous instrument. Arnold may be Eliot's Hamlet, unable quite to get a grip on an emotion he is doomed to keep repeating precisely because his sense of self-worth depends on achieving closure. So an analysis of the affects in this poem helps us appreciate from the inside how a Victorian ego tries to build up its sense of identity through affect, and how in the process it reveals serious problems with the imaginary projections of agency inherent in that process. This analysis also shows us why Modernism had to pursue very different affective priorities, priorities that in turn require contemporary recastings of that modernist heritage.

In my view Arnold's is a great poem because it does not hide the raw pain and desperation underlying the text's effort to achieve resignation in self-pity. Even the basic structuring devices seem shaped by that pain. The poem opens with a remembered "we" instantly displaced into a needy "I" who has to serve as his own interlocutor.

The poem is the mind's dialogue with itself trying to convince itself that this is nature's law for man. There are also two quite different past tenses, one caught up in the life now only remembered, and one, entering in the second stanza, that presents the speaker haunted by subjunctive possibilities that he has to fight off. Confronting those pasts is a bleak present threatening to swallow the future within it: "Thou hast been, shall be, art, alone." Being true to himself is inseparable from utter loneliness.

Yet Arnold's poem cannot stop with that absolute condemnation. Why? One reason is structural. The poem's first three stanzas move from the initial memory of a relationship to the pure acceptance of solitude, now having learned not to "haunt the place where passions reign." The last three stanzas go in the opposite direction, as if Arnold could not be content with the personal resolution without also universalizing the significance of his emotional state.

Where stanza three ends by encountering the apparent truth of his personal plight, stanza five ends with an abstract generalization about that solitude. And even then the poem remains restless. It may have arrived at the truth but it has not yet contextualized that truth in a way that the ego can accommodate. So Arnold adds two compensatory complications. He can reach some connection with the unmating things that accompany his loneliness. And, more important, he can position himself by an elaborate contrast with those who though unmating still dream of two hearts blending into one.

His dazzling play on the boundaries of what can and cannot be shared in loneliness makes his disappointment seem to him ultimately ennobling. After all he learns from his suffering. In fact he not only learns abstract truths, he also masters a new position for himself in relation to nature. He in effect learns to occupy its core, the one truly disillusioned person willing to accept fully the loneliness to which we are all condemned. My students find this final self-congratulatory move appalling. But, older and lonelier, I want to keep sympathy for Arnold while recognizing just how deeply self-deluding this bid for an ennobling lucidity is. In effect we have now to read the poem backwards, recognizing how much he works to secure a self-image and tracing the moves that in seeming to make this possible also make it almost reprehensible. We have to appreciate how a sense of pathos seems to haunt this particular self-expressive process.

So rather than see the situation entirely through the speaker's interpretations we will shift to how the speaker goes about constructing the self that for him seems capable of providing a satisfying resolution to his pain. For that we should turn to those moments when the expressive activity tries too hard or falters—quintessentially in the poem's repetitions and in the central fourth stanza which I passed over in discussing the structure.

Why the repetitions? The first one is pretty easy to handle. Our speaker wants simply to say "farewell" to love, but he cannot because something important would not be resolved by that gesture. The obvious candidate for non-resolution is the state of his ego. The "might have known" is not a sufficient ego position from which to walk away. So he has to keep reworking the situation until it seems that it was not she who chose to leave so much as it was he who was helped to realise that he had given into illusion. She tested and brought to the fore his ability to live with a full grasp of loneliness as an absolute condition. So "farewell" opens a condition of dialogue with himself and enables him to relegate to a mistake his leaving his solitude for the life of passion. From this new perspective her act of breaking their bond becomes almost irrelevant. The important romance is with himself.

But there is not yet a self sufficient for him to cathect to in the way that he had cathected to her. To get to that lovable self he needs another, this time quite revealing repetition generating the fourth stanza.

Here he moves beyond recognition to fantasy, so that he participates in the romance imagination at the core of passion, but only insofar as he becomes the focus for those romance energies. To accomplish this he recasts his shame at being rejected into shame at having given way to this very way of imagining in romance terms. Yet we also realise that the shame he postulates is not all the shame that he feels. For his mistake was less in yielding to passion than in putting himself in a situation where he could be rejected, where his own strange sense that one can treat the heart as duty bound might not be sufficient grounds for securing another's passion.

I cannot tell whether Arnold intended this level of exposure for his speaker. I suspect he did not. But his third repetition offers perhaps the most brilliant and most touching moment in this occluded drama. For at the end of the fifth stanza the speaker reaches his ultimate nadir—the realization of loneliness in past, present, and future.

No wonder that this repetition seems somewhat different. Rather than simply echoing the previous expression this one seeks a slight escape: some companionship is possible. For this speaker, however, even that glimpse of weakness seems vulnerability, so we get a fourth repetition which uses the figure of happier men as his contrast to his own freedom from illusion. Partial concession makes possible absolute repudiation. And here absolute repudiation turns out to be both true for the speaker and false as an analysis of his situation. At his most intense acceptance of loneliness, the speaker is in fact desperately crying out for some kind of pity, or at least some recognition of a nobility that depends on his pain over these flimsy and needy contrasts.

The poem's expressive intensity enables the speaker to assert an independence entirely belied by the rhetorical manipulations showing how badly he needs not only the posture but someone to convince of the posture. The I produced by passion seems an I desperately seeking a reflection, while in the process undermining the possibility of getting mirrored back what it wants to have seen.

History enters our story when we realise that our own readings quite likely echo those for whom struggle against Victorian poetry was necessary for survival. As readers become familiar with the poem they have to experience the speaker's pathos along with his power. They are allowed the gestures of nobility only with an accompanying consciousness of all of the dependencies and pains such gestures must try to ignore. From this perspective then it is not surprising that Arnold's speaker becomes Eliot's Prufrock, forced to confront the displacing force of his own need for passions which might produce desired imaginary identities.

Nor should it be surprising that one of Eliot's basic theoretical concerns was to make sharp distinctions between emotions and feelings, the former dependent on self-staging plots while the latter afford affects more closely woven into the rendering of sensations. In that concreteness one can hope for intensities and attachments much less bound to the illusory project of constructing individual egos.

For heuristic purposes, the best quick way to indicate what this cultural shift involves is to turn to the lyrics of William Carlos Williams. For much of the power of these poems consists in their knowing how to resist becoming vehicles of emotion, and hence of plots involving imaginary identifications.[2] In Williams readers have to learn to accept what the moment gives, and to have the discipline to engage the moment without attempting to build upon it. Correspondingly, Williams shows how and why modernist constructivism tries to keep the focus on how the art composes the event rather than on how selves interpret and transform affect into "meanings" and roles. The idealized imaginary individual self has to give way to the floating modes of consciousness that can be composed by an impersonal constructivist intelligence.

I will concentrate on two short poems, one stressing how the composition of feeling thrives in its refusal of emotional build-up and the other articulating Williams's very unArnoldian rendering of personal identity within the lyric. "The Young Housewife" opens with the speaker alone in his car passing a housewife who "moves about in negligee behind/ the wooden walls of her husband's house." The poem ends:

Then again she comes to the curb

to call the ice-man, fish-man, and stands
shy, uncorseted, tucking in
stray ends of hair, and I compare her
to a fallen leaf.
The noiseless wheels of my car
rush with a crackling sound over
dried leaves as I bow and pass smiling.

On the most general level the poem's energies are gathered in a contrast between what leads him to compare the wife to a fallen leaf and the sound of dried leaves marking his departure and somehow contributing to his smile. But I don't think we are intended to dwell much on this general level. The poem's energies are focused on the possibility of establishing concrete affective relations that depend on not letting the scene become metaphoric. Instead we have to let the juxtaposition of details do all of the work, without our irritable reaching for dramatic or thematic models.

Mention of "her husband's house" somewhat melodramatically sets the stage. In the first stanza everything is arranged, almost ceremonious. The second stanza then shifts to quite particular feelings gathering around the ways that her body contrasts with that order. Each detail complicates the picture. Her shyness defines an attitude; her uncorseted fleshiness indicates a simple voluptuousness; and her stray ends of hair mark a minimal rebelliousness or at least freedom to be something other than her husband's possession. Yet her freedom is severely limited and not internalized at all, the freedom one might say of a fallen leaf, attractive in its pure contingency and marginality.

It is crucial in developing this picture not to let the details add up into some kind of traditional snap photograph rendered in words. The details can be made to cohere. But we honour them best by keeping a distance between them so that all seem stray hair momentarily taking a particular pattern. Each detail then peeks out at us like an aspect of the woman's spirit, unpossessed but also undirected and unable to reach out to passers-by or to return whatever desire the watching generates. And the watcher knows that the desire cannot be returned. Accepting that is part of the texture of feeling preparing for the speaker's final return to his own version of contingent and frustrated freedom. We have to ask why the speaker smiles as he goes away. But we also have to be satisfied with an explanation as partial as the speaker's knowledge of the woman he watches.

In some respects the smile is ironic, or at least ruefully accepting. Whatever elicits the metaphor of a fallen leaf turns out to be reduced to the actual dead leaves filling the street. Contingency reigns. But the smile also has a self-reflective dimension. The speaker finds satisfaction I think in recognizing the pure momentariness of his vision. His glimpse is not unlike her uncorseted presence, a slight escape from being possessed.

Yet one can trust that freedom, just as one trusts the smile, so long as nothing more is asked of it. Any effort to base meaning on the scene or to expand the self's role would destroy this minimal freedom and reimpose the order in which husbands own houses and others comply with the rules of ownership. Any effort to make an emotion of this feeling would destroy what freedom is possible and put in its place a problematic self having to play out a doomed Arnoldian project of self-construction.

Williams's "Danse Russe" offers a more pronounced version of this effort to redistribute affective energies so that self is much less burdened than Arnold's by the need to rely on elaborate imaginative constructions. The speaker hypothesizes dancing naked in front of a mirror while everyone else in the household sleeps, singing to himself: "I am lonely, lonely,/ I was born to be lonely,/ I am best so!" "Danse Russe" ends:

If I admire my arms, my face,
my shoulders, flanks, buttocks
against the yellow drawn shades,—
Who shall say I am not
the happy genius of my household?

I will confine myself to two observations about this marvelously intricate poem. One involves how the poem empties out the form of traditional emotions, the other how it focuses energy instead on something like the immediacy of feelings won by holding off the demands of the imaginary ego. Our speaker is clearly a solipsist, not unlike Eliot's Prufrock. Yet he has found an intriguing way of living with that solipsism. When he turns to himself in the conventional lyric space of self-possession, the only self he cares about is the one that manages not to be beholden to some examining eye or possessing spouse. Williams stresses the "not" because he is more interested in freedom or unsponsoredness than he is in attributing any clear judgment or even identity to his activity.

This morning ritual is in the service of anti-identity, of being able to play out a momentary self precisely because he is beholden to no judges. And, as Gertrude Stein might say, perhaps sheer commitment to one's impulse without fear of judgment is precisely what it means to be a genius. But it cannot suffice to base genius on negativity.

Hence the importance of my second observation. Williams's lineation is called upon to play a fundamental role in the poem. It has to provide affective intensity for a series of gestures that have little significant symbolic or imaginary force. These acts, qua acts, will not sustain a rhetoric of genius or even of lyric significance.

But this lineation holds them over against pure banality just enough to let them emerge as capable of bearing attention and hence of becoming fascinating in their own right. What merely passes has the capacities to behave as if it composed a picture, to invite dwelling on different rhythms of attention, and to give the body a passing delight in its own ordinariness. Making all of that possible, without a plot or deep psychology or promise of consequence, may be just what genius has to do in our secular century and in the speaker's otherwise orderly domestic life. Contemporary American radical poetics has obviously learned a good deal from Williams about resisting the culture's primary modes of symbolic and imaginary identification. Yet the various orientations within this poetic also have to establish substantial differences from his characteristic lyric gestures. From those perspectives Williams is far too scenic. The sensations basic to his poems are organized by a dramatic sense of the world, with insufficient attention paid to the affects organized within the activity of writing. We are asked to identify with phenomenological stances by embodied characters rather than with the authorial activity, even though the constructive force of that activity is quite pronounced.

We feel the effects of lineation, but as an intensifying of the scene rather than as a presentation of authorial engagement. Correspondingly, radical poetics is not quite satisfied with how authorship is represented in Williams. He turns out to be at least as impersonal as the poet Eliot fantasized, with the author somewhat aloof from the perspectival energies organized within the work. No wonder that Williams projects the poet as composer-antagonist, standing out as a vertical force in a horizontal landscape.

A new poetry would have to explore authorial subject positions more committed to challenging boundaries between subject and object as well as between subjects. The poet could not rest in the safety of the composer position but would have to risk the range of sensual attachments available for the medium of writing. In taking those risks it might be possible to stage writing as an activity with exemplary social force because it can envision a version of affect capable of organizing shareable resistance to dominant cultural habits for orienting affective engagement.

I cannot here survey various styles within the poetic position I am characterizing in such general terms. Instead I am going to focus on one particular example of work that foregrounds its own self-conscious responsiveness to the concerns about affect and authorship that I have been summarizing. On the topic of affects elicited by self-consciousness about writing there is no contemporary work more suggestive than Sight, a collaboration between Lyn Hejinian and Leslie Scalapino. For the collaboration itself takes on all sorts of exemplary qualities. Most collaborations try to fuse authorial energies, and so in effect pursue a synthetic version of the Arnoldian ego.

But by taking turns responding to one another's brief

units of two or three paragraphs based on some aspect of sight, Hejinian and Scalapino take turns insisting on the pressure of differences that arise as each disposition expresses itself and as each contribution reorganizes the imaginative field the writing has to enter.

All the major LANGUAGE writers share this concern for foregrounding the activity of writing over the illusionary worlds it manages to project. Writing seems the thing in itself behind the appearances being reflected on the surface of our cave. But substantial differences emerge when we examine how this focus on writerly presence can fold affect into sensation and give the compositional energies exemplary social force. Poets like Charles Bernstein and Bob Perelman, for example, take what we might call a fundamentally ironic attitude toward all expressivist ideals.

They do not dismiss affect, but they also are very careful not to let ideals of intensity or depth seduce them into postures that lose sight of the irreducible writtenness, literal or figurative, of all our affective identifications. So they emphasize writerly engagement with and against the modes of affect inscribed in the social registers of our language. Instead of the mind's dialogue with itself, these poets stage writing as dialogue with those registers of language. Lyric energy resides in the efforts of intelligence to hear its situatedness and to develop a little freedom for itself and the community it addresses, usually in the form of ironic play ranging from fierce opposition to reluctant complicity.

Hejinian and Scalapino have other ambitions. While they share Bernstein's and Perelman's suspicions about the rhetorics of sensibility, their work has been more phenomenological, more attentive to writing as a direct engagement with the dynamics of sensation and the projection of intimate desire. With Sight I think they have discovered a marvelous vehicle for foregrounding these differences, primarily because the dialogue form gives the writing a literal stage on which to play out through textual time complexities pervading the personal and transpersonal aspects of expressive activity. To frame these differences I will begin with an extended passage from the

"Introduction" to Hejinian's collection of essays, The Language of Inquiry:

This is not to say that poetry is about transitions but that "aboutness" (in poetry, but, I would argue, also in life) is transitional, transitory; indeed poetry (and perhaps life) calls conventional notions of "aboutness" into question.... The language of poetry is a language of inquiry, not the language of a genre. It is that language in which a writer (or a reader) both perceives and is conscious of the perception. Poetry, therefore, takes as its premise that language is a medium for experiencing experience.... It is at points of linkage... that one discovers the reality of being in time, of taking one's chance, of becoming another, all with the implicit understanding that this is happening (The Language of Inquiry 2-3)

There are here three concepts at the core of a poetics that Hejinian and Scalapino share, even though their particular projects usually pursue quite different emphases and tones. The most fundamental belief is this insistence on a pervasive critique of conventional ideas of aboutness—not only in relation to how fictions portray worlds but also to how persons engage one another. Traditionally aboutness is conceived in terms of representations. Language pictures events and agents provide accounts of themselves. But if one emphasizes writing as the locus of affective events, then the feelings become literal states. Writing does not comment about what one is feeling but makes articulate the actual event of feeling as it takes place, or makes a place for itself.

Radical as this claim sounds, I think all the great modernists would sympathize with it, if not subscribe to it. Hejinian pushes the resistance to aboutness in fresh directions when she adds a second claim insisting that the event becomes a vehicle for the experience of experience. Here all descriptive and dramatic and ironic notions of writing yield entirely to phenomenological ones. Writing does not so much present a world as present the sensation of sensation or the experience of experience. This shift substantially alters what we can say about affect in poetry.

For where Williams still locates affect in the rendering of

a scene, and where Bernstein and Perelman tend to locate affect in various kinds of resistance to the public textures of language, Hejinian projects affect as itself the most fundamental of phenomenological states. Indeed one cannot imitate or describe the affects basic to lyric because the affects are inseparable from the qualities of self-consciousness one brings to the events taking place within the writing.

Finally, Hejinian suggests that this particular kind of affect has a distinctive social and ethical force because as event, as happening, the writing so involves the self that what appears is to some degree or another different even from the intentions that got one going in the first place. The logic of event is inseparable from the logic that bases the possibility of ethical thinking on an irreducible responsiveness to the otherness of the other. For then we have no basis for imposing our own preconceptions. We are left only with the options of feeling our own emptiness or attempting to attune ourselves to the very processes by which that otherness emerges and takes on its own directions.

Sight seems to me a superb realization of all these possibilities because the affective texture is entirely woven into the structure of call and response. There are no imaginary selves invoked to explain emotions, since the affects only emerge at the intersection of selves. And there are no affects that the text gestures toward while keeping its aloofness. Hejinian and Scalapino share Williams's concern to keep the affects from taking on some separate reality apart from the specific modalities of perception and expression. But now the reality they do compose is not in some world over against the author but in the author's own articulated processes of sensation.

Here the author is always already audience. Writing becomes a constant process of recognizing the presence of others, of positioning oneself simultaneously in relation to another person and to various topics that arise, and of working constantly at the boundary between understanding and misunderstanding or sympathy and turning away toward the recesses of private obsession. Moreover because this process controls an entire volume, the poets manage also to capture the importance of repetition as a concrete index of those feelings which seem fundamental or unresolved or obsessive to the individuals.

However the individual is not asked to explain or interpret those feelings, nor is the interlocutor invited to play therapist. Feelings are not expressed to be interpreted so much as to be pursued so that one finds where they lead and tests what transitions their articulation makes possible. In fact the text suggests that we most fully respond to others not when we try to find words for what has been said but when we treat the other's expression as a provocation enabling us to change directions and try other routes of engagement. This enables us to avoid attributing the kinds of causes that turn feelings into emotions and dialogue into therapy. Stressing writing as the locus of affect keeps the entire affective field fluid so that we are constantly aware of how our own self-reflection depends on what the presence of the other opens up for us. Friendship becomes a structure based on a dance of difference and realignment. I have space only for one example, so I can illustrate only a very limited range of the complex play of writerly effects and affects made present within the text as a whole. The relevant sequence begins when Hejinian takes up an anxiety about the aesthetic being a means of evading the fact of actual wrecks. She tries to convince herself that instead of being an evasion this focusing of consciousness serves as a means of evaluation.

But the two poets do not easily rest with that formulation. Memories of pain and fears of death occupy the text, until Hejinian turns from their dream-laden abstraction to the following passage, the only one in this section rendered as verse: One is happy in one's susceptibility to chance, accident, hazard So a descriptive sentence (being an account of what unfolds to sensibility) may be precarious and must be careful

As something's happening
The sentence says so with felicity — that's what one might get when writing in sight with happy exactitude

In the realm of death, too Each thing, no matter how

happy in its word, is ('only') floated In the realm of life, too A hummingbird in the morning flies right up to me at the door and stays in the air

I am moved in part by the ways that this passage resists my efforts to cite it as somehow a privileged example for the text. Each gesture here toward lyric closure suddenly lapses into something like prose, with its resistant wordly flatness and its utter openness to contingency. Hejinian probably wants us to feel how fleeting and ineffective our capacity for aestheticizing is in relation to the world of fact and disaster. Yet at the same time she wants that concern with aestheticizing to pervade the entire reflection so that we find ourselves strangely empowered by this particular overall attitude toward our own contingency and impotence. We sense the sensation of impotence and fear made articulate, so that we cannot rest simply in those all too standard states, but we have to explore the complexity of feeling which the self-consciousness brings.

Hejinian's refusal of elaborate metaphor keeps her close to Williams. But that proximity serves primarily to set off basic differences between his subtle play of dramatic affect and her concern for the sensation of sensation as itself affectively charged. In one respect she is even more respectful than Williams of the limitations fact imposes on imagination. Not only is there no synthetic work of the interpretive imagination, there is not even the faith that particular feelings provide moments of attention satisfying the speaker's desires.

All the details up to the emergence of the hummingbird lead consciousness back to death and to chance. But the mind's play upon, or, better, within, those sensations opens a quite different space for feeling. (Relations between inside and outside are fundamental motifs in the volume as a whole.) We are asked to experience strange investments in the very process of recognizing the problems of chance, accident, and hazard. For "happening," "hap," and "happiness" become here closely allied.

This effect is not mere linguistic accident, but neither is it a Heideggerean attempt to put authority in etymology. Hejinian wants to earn the connection by making the feeling for the one merge with the feeling for the other, as if the very conditions generating fear were inseparable from what makes for happiness. More important, one cannot read the poem carefully without experiencing the sense of constant movement between the registers of "happening" and "happiness," as if recognizing this fluidity could provide a basis for pursuing the satisfaction the poem seeks.

Then we can speak of happiness without any need to speculate about moving from facts to values. Satisfaction comes not in what we believe but in how we go about processing our sense of what those facts involve.

Once we stress the feeling for feelings in the passage, many of its details begin to resonate, again without in any way being metaphorically transfigured. Notice how the second sentence has to bring some kind of concreteness to the initially vague and intuitively silly opening statement. Why is one happy in such susceptibility? Wouldn't one be much happier if there were no such problems?

The resulting "so" has a lot of work to do in establishing an answer. But our grasp of the difficulties can lead directly to an appreciation of how the specific choices here respond to the pressure. The contrast between "may" and "must" echoes and reverses the syntax at the end of Stevens's "Of Modern Poetry": "It must/ Be the finding of a satisfaction, and may/ Be of a man skating, a woman dancing, a woman/ Combing." For Hejinian the specific permissions do not matter. Everything rides on the imperative to be "careful."

In my view this imperative both describes and enacts the overall texture of feeling that the poem sets against its fears concerning contingencies of all sorts. "Careful" refers to all those fears. The poem bears the weight of cares that constantly resist aestheticization.

Yet "careful" also refers self-reflexively to the poem's efforts to embody a mode of activity that can be responsive to such weight. And this doubling of meaning prepares a specific model of reflexive action soon to be further elaborated when the relation of "happening" to "happiness" becomes explicit. That doubling in turn is framed by a more complex invocation of the way feelings or framing can pervade the effort at self-description.

For Hejinian relies on the Stevensian resources of the "as," in order to show just what care can bring about. At first this "as" seems consumed simply in its temporal function: when something significant is happening pay attention to it. But my paraphrase seems to miss the mark on many levels. One might also say that the care is necessary because something is happening. But this reading also keeps the care simply as something parallel to the happening. I think we also have to see care as continuous with the happening, perhaps an adverb modifying the very conditions that allow the happening entrance to consciousness. "As" here thickens the sense of two orders at work—one descriptive and one involving the ways that the mind finds itself an invested participant in the very possibilities of description.

It is not a large leap then to the next line, where self-reflection becomes explicit and the sentences become visible actors on the scene. But here Hejinian produces another surprise. She is not willing to let the self-reference flow smoothly into the practical situation or have its realization constitute a moment of triumph.

The sentence's power to abstract itself from the particulars returns consciousness to all the fears circulating around death. It too shares with these multiple meanings a frightening weightlessness. The very doubling of meanings linking hap to happiness and fear to concern also keeps present something like an awareness of the unbearable lightness of being.

And so we get our hummingbird. On one level, or better on all levels, this is just a moment of happenstance. Certainly no guardian spirit sends the bird and its hovering is not a symbol of grace. Yet the bird does take on many of the properties of grace simply because its concreteness brings all the strands of the poem into momentary coexistence. And that coexistence is insistently concrete.

The bird's most important action is simply its manifesting its power to stay in the air. This cannot provide a thematic resolution except for something clunky and moralistic. Yet the bird does bring back the motif of care and establishes a situation where we see that not only words float in the air. And not all things that stay in the air need remind us (only) of death. The hummingbird offers a parallel to the poem's own effort to keep reflective distance while hovering very close to worlds exhausted by description.

So its hovering participates in the same basic forces as the double meanings that prevent key terms like "happening" from being reduced to the world of pure contingencies. In fact this hovering so perfectly matches what the mind has been doing that it allows author and readers to engage in self-reflexiveness without postulating any kind of empirical subject. The hovering itself constitutes a version of engagement that all subjects can take as their own, without the mediation of personal plots.

Satisfying as it is, this moment too must immediately pass, here into Scalapino's reply with its intense questioning of the effort to let the hummingbird serve any kind of resolving function: even if she wasn't [past] where at dawn on gorges burning the tar — migratory labour on roads — as it being at dawn 'only' there 'accident' of birds [that are] being in space. — singing too only floating in the realm of life too — are they at [their] present and past (at the same time) — and separately which is the space [them] — the figures the same as space, no other phenomena — 'something's happening' is this too these blossoms purple-white-fringed blooming in the time away from them — and before — at the same time as 'one' is happy

The abstractness that had existed only in affect organized by the doubleness of meaning now takes on something like an existence of its own. In fact the feeling of space as an abstracted floating becomes so intense that it works its effects on the very form of the sentence. This mode of consciousness seems to need these brackets because all claims about existence and identification have to be bracketed. Just as one hummingbird must become many, one moment of satisfaction must be placed in a larger context where even the realm of life begins to float. Even the hummingbird gets abstracted into the bird song that dissipates into the atmosphere.

However even this level of abstraction generates a countermovement. The text modulates back to an awareness that in this space too "something's happening." For one is prepared to return to appreciate how blossoming flowers themselves offer something like a parallel to verbal abstraction, anchoring its ways of organizing sensation while itself taking on force as an overall field of relations. But Hejinian is not content. Her response repudiates all this abstractness for this prosaic passage:

The hummingbird is busy with the mass of sensations, 'up' and 'down,' advancing and receding, among cascades of accidental purple morning glories hanging (where they weren't meant to be) from a tree.

Perhaps it is better to say what seems repudiation is really an effort to right a balance and to use abstractness as a frame for bringing the aesthetic back into the world, ironically where it too is not meant to be but where it melds perfectly with strange contingencies in nature.

On the basis of this new concreteness, now charged with affect, Hejinian's passage returns to abstraction, but this time with all the sensations of floating beautifully anchored—in nature and in the mind's appreciation of the kinds of composure self-awareness can bring:

Still the air sustains the sensation of relevance — that this is ' meant to be' — but the hummingbird flying about in it seems to go to one side Then the tree acts as an 'anchoring point' so the garden has 'top' and 'bottom' The hummingbird makes a 'correction' — backs "I" am still, so this is a still — in motion, blooming, and fringed, in continuation While this vocabulary, which is still, for seeing — another at the same time — we pass Here anchoring is inseparable from adjusting to how fluid movement creates a range of stills, each allowing for correction and readjustment.

Wordsworth haunts this passage, since it seems desperate for a resolution of the mind's needs in natural process. But Hejinian uses this dependency to keep the mind foregrounded and to re-appropriate nature into mind. What matters is not so much the scene as the sense of activity it rewards and returns as an emblem for what can be involved in the sensation of sensation. Wordsworth's glorious "I am still" in "Tintern Abbey" is followed by a long list of predicates, all there establishing credentials for the self as poet and interpreter of nature. For Hejinian the "I" appears only momentarily, to be quickly subsumed into a care for how the self's stillness provides a concrete focus for the use of a vocabulary of photography.

The "I" manages a point of rest that is compatible with constant change. Contingency need not provoke the same anxieties as it did in the earlier passages because it is inseparable from the formation of a vocabulary for seeing and appreciating what engages our care. The fact that this scene must pass proves inseparable from an eagerness to go beyond it to other possible scenes and, most important, to other configurations of consciousness in which both the "we" and the fact of passing seem entirely acceptable conditions. And yet nothing has changed at all except how the writing comes to a different sense of its own sensations and grounds its thinking about that sense in its awareness of its own resources.

The steps are simple ones. But the world we come to inhabit is a long way from the one oppressing Arnold's efforts to give individual meanings to what has to pass.

Chapter 16

Study Questions

Q. Write essay on the Solitary Figures of William Wordsworth?

Most of the characters who appear in the poetry of William Wordsworth (1770-1850) are solitary in some way; there are none who appear to be the sociable type which can be found in the poems of other Romantic poets, such as Byron's Don Juan, and Childe Harolde. The reason for this is perhaps that Wordsworth himself was quite a solitary person; although he appeared to enjoy the company of a select few, for example his beloved sister Dorothy, he seemed to be happiest when he had only Nature for company.

Wordsworth's preference for his own company seems to have been a characteristic which began in early childhood. In his writings about childhood experiences in The Prelude he was often alone, as in the incident of the stolen boat (1. 356-400), or if he was in company, would stand apart for a while to consider nature, as in the ice skating incident (1. 415-462). Further examples of his solitary nature as a child are provided by the poems Nutting and Expostulation and Reply.

It appears that even as a young boy he would take time to consider nature and beauty. He writes in Nutting as he stands in 'one dear nook':

A little while I stood,
Breathing with such suppression of the heart
As joy delights in

And in Expostulation and Reply when the young Wordsworth is reprimanded by his good friend Matthew for apparently sitting on a stone doing nothing, he replies:

Nor less I deem that there are Powers
Which of themselves our minds impress;
That we can feed this mind of ours
In a wise passiveness.

It seems that Wordsworth thought it important to consider and appreciate nature fully, and he often liked to do this alone. Perhaps this is one of the reasons why he appears to have such great respect for many of the solitary figures about whom he writes in his poetry.

Most of the lonely characters Wordsworth writes about are ordinary rustic people. He explains his reasons for this rather unusual choice of subject matter at great length in his preface to Lyrical Ballads. He writes that within rustic life:

The passions of man are incorporated with the beautiful and permanent forms of nature.

He also writes that these rustic people are: Belonging to nature rather than manners As Wordsworth believed nature to be of such importance, he had great admiration, and perhaps even envy of those people who lived according to the rule of nature rather than the social constraints imposed by man. He admired their simplicity, and also seemed to believe that more sophisticated people could learn a lot from them. Their emotions appear more pure, as they seem less worried about other people's opinion of them.

Although Wordsworth's solitary characters are all rustic, they are extremely varied and Wordsworth admires them all for different reasons.

An emotion which Wordsworth appeared to be particularly interested in was that of maternal passion, and he illustrates the power and importance of this through various poems, including The Thorn, The Mad Mother, and The Complaint of a Forsaken Indian Woman. These three poems all deal with a solitary mother and Wordsworth's wonder at the mother-child relationship and its uniqueness. The poem The Mad Mother describes a mad woman who sits underneath a hay stack (close to nature) with just her baby for company. She says:

Sweet babe! they say that I am mad,
But nay, my heart is far too glad;

Wordsworth suggests that she has been cast aside by society, abandoned by the baby's father, but remains happy because she has her child. He also suggests that the baby has a calming influence on the woman when she says:

Suck little babe, oh suck again!
It cools my blood; it cools my brain;
Thy lips I feel them, baby! they
Draw from my heart the pain away.

Throughout the poem the woman emphasises and reiterates the fact that she cares deeply for her baby, is greatly concerned that he does not come to any harm and, although she has been looking for the baby's father, it is strongly suggested at the end of the poem that she will be happy without him, as long as she has her baby. The poem ends:

Now laugh and be gay, to the woods away!
And there, my babe; we'll live for aye.

Wordsworth illustrates in this poem that it is possible for someone to be alone but entirely happy, as she has her baby and nature for company. It is necessary that the mother is alone in order for the poet to show how fulfilling maternal passion can be, and how it can even be a calming influence in the instance of madness.

This idea is continued in The Thorn. This poem's central character is Martha Ray, who Wordsworth deşcribes thus:

A woman in a scarlet cloak,
And to herself she cries,
Oh misery! oh misery!
Oh woe is me! Oh misery!

Through her deep melancholy Wordsworth shows the trauma of losing a child. Martha Ray was also considered mad so it must be noted that Wordsworth wrote of her when it was almost time for her to give birth:

And when at last her time drew near,
Her looks were calm, her senses clear.

The significance of Martha Ray's solitude is slightly different to that of the mother in The Mad Mother. While The Mad Mother illustrates a mother's joy at possessing a child and The Thorn a mother's despair of losing one, it is possible that the latter also illustrates the cruelty of society. Martha Ray mourns alone, no one comforts her. Instead, they speculate about what might have happened to the child:

... but some will say
She hanged her baby on the tree,
Some say she drowned it in the pond

There is, of course, no evidence whatsoever that she killed her baby; Wordsworth himself comments 'I do not think she would'. In this poem he appears to be illustrating not only a mother's sorrow at losing her child, but also the often unsympathetic nature of society.

The Complaint of a Forsaken Indian Woman makes the point that the woman seems less concerned about the fact that she is about to die than about her child. In the final stanza of the poem she despairs that:

My poor forsaken child! If I
For once could have thee close to me,
With happy heart I then would die,
And my last thoughts would happy be.

In these three poems Wordsworth illustrates that the happiness of the three mothers rests almost entirely on their child. This message is achieved much more effectively by portraying the mothers as solitary, thereby suggesting that nothing in their life is more important than the child, and thus illustrating the intensity of maternal passion.

Wordsworth also writes about rustic characters who do not have a particular story to tell, who he appears to admire merely for their rusticity and simplicity. The best example of this is probably Simon Lee, the Old Huntsman. In this poem Wordsworth explicitly tells the reader:

It is no tale; but should you think,
Perhaps a tale you'll make it.

His admiration for the man's gratitude is the key point of the poem. Wordsworth is once again making the point that he greatly admires the fact that these solitary, rustic people are unashamed to show their emotions. This idea is furthered in The Last of the Flock, in which the poet writes:

In distant countries I have been,

And yet I have not often seen
A healthy man, a man full grown,
Weep in the public roads alone.

Wordsworth appears to admire both the shepherd's display of emotion and his solitude, suggesting that the man does not wish to burden his family with his sorrow. Wordsworth is also impressed because the man is selling off his sheep despite the fact that, as the man says:

Sir! 'twas a precious flock to me,
As dear as my own children be;

He is selflessly selling his last sheep in order to support his family, and bearing his sorrow alone, emphasising his generous nature. Wordsworth seems to have written this poem to show the lack of selfishness of many rustic people, perhaps so that others may learn from it. Simon Lee is one of the less content rustics. A much happier solitary figure is the little girl who Wordsworth meets in his poem We Are Seven. This girl does not feel lonely despite the fact that two of her siblings have died and the others have moved away, leaving her alone with her mother. She constantly reiterates 'We are seven!' and even goes to the graves of her dead siblings and sings to them. This girl is happy and does not feel alone, despite her solitude. Wordsworth greatly admires her happiness, contentment and complete lack of feeling of alienation. This poem seems to illustrate both the innocence of children and the fact that we can learn from it, and also that loneliness is entirely due to a person's attitude. This girl is alone, but does not feel as if she is.

A stark contrast to this is The Female Vagrant. This woman, who started out like a happy and well provided-for has been forced into the mendicant life by a series of unfortunate circumstances. She is so distressed by her situation that she breaks down in tears as she finishes relating her tale. She is an example of someone who is alone and unhappy about it. Perhaps this poem is a criticism of society in the same way as is The Thorn; no one now shows this woman any generosity or friendship. She is forced into a life of poverty, solitude, and unhappiness, through no fault of our own.

A contrast to this woman is the hermit described in Lines

left upon a Seat in a Yew-tree. He has chosen a life of solitude because he cannot relate to people. Wordsworth writes, after describing the hermit, and his unhappiness:

Stranger! henceforth be warned; and know, that pride,
Howe'er disguised in its own majesty,
Is littleness; that he, who feels contempt
For any living thing, hath faculties
Which he has never used; that thought with him
Is in its infancy.

Although Wordsworth seems to feel pity for this man, he does not feel admiration. This man's loneliness and unhappiness were self-induced, and he warns his reader against it by making an example of this hermit. However, he also makes it clear that the hermit feels more at home in nature than among people, but Wordsworth seems to suggest that a balance should be found between the two; although appreciation of nature is important, it is also desirable to relate to people. The characters about which he writes who are in a permanent state of absolute solitude, rather than a temporary one, are rarely happy, for example, Martha Ray.

The solitary characters often find a certain amount of solace in nature, as did Wordsworth himself. Examples of this are the reaper in The Solitary Reaper, and the child in We Are Seven. Wordsworth believed nature to be a great comfort. A poem which fully illustrates this is The Dungeon. In this poem he praises nature's virtues by contrasting the destructive solitude of a dungeon:

... uncomforted
And friendless solitude, groaning and tears,
And savage faces, at the clanking hour,
Seen through the steams and vapour of his dungeon
By the lamp's dismal twilight!

to the to the much more beneficial influence which he feels nature would be:

His angry spirit healed and harmonized
By the benignant touch of love and beauty.

In this poem he uses the solitary figure to illustrate not only the healing power of nature, but also to criticise society for its unsympathetic attitude towards convicts. There are numerous other solitary figures in Wordsworth's poetry and there is not room to describe them all. However, there is one other character who is worth mentioning as he displays an entirely different type of solitude. This is the boy in The Idiot Boy. He is entirely content, but mentally lives in a different world, as we see from his description of the moon and an owl:

The cocks did crow to-whoo, to-whoo,
And the sun did shine so cold

His view of the world is different to that of others, but he is happy in this solitude.

It is evident that Wordsworth placed great importance on his solitary characters, as he so often wrote about them. Wordsworth wrote in the preface to Lyrical Ballads: Poems to which any value can be attached, were never produced on any variety of subjects but by a man who being possessed of more than usual organic sensibility had also thought long and deeply. Wordsworth obviously saw himself as this man described above, and believed he had seen the worth and importance of these ordinary, solitary figures.

They are all important for different reasons, but often Wordsworth admired their solitude because it gave them more time to think about nature and their general being. The emotions of a solitary person are generally more intense as they have no one to share them with, so this is perhaps another reason why he often wrote about people alone. However, it seems that many of these solitary people represent aspects of himself. He seems to enjoy his own company, or rather, the sole company of nature. Undoubtedly his first concern is expressing the pure emotion of these people to the reader, but it is possible that his writing was an escapist technique, and perhaps to an extent he envied his lonely creations, living in their rustic fictional simplicity.

Q. Write a character sketch of William "The Interminable" Wordsworth.

Or

Q. Discuss William Wordsworth as The Interminable.

William Wordsworth was born on 7 April 1770 in

Cockermouth2, Cumberland, the second of five children. His father, John, a lawyer, was very educated and liberal for the time, and encouraged all his children to be the same. William was definitely the wild one of the family, and his sister Dorothy, a year younger than him, was usually his only ally in the family. The Wordsworth children had a pretty happy childhood on the whole, at least until their mother, Ann, died in 1778. William was sent away (I think maybe his father couldn't handle him very well) to a grammar school some distance away. William was allowed to run wild, and became quite the young sportsman.

When John Wordsworth died in 1783, the outlook for the children became really bleak. Though theoretically John's estate was worth £10,485, that amount included many debts which people owed him. The largest debt, that owed by John's employer, the Earl of Lowther, amounted to nearly £5,000 of that sum, and would not be paid to the Wordsworths for 19 years. The kids were foisted on two uncles6 who were very peeved at having to take care of them.

They paid for William to go to Cambridge, where he did very well in his first year, but soon realized Cambridge was no place for him. He chose his own course of studies from then on, and though he did graduate, it wasn't what you would call a real degree8.

After graduation, William wandered aimlessly through France for a time. The country was then in the early, glorious stages of the French Revolution, and William was only one of many Englishmen who were fascinated by its Republican ideals. In the city of Orleans, he met a young woman named Annette Vallon. She was a Royalist and a Roman Catholic, but you can't fight chemistry. They had an affair and Annette became pregnant. Before the child was born, however, William had to go back to England. He needed to earn money somehow, and in any case, the Revolution was starting to turn into the Terror. He returned to London with every intention of marrying Annette or `> things had settled, politically and financially10.

He tried to raise money by publishing two poems he'd

written, mostly for his own amusement. These were Descriptive Sketches, a very pro-revolutionary piece, and An Evening Walk. They weren't very good, and sold accordingly. But some saw potential in them, most notably an old school friend of William's who arranged for a legacy of £900 so William could concentrate on his poetry. William was very grateful for the bequest, and between the income from that and some money he got from another friend (a widower) in exchange for watching the friend's young son, William and his sister Dorothy were able to live together in a little cottage. About this time, William met Samuel Taylor Coleridge and Robert Southey, two young poets who were planning a great socio-political experiment.

Robert and Coleridge soon had a terrible quarrel13, the scheme died, and Coleridge became William's friend. In 1798, they published a joint volume of poetry called Lyrical Ballads. No one quite knew what to make of it14; it was really nothing like what the reading public was used to. It was Romantic, though at the time everyone called it poetry of the Lake School, since William was froom the Lake District.

In 1800, Lyrical Ballads was reworked and a second volume added. William also wrote a preface expounding his theories of what made good poetry. Two years later, the Wordsworths discovered they were at last to get the money owed to their father. Perhaps because of this, William asked Mary Hutchinson, a friend since childhood, to marry him. After a quick visit to Annette to straighten everything out, William and Mary were married in a quiet ceremony. William, Mary, and Dorothy all lived together in their little cottage.

In 1807, William published a two-volume set containing 113 poems, which was again given a very bad review by everyone who bothered to review it, including Lord Byron, then 19 and just getting started in the business of slamming poetry. William tried to take it all in stride, but it was probably no coincidence that he changed his mind about publishing some long poems he'd just finished. He also started writing more prose, at least partly because Coleridge had recently started a magazine that needed articles. But Coleridge's growing drug addiction and paranoia soon put a stop to that literary endeavour, and, unfortunately, his friendship with William as well.

William's home life, generally happy, was nearly shattered in 1812. In June of that year, Catherine, his fourth child, died of convulsions at age 3; in December, the third child, Thomas, died of pneumonia. Mary herself came close to dying from grief, and Dorothy was little better. William wrote a very touching sonnet on Catherine's death some years later, called "Surprised by Joy" The following year, realizing that the family's finances were suffering, William begged and pleaded and called in a lot of favors to get the appointment of Distributor of Stamps for Westmorland19, with an income of £200 per year. A couple of years later, he started cautiously publishing some poems again, and actually got a few good reviews. Some even went so far as to compare him favorably with Robert Southey20. He was much more popular with the general public—tourists actually came to the Wordsworth house in hopes of seeing William.

Though he published a few of the poems he'd been afraid to before, William didn't write much over the next few years, concentrating instead on his family. 1822 saw the re-release of a travel guide to the Lakes which he had earlier printed anonymously; it was an immensely popular guide21. In 1829, William returned from a jaunt (he was forever going off on jaunts, usually with Dorothy or his daughter Dorothy, commonly called Dora to avoid confusion) to find his whole household stricken with influenza. Sara Hutchinson, Mary's sister, who had been staying with them, died. Dorothy, already in somewhat precarious health, recovered from the influenza physically but not mentally. For the rest of her life she suffered continual ill-temper and was mostly incoherent, except when quoting poetry.

In 1839, William finshed The Prelude, a poetical autobiography of his early life which he'd been working on for years. He sealed it away, to be printed only after his death22. By 1840, Robert Southey23 was beginning to deteriorate, both mentally and physically. He died in 1843, and William was asked to be Poet Laureate in his place. Though he initially refused on grounds of age (he was 73), William eventually agreed as a personal favour to a man named Sir Robert Peel, who had gotten a government pension for William to live on24. William died (finally) on 23 April 1850, of pleurisy, an infection of the lung cavity.

His daughter Dora died of tuberculosis in 1847, but his two remaining sons, John and Willy, both married25 and had children, as did his illegitimate daughter Caroline, so there are still direct descendants of William's around today. No signs of any more poets in the family, though. I guess one's enough.

Q. Analyse the works of renowned English Poets: Wordsworth, Cowper and Clare.

Clare's 'To a Fallen Elm' has been recognized as one of his best poems, one still powerful in the way it develops a discourse of political protest from a personal response to a local landscape. In this article I want to read the poem in two related contexts. One is that of the poetry of Cowper (in particular 'Yardley Oak') and the politics of nature articulated by that poetry. Clare, I shall suggest, can be seen like Wordsworth to have been sharing Cowper's concerns and developing his language - a point sometimes neglected by critics of Wordsworth who overlook both Cowper and Clare in their discussions of Romanticism.

The other context in which I shall place Clare's poem is that of debates about the need for a form of government capable of securing liberty. Both radical opponents and conservative defenders of Britain's unreformed constitution employed nature-imagery to render their arguments appealing. Trees figured prominently in that imagery: their longevity, rootedness and strength made them suitable emblems for writers who portrayed an ancient constitution capable of gradual change as a growth of English soil. Edmund Burke depicted Britain's form of government as tree-like, of ancient growth: it 'moves on through the varied tenour of perpetual decay, fall, renovation and progression' in 'the method of nature'. Burke was opposed by Thomas Paine and other radicals who employed the political iconography of the

French Revolution, in which the Liberty tree was an emblem of the new growth possible once ancient injustices had been uprooted. Like an oak Burke's constitution was organic, time honoured, slow to change and grow, protective of the subjects who sheltered beneath it. Wordsworth characterized Burke himself as an oak tree, acknowledging the power of his symbol as an anti-revolutionary naturalization of conservative politics:

I see him, - old, but vigorous in age,
Stand like an oak whose stag-horn branches start
Out of its leafy crown, the more to awe
The younger brethren of the grove...
While he forewarns, denounces, launches forth,
Against all systems built on abstract rights,
Keen ridicule; the majesty proclaims
Of Institutes and Laws, hallowed by time;
Declares the vital power of social ties
Endeared by Custom; and with high disdain,
Exploding upstart Theory, insists
Upon the allegiance to which men are born.

Wordsworth wrote this tribute in his later years when a political supporter of his patron, the landowner and political magnate Lord Lowther.

Landowners and conservative moralists exploited the political symbolism of trees in an attempt to show liberty to be more truly rooted in the British constitution than in the French Revolution. Uvedale Price, the Whig squire and theorist of the picturesque, put such ideas into practice. He designed his estate at Foxley as a display of paternalism. Cottagers were not cleared from his park but included within it, their rustic dwellings sheltered by the oak and ash trees which Price spent his life planting. His tenants were visibly under his protection in a symbolic ordering of the real landscape which emphasized that order and liberty depended upon the mutual duties owed by rich and poor.

Price's fellow theorist Richard Payne Knight, also a Herefordshire Whig squire, both planted oaks and poeticized about their political significance. He portrayed the oak tree as a symbol of a constitutional British monarch paternally sheltering lesser trees grouped around it: 'Then Britain's genius to thy aid invoke/ And spread around the rich, high-clustering oak:/ King of the woods!' The cedar by contrast was shown to resemble an Eastern despot, destroying everything in its shade.

For traditionalist moralists the greatest danger to Britain's parliamentary monarchy lay in the landowning classes themselves. If they abandoned their paternalist care for their country estates the basis of their legitimacy - their claim that they represented the people - would be undermined. Discussion of landscape, and of tree-felling in particular, became a thinly coded way of recalling the gentry to its duty so as to prevent the further spread of disaffection amongst the labouring classes.

In his Moral Contrasts: Or, The Power of Religion Exemplified Under Different Characters (1798) the clergyman and picturesque theorist William Gilpin wrote a parable of two young men who inherit country estates. One, Leigh, squanders his inheritance remodelling his park, abuses his servants, drinks and gambles and ends in failure Đ rejected when he stands for election to parliament.

The message is clear: gentlemen who renounce their paternalist duties deserve to lose their power to represent the people. Leigh's tyranny is symbolized in a style of landscape improvement that ignores the local history and geography of the estate. Ancient trees are wantonly cut down, hills removed. On the other hand Willoughby, the dutiful squire, makes no hasty alterations, having resolved 'never to fight with nature'. He works with the social landscape he has inherited too, employing local labour only when it can be spared from the farms, personally paying allowances to the children of deserving tenants, ensuring that cottagers' rents remained fair and that their dwellings remained within 'the precincts of his park'.

Similarly Southey, admirer of Burke and editor of Cowper (responsible for the publication of 'Yardley Oak'), claimed the order of the nation to depend on men 'whose names and families are older in the country than the old oaks upon their estates'. In the England of 1814 in which bad harvests and enclosure had further impoverished the rural poor, Jane Austen criticized extravagant and foolish landowners in similar terms. In Mansfield Park Fanny Price cites Cowper as she quietly questions whether Rushworth's intended destruction of an avenue of trees to make way for a fashionably remodelled park is proper: 'Ye fallen avenues, once more I mourn your fate unmerited'. Her taste (and that of Cowper's The Task) is vindicated: she marries a gentleman-clergyman determined to protect the landscape and the parishioners under his care.

In the charged political atmosphere of the 1790s and 1820s, with alarm over possible rebellion by the labouring classes gripping landowners and ministry, quiet repair of the landscapes of paternalism seemed to many to be insufficiently repressive. Price and Knight found themselves accused of Jacobinism for advocating a degree of wildness in landscape gardening. Cowper, Clare and Wordsworth had greater reason to be jacobinical: each was a victim of the power of landowners. Each suffered from the destruction of a familiar landscape by owners who were seeking greater agricultural efficiency in order to increase profits.

Like the labourers driven by such destruction towards rebellion, they protested. They did so in poetry which made sophisticated use of the real loss endured as the local landscape was drastically altered. Cowper and Clare in particular employed the symbolic value traditionally placed upon trees to give their evocations of familiar scenes political implications. They were able to turn traditional tree-symbolism against those who benefited from it. The sheltering oak had been used to naturalize landowners' monopoly of power. Oaks had symbolized the independence given by landownership, an independence landowners claimed to use to secure Britons' liberty in Parliament.

Oaks symbolized the shelter which that independent authority afforded to the weak - the landless labourers under the paternalist eye of the squire. Cowper and Clare, showing trees cut down by landowners in the name of taste or profit, depict this paternalist rhetoric as a sham. As landowners are revealed to be paternalists in name only, the legitimacy of their constitutional power is questioned. And at the same time the poet's own relationship with the trees is shown to be far closer and more complex: he (and, vicariously, the reader) is made a more rightful possessor of the land because he is more familiar with it.

The poet's understanding of value, based on a lived history of local knowledge, is made to supersede that of the landowner's, which is shown to be commercial, based on greed. The poems thus suggest that freedom lies elsewhere than in the language and the actions of those who claim to uphold the nation's liberty.

A gentleman who had retreated from public life, Cowper found in the landscapes of Buckinghamshire the virtues he had sought and failed to find in polite society. They were for him places from which order, morality, even love could be derived when it could not from the actions of gentlemen. They became a foundation of Cowper's self, essential standing-grounds as the only places in which God's order seemed to exist.

They were essential to his poetry too, since only by description of them could he find a language properly rooted in virtue. Once in possession of that language he could call upon his fellow gentry to purify themselves, their language (the corruption of which in Church, Law, and Parliament he attacked) and the society they governed. Cowper's retreat to the rural margins gave him great critical authority. It also left him vulnerable: like a hermit his choice of seclusion, relative poverty and powerlessness exposed him to many of the dangers usually only experienced by the rural poor. Whilst his capacity to suffer these dangers increased his moral authority it also pushed him - like Clare later - towards madness.

As Cowper saw his beloved landscape destroyed by fellow gentlemen in the name of the national order they claimed to uphold (and from which they benefited disproportionately) he not only lost the ground on which his identity was paced and measured but also lost his faith in the capacity of gentlemen (however he exhorted them) to uphold the virtues for which a gentleman was supposed to stand.

In July 1785 a local landowner felled trees, removed scrub, and re-organized as an orderly plantation a wood near Olney through which had run one of Cowper's favourite walks. He mourned for its loss in terms that make of the picturesque glade a sanctuary of spiritual community shared between Cowper and his domestic circle:

> myself that I will never enter it again. We have both pray'd in it. You for me, and I for you, but it is desecrated from this time forth, and the voice of pray'r will be heard in it no more. The fate of it in this respect, however deplorable is not peculiar; the spot where Jacob anointed his pillar, and which is more apposite, the spot once honoured with the presence of Him who dwelt in the bush, have long since suffer'd similar disgrace, and are become common ground.

This letter tries to locate the holy language of prayer in particularly loved scenes. Rural beauty, it implies, is sacramental, an earthly form in which spiritual presence can be encountered. Despoilation of nature is made to seem sacreligious. And despoilation also threatens the self. Cowper proclaims that he will never enter the wood again, heralding the growing sense of exile from God that led him to despair and insanity. The letter is prophetic in that it predicts the form of this exile - a gradual exclusion from the only landscapes in which he could discover spiritual meaning.

This exclusion is evident in the change from the 'Olney hymns' with their awed discovery of God's 'mysterious ways' in nature, to 'The Castaway', in which nature is represented by the undifferentiated desert of the sea. A named local landscape is replaced by a sea in which the only refuge is that of the 'deeper gulphs' in which Cowper imagines and wishes himself drowned. Destruction of rural beauty threatens Cowper's selfhood with the loss not just of a place of security but of the very ground on which its ability to discover a language of redemption depends. To lose a familiar and therefore meaningful landscape is also to lose a saving language.

In The Task Cowper takes up arms against the

despoilation of rural refuges, transforming his anger at the loss of his own sylvan retreat into an indictment of the political values and cultural fashions of his contemporary Britain. He views the removal of woodland as a symptom of the triumph in the nation of commercial greed over traditional paternalism:

Mansions once
Knew their own masters; and laborious hinds
Who had surviv'd the father, serv'd the son.
Now the legitimate and rightful lord
Is but a transient guest, newly arriv'd,
And soon to be supplanted. He that saw
His patrimonial timber cast its leaf,
Sells the last scantling, and transfers the price
To some shrewd sharper, ere it buds again.
Estates are landscapes, gaz'd upon a while,
Then advertis'd, and auctioneer'd away.

For Cowper such a gaze is exploitative and it uproots not only the trees but the landowning classes, to their own detriment and that of the rural society of which they had been masters. They are lost to gambling and luxury; it is without government or care. Richard Feingold comments 'in the new polity of power and wealth... the moral basis of politics is destroyed along with the old order of society because the former guardians also now join in the new riot of luxury'. Cowper reveals the hollowness of the ideals of gentlemanliness that such men claimed to embody and so attacks the authority of the ruling class by undermining its ideology.

It is in 'Yardley Oak' that Cowper best fuses the personal with the public. He wrote this poem after reading Burke's defence of the constitution in Reflections on the Revolution in France. And he responds to the symbolic use Burke had made of the oak as he derives a political and moral sermon from the tree. He gains the authority necessary to sermonize because he is close enough to the particular named tree to make it a measure of himself. In speaking solemnly to it he speaks his own being, finding his own vulnerability and decrepitude in its decayed trunk:

Survivor sole, and hardly such, of all
That once liv'd here thy brethren, at my birth
(Since which I number three-score winters past)
A shatter'd veteran, hollow-trunk'd perhaps
now, and with excoriate forks deform,
Relict of ages!

The tree is then made an object of worship, a living monument to a shared sense of common ancestry, a totem rooting poet and readers into the English past: 'It seems idolatry with some excuse/ When our forefather Druids in their oaks/ Imagin'd sanctity' (ll. 9-11).

The poem's style is Miltonic, biblical. Cowper addresses the tree as 'Thou', risking bathetic disproportion between diction and subject-matter in an effort to convey the religious awe he feels at the sublime oak. By so doing he is able to turn a local description into musings on the common fate of all nature in the post-Edenic world - Death. The oak's slow growth and slower decline make it a humbling reminder of mankind's greater vulnerability to time. It is a funerary monument, a living Death-in-nature. It is also a political symbol. Hollow, aged yet 'still erect' (l.119) it stands for England - diseased by corruption yet sustained by its rootedness in history:

So stands a kingdom, whose foundations yet
Fail not, in virtue and in wisdom laid,
Though all the superstructure, by the tooth
Pulveriz'd of venality, a shell... (ll. 120-23)

Cowper speaks on its behalf for an organic constitution, ancient and slow to grow and change - unlike the sudden innovations of the French revolution. Yet unlike Burke's, Cowper's Whig tree stands against a policy of war:

But the axe spar'd thee; in those thriftier days
Oaks fell not, hewn by thousands, to supply
The bottomless demands of contest wag'd
For senatorial honours. (ll. 100-103)

Here to waste the nation's trees is both to squander its men and to endanger the oak-like constitution upon which its independence has historically been based. Cowper's lines contrast with Pope's 'Windsor Forest' in which oaks are resources for the navy by which Britain's commercial and imperial dominance would be achieved. Cowper's oak is a critique of public policy as well as a monument to shared Englishness and an object through which the inevitability of decay and death is brought home to the poet.

From this public verse the poem returns to troublingly personal images of dismemberment; 'Thine arms have left thee. Winds have rent them off... ' (l.125). It ends by placing the tree and fallen man, crippled and vulnerably mortal, in opposition to Adam in Eden. Adam was moulded at once, not subject to time or Death. His language exactly named the new-created world:

survey'd
All creatures,... assign'd
To each his name significant, and fill'd
With love and wisdom, render'd back to heav'n
In praise harmonious the first air he drew (ll. 173-78)

Adam's paradise is one of security and exactitude. It is a paradise of language in which words not only fit things precisely but are a gift given to God in return for the gift of breath. It is a paradise too fragile to be sustained, watched by 'History' and 'Time' - and by Cowper, whose poem fades into uncompleted silence at this point. His own text, like the oak which he resembles, is dismembered, lacking a resolving conclusion. It, like the tree and all in the post-Edenic world, is shown to be acutely vulnerable to loss. Outside Eden language like the oak and the man who speaks of it is felled by the consequences of the first fall - Sin, Death and Time.

In 'Yardley Oak' Cowper's landscape-poetry becomes not simply a protest at the destruction of landscape (and lives) by men of political ambition; it becomes an exemplification of the human fragmentation that occurs when all available linguistic sources of moral reparation have been destroyed. Faced by a landscape and a culture in which he finds decay, Cowper finds no compensating 'strength in what remains behind' in his own imagination (as does Wordsworth in the 'Immortality' ode). In 'Yardley Oak' - as in Clare's poetry - it is the lack of a unifying and resolving language, the loss rather than the discovery of a coherent self that is effective. And it is effective politically: rather than simply preaching about social evils Cowper makes readers experience their cost as a linguistic dislocation. Description can memorialize but not compensate for the tree's decay, for the cultural corruption it symbolizes and for the self left by that corruption without faith in the contemporary language of public life.

Cowper's influence on Wordsworth was profound. Wordsworth wrote 'Yew Trees' after reading 'Yardley Oak'. This poem displaces the poet's voice into that of the trees which become, as in Cowper, monuments that show nature to be a living death. Here Wordsworth is not the sublime egotist recoiling from nature who is praised by many Romantic critics.

There is a Yew-tree, pride of Lorton Vale,
Which to this day stands single, in the midst
Of its own darkness, as it stood of yore:
Not loth to furnish weapons for the bands
Of Umfraville or Percy ere they marched
To Scotland's heaths; or those that crossed the sea
And drew their sounding bows at Azincour,
Perhaps at earlier Crecy, or Poictiers.
Of vast circumference and gloom profound
This solitary Tree! a living thing
Produced too slowly ever to decay;
Of form and aspect too magnificent
To be destroyed.

The poem turns the local tree into a patriotic symbol, into a guarantor of the deep-rooted and thus enduring strength of Englishness. The references to Agincourt were significant in a period of war with Napoleonic France.

Wordsworth's patriotic vision of the English landscape owed much to Cowper. So too did Clare's and he acknowledged Cowper as an influence on his political verse. His 'England my country among evils enthralling,' takes Cowper's 'England with all thy faults I love thee still' as its epigraph. Like Cowper, Clare assures readers of his loyalty to England before venturing to criticize its faults and injustices. The 'Lines on "Cowper"' acknowledge the debt by idealizing the poet of The Task as the kind of poet Clare wished to be. He 'found the muse on common ground' (l. 2). His songs 'share the peoples talk' (l. 7). Most importantly his voice is present in nature, articulate in its motions:

Birds sing his name on every bough
Nature repeats it in the wind
And every place the Poet trod
And every place the Poet sung
Are like the holy land of God
In every Mouth on every tongue (ll. 23-28)

Here Cowper is shown to have sanctified nature; his words like those of scripture are alive because they are a shared part of common speech - written become oral. It is a powerful tribute, poetic justice for a poet whose own linguistic identity fractured and fell into silence.

Clare possessed several editions of Cowper's poetry. He also possessed a selection of verse which included the posthumously published 'Yardley Oak'. (And his 'To a Fallen Elm' develops a politics of nature similar to Cowper's poem. It too was prompted by the threatened loss of actual trees. Clare protested in a letter which his publisher Taylor subsequently included in his introduction to The Village Minstrel. My two favourite elm trees at the back of the hut are condemned to die - it shocks me to relate it, but 'tis true. The savage who owns them thinks they have done their best, and now he wants to make use of the benefits he can get from selling them. O was this country Egypt, and was I but a caliph, the owner should lose his ears for his arrogant presumption; and the first wretch that buried his axe in their roots should hang on their branches as a terror to the rest. I have been several mornings to bid them farewel.

In this letter Clare suggests that he had an individual, almost human, relationship with the trees. He opposes this relationship ('bid them farewel') to that of the 'owner' which is defined by profit. In the poem itself this opposition is used tactically: Clare aligns his relationship with that of birds and children, the owner's with that of men who seek money and power at others' cost. The elm is made a landmark for a community: 'The children sought thee in thy summer shade' (l. 23). It is a bastion against the hostile world, protecting Clare's cottage 'like a friend' (l. 12). In a line Cowperian in its intimation of insecurity Clare makes the elm's rooted strength a source of reassurance: 'It seasoned comfort to our hearts desire' (l. 11).

Here seasoned is the crucial word: in a complex image Clare uses it as a transitive verb referring to the seasoning of food: like honey the elm's 'sweetest anthem' turned a domestic retreat into a comfort to be enjoyed (l. 2). And he also suggests another more unorthodox meaning - that it was the elm's seasoned timber, strong through its growth through many seasons, that strengthened with comfort those who had known the tree through many seasons (and known themselves by dwelling in its shade).

Clare makes the tree a self mark as well as a landmark. He describes himself in words normally applicable to it and it in words normally applicable to himself: 'Thou ownd a language by which hearts are stirred/ Deeper than by the attribute of words/ Thine spoke a feeling known in every tongue' (ll. 31-33). As in the 'Lines on "Cowper"' the poet's communication (and this poem is a conversation with the tree) is grounded on his perception of an inarticulate language of nature - a truly Wordsworthian perception.

Yet Clare does not develop this perception into a discovery of the sublimity of the poet's mind. Instead he moves like Cowper in a political direction. He attacks the men who were changing the landscape in the cause of improved farming. But his poem is also charged with the tension these changes produced in Clare himself: he knew that the literary form in which he wrote would be associated with the gentlemanly classes who organized agricultural 'improvement'. His local patron Lord Radstock demanded that he suppress poems that displayed 'radical slang'. His gentlemanly readership wanted a peasant who could respond with sensitivity to natural beauty, not one who developed that response into political protest. Clare protested nevertheless and made the hypocrisy of contemporary discourse his subject as Cowper had done.

Thoust heard the knave abusing those in power
Bawl freedom loud and then oppress the free
Thoust sheltered hypocrites in many a shower
That when in power would never shelter thee
Thoust heard the knave supply his canting powers
With wrongs illusions when he wanted friends
That bawled for shelter when he lived in showers (ll. 41-47)

'To a Fallen Elm' is a narrative of imprisonment. Like Cowper in 'Yardley Oak' Clare reveals in it his sense of being trapped in corrupted languages: the elm, for all its strong indifference to the 'wrongs illusions' it hears cannot survive their power to effect change; nor, therefore, can the heart-stirring language 'deeper than... the attribute of words' which the poet derives from it. And neither the cant of popular agitators nor the language of gentlemen with its self-serving justification of the tree-felling can be trusted. Neither is adequate to the needs of the self for a verbal source of truth and honesty. Yet neither can be avoided. Clare's literary form aligns him willynilly with gentlemen patrons, his status as a rural labourer with popular agitators ('knave[s] abusing those in power'). And since the ancient trees he so loved were being felled, he no longer had a home ground, a piece of England from which he could derive himself and for which he could speak with an untainted authority of love. He did have a tradition of radical invective at his disposal; the angry rhetoric of the poem's attack on enclosure borrows from that republican enemy of the monarchical constitution, Milton - as Wordsworth and Coleridge also did in their radical verse. And yet, as Peter J.

Kitson has argued of radical rhetoric in the late 1790s, Clare's words are imbued with the expectation of defeat by the words and deeds of men of power. Neither the heart-stirring murmuring of the elm (the inarticulate language of nature) nor the Miltonic jeremiads of radical tradition will deflect the 'force of might' and the hypocritical language used to justify that force (l.54). Clare anticipates a linguistic as well as physical destruction, a mental as well as agricultural enclosure:

Such was thy ruin music making Elm
The rights of freedom was to injure thine
As thou wert served so would they overwhelm
In freedoms name the little that is mine (ll. 65-68)

In face of the power of a perverted language in which 'wrong was right and right was wrong' (l.63) Clare can protest but cannot win. His own source of verbal and moral authority may remain, but it is likely to be obscured by the overwhelming language of men of power - left to speak for a landscape and community that no longer exist. The experienced meaning of freedom will, in the poem's last grim phrase, be devoured in 'freedom's' name.

On the evidence of these three 'tree poems' Clare's and Cowper's politics of nature are more troubling than Wordsworth's. Although all three poets treat a local landscape as a testing-ground for the state of the nation, Clare and Cowper dramatize loss and destruction without a compensatory discovery of a remaining power and unity in their own minds. They reveal in their tree-poems what Coleridge revealed with terrible force in 'The Rime of the Ancient Mariner' - the appalling fragmentation of language and meaning that results from the destruction of an interpretable landscape on which the self is founded. Theirs is a kind of poetry in which language is left on the point of breakdown and the poet at the edge of madness rather than one of sublime egotism.

It is one in which the poetry of retirement, political protest and the traditional symbolism attached to landscape fuse. It is one transformed by Cowper's and Clare's ability to find a language able to anticipate its own destruction, to prophesy its own silence. It operates according to an aesthetics of weakness - an intimation of loss, dismemberment and oblivion rather than immortality.

Q. How does Wordsworth excursion ravel between memory and history?

Or

Q. Write an Essay on William Wordsworth's Excursion.

Despite—or perhaps, because of—its own mixed reception

history, The Excursion remains an interesting comment on the process of historical and cultural change. Like The Prelude (1850), the poem addresses the status of the self, the passage of time, and memory—issues that have revived critical interest in the poem over the last two decades. As the arguments of critics like William H. Galperin and David Simpson have implied, The Excursion engages with these issues by "displacing" them as symptoms or "anxieties." The poem seems to indicate Wordsworth's revision, or at least his questioning, of assumptions about self, imagination, and memory on which The Prelude operated. Instead of undertaking a further interrogation of the poem's "anxieties" in this essay, I want to suggest another way of reading them—a reading that also suggests a schema for re-reading critical and editorial interventions that seek to determine any poem's meaning.

"The history of ...memory is the history of its transmission." While considerations of Wordsworth and memory are nothing new, such readings have usually sought to interpret or critique Wordsworth's own relationship to memory, with regard to language, landscape, or an apriori concept of historical "truth." But these investigations do not, usually, read Wordsworth as memory—that is, as a mode of knowledge, that responds to, draws from, and narrates historical events, but has no necessary allegiance to history. All narrative genres, whether documentary or fictional, create "typical patterns in which we experience and interpret events".

As we know, these patterns always operate in terms of a particular discourse; comprising a grammar of conceptualized images and figures, all narratives are purely rhetorical at some level. Impure Conceits, Alison Hickey's recent book-length study of The Excursion, provides an in-depth examination of such rhetorical figures, and how they structure meaning in the poem. These rhetorical figures also structure memory; and this suggests that memory is less a corollary to history than a system of meaning unto itself, albeit one that draws its material from history. But Hickey's reading is important to my discussion for another reason: she focuses her attention on the failure of tropes in The Excursion. It is this failure—a failure of memory, in a sense—that leaves the poem caught between memory and history, and ultimately questions the power of memory to sustain and nourish the modern imagination.

Hickey notes that The Prelude's unified force of memory—the narrative authority of an "imperial self"—is almost entirely absent in The Excursion. Instead, The Excursion presents us with far more uncertain "gaps and strayings...plots of deviation and deferral, usurpations and broken lineages, and unfulfilled promises".

What The Excursion demonstrates is not a memory that recreates or in some way reenacts the past, but a memory that can only represent, by signs and figures, the broken narratives of a past that is and always was irretrievable. In many ways, the poem revises Wordsworth's former, more hopeful view of memory as a redemptive, restorative, and absolute power—a view that informs The Prelude and poems like Tintern Abbey.

"Memory has never known more than two forms of legitimacy: historical and literary," writes the historian Pierre Nora. Nora, who recently published his decade-long collaborative historical study, Les Lieux de Mémoire, or "Realms of Memory," is concerned with the way in which cultural or collective memory is "in permanent evolution, open to the dialectic of remembering and forgetting... vulnerable to manipulation and appropriation, susceptible to being long dormant and periodically revived". Echoing Nora, Hickey's focus on The Excursion's "gaps and strayings" would support a claim that this poem is remarkable for its very problematic relationship to memory, and for the way it sketches out the boundaries between memory and history.

"The ages live in history through their anachronisms"
Oscar Wilde

Nora writes that memory and history, "far from being synonymous, appear now to be in fundamental opposition". The Excursion was written during a process of cultural change; demonstrating the beginnings of this opposition, the forces of memory and history struggle within the text like conjoined twins. Contemporary critics' persistent and well-intentioned efforts to reclaim or reallocate memory—to wrest the displaced "truth" from historical or literary narrative—suggests that Nora's theory of a once-organic relationship between memory and history is correct. Such critical trends also attest to our difficulty, now, in comprehending such a relationship. Moreover, it demonstrates that the formerly recreative act of memory Nora postulates has mostly survived as an object: a product, itself, of history.

It is not surprising then, that one of "the costs of the historical metamorphosis of memory has been a wholesale preoccupation with the individual psychology of remembering," creating a new "economy of the identity of the self, the mechanics of memory, and the relevance of the past". His argument entails the very conditions which appear, now, to have shaped Wordsworth's poetry, and by which we generally characterize the poet himself.

The Excursion strikes me as a text under extreme historical pressure. Whereas The Prelude attempts to trace the development of a consciousness in the grip of, but not entirely "besieged" by history, The Excursion repeatedly, and defensively, invokes the name of memory against history. It attempts to stave off what is perceived as time's destructive nature, by establishing memorial sites and appealing to an apparently immanent desire for their preservation. In this sense, The Excursion strives to be not a witness to change, nor an occasion for historical speculation, but a book-length elegy. An elegy for what? For memory itself.

Nora's introduction to Realms, republished in the Spring 1989 issue of Representations, has already found its way outside of the historical field, perhaps because the essay establishes a useful critical schema for examining the familiar binary of "memory vs. history." For this reason I think it successfully illuminates a text like The Excursion. Like Fentress and Wickham, Nora treats memory not as an alternative to history, but as an affective and unpredictable mode of truth in itself, one which "only accommodates those facts that suit it" . Above all, memory is always in movement; it is a process that "nourishes recollections that may be out of focus, or telescopic, global or detached, particular or symbolic— responsive...to every censorship or projection". Likewise, his definition of history implies an equally selective (or defective) function: History, even as idea, is "the reconstruction, always problematic and incomplete, of what is no longer... [It is] a representation of the past").

While some historicist criticism—especially of Romantic literature—has called attention to memory's telescoping, projecting and censoring functions, it has tended to posit a very deterministic relationship between literature and the historical record. Even the title of David Simpson's book, Wordsworth's Historical Imagination: The Poetry of Displacement, implies a kind of literary text that could be entirely "in place." Yet this concept of displacement invokes the very terms by which memory operates.

And like literature, history is also a text, with its own uncertain gaps and strayings, its own rhetoric, and its own memory. In this light, I would argue that what appear to be historical "truths" breaking through the surface of a literary text are more often than not "memorial" truths. However, if we choose not to hold texts responsible to history, neither can we make them answer to the fugitive authority of memory. Perhaps we can read any historically conscious text as a means of mapping out a realm between them.

Whereas historical narrative is, generally speaking, "bound strictly to temporal continuities, to progression and relations between things," the narrative recreated by memory "takes root in the concrete, in spaces, gestures, images and objects". Realms, or sites of memory, "are created by a play of memory and history, an interaction of the two factors that result in their reciprocal over determination. To begin with, there must be a will to remember" As this "will to remember" increases under the pressure of an historical consciousness (a will to write history, in a sense), it produces sites of memory—narratives, monuments, and cultural artifacts.

These sites begin to constitute one's experience of the past, until it is reduced ultimately to a history of ideas, and the scars or traces left by those ideas upon a culture and the landscape it inhabits. Nora argues that, with the "acceleration of history" in the industrial era, temporal continuity in traditional societies experienced a division—between memory, "social and unviolated," and history, "which is how our hopelessly forgotten modern societies, propelled by change, organize the past").

The Excursion "opens onto profound societal shifts in whose midst it is located"; the poem is also notable for the way it addresses the problems of individual versus collective memory, natural process versus historical change, and nature versus culture. Reading The Excursion with these issues in mind, the poem demonstrates a change in Wordsworth's relationship to memory, and perhaps narrates the process of a larger cultural change—more or less contemporaneous with the poem—from a tradition or ritual practice of memory, to a history or narrative of such practice.

Each of The Excursion's narrative "clusters" attempts to make the processes of time intelligible; each of its four principle characters—the Wanderer, the Solitary, the Pastor, and the Poet—engages the others in a "dialogue of perspectives" on memory, and on its role in individual, communal, and national consciousness. The Wanderer is the threatened voice of tradition; he represents a (nearly outmoded) relationship to nature and time which allows him to transcend the impulse to memorialize. The Solitary is the Wanderer's antithesis—an example of the alienated, "modern subject"—a figure for memory that has become utterly transformed by history.

The Pastor, appearing in Book Six, is the producer and transmitter of a community's memorial sites. The Poet, Wordsworth's ironically silent narrator, is the ostensible author of The Excursion's lengthy realm of memory. The Poet's "silence," and his deferral of (narrative) authority to the Wanderer in Book First, already indicates that Wordsworth was somewhat skeptical of memory's power. As William Galperin argues, this deferral suggests that the poetic stance is inadequate "to order nature in a secularized, unorthodox way". For poetry must draw on previous models to fashion its "own" patterns of narrative and imagery. It must defer to preexisting modes of social and intellectual order to create its own rationale for ordering, conceptualizing, and remembering.

'I would enshrine the spirit of the past for future restoration'

In most of Wordsworth's writing, poetry and prose, a sense of the past is embedded in and extended by landscape, which becomes an analogue for memory or, as Christopher Salvesen described it, "a kind of reservoir...of mystically diffused memory." Within The Excursion the interactive cycles of natural, geologic time and the span of human lives reach a point of crisis. Human memory, once bound in a symbiotic, metonymic relationship to the land, now interferes with the memorial landmarks it created, or is itself erased by natural and social processes.

This sense of crisis is evident, especially, in work from the latter half of Wordsworth's career. In his essay "Description of the Scenery of the Lakes", and pamphlet "Kendal and Windermere Railway" Wordsworth complains bitterly about technological and "picturesque" incursions of man on his beloved, wild landscape. While a similar apprehension of crisis operates throughout The Excursion, it transforms the poem into something more than the historical portrait of a rural community, or a protest of its inevitable modernization.

In Hickey's words, "The Excursion is a vast landscape of epitaphs...but such [literary] objects, and the truths they yield to those who invest their interpretive labour in them, are held in the balance as the spread of industrialism changes the face of the signifying landscape, raising the disturbing possibility that the entire epitaphic poem itself may mark the demise of the actual landscape in which epitaphs have borne meaning...An epitaph for epitaphs...[and] for a way of life..."(103-4). To read the poem in this way means to name it, for ourselves, as a site of memory.

As an epitaph serves to perpetuate a community's memory of an individual, The Excursion attempts to re-order the "diffused" memory of a landscape and community, thereby ensuring its futurity for individuals (characters and readers alike). Hickey rightly characterizes the poem as an epitaph—at once a "lament" for memory, and for the very need to elegize the once-organic, mytho-poeic practice of memory. In its lamentation, the poem calls attention to the relationship between "signifying object and plot"—the site and the story - "stressing the difficulty of interpretation and the threat of error".

It lays bare the hybrid function of a site, as well as the inherent problems of authority that arise in the process of interpreting memorials. Yet the poem-as-epitaph must also mourn "its own erasure, which has already begun".

The voices of memory that speak throughout The Excursion seem to anticipate many of Nora's claims. In Book I ("The Ruined Cottage"), The Wanderer explains to the poet that as lived experience recedes in time, it is the self-conscious "will to remember" that constitutes memory, effecting its transmission through the ages, for

...we die, my Friend,
Nor we alone, but that which each man loved
And prized in his peculiar nook of earth
Dies with him, or is changed; and very soon
Even of the good is no memorial left. (I, 469-474)

The Wanderer was a "peddler" earlier in life—already an antiquated occupation by the time he relates this story to the Poet. Despite Francis Jeffrey's objections, it is this status which grants the Wanderer authority to speak for the memory of an agrarian, pre-industrial society. The story of Margaret's dilapidated cottage seems to be a product of his spontaneous memory that is, not produced by specific pressures of history. While war and economic instability are primary catalysts in this narrative, such events are related as "history sought in the continuity of memory," rather than as "memory cast in the discontinuity of history".

As his narrative progresses, the Wanderer builds an argument for the relinquishment of "the will to remember," showing how the monuments or ruins by which memory can transcend individual lives cannot themselves escape effacement by nature and "natural time." Yet the cottage, even in its gradual disappearance, has become the Wanderer's site of memory, a way to generate narrative and tap into a stream of remembrance.

A site of memory exists between "living memory"—spontaneous, repetitive—and historical memory: "that which has already happened." As a sign or relic of the Wanderer's past, the ruined cottage consolidates his relationship with Margaret, her tragedy, and the years he spent as a pedlar in a world that has since changed. But as it is also a place of natural process—of death and reintegration—the physical site itself is analogous to the Wanderer's relationship to the past.

Rather than struggle against the forces of nature and time to erect a more permanent and artificial monument—to consciously fix this memory— he puts his faith in the life cycles of weeds and spear-grass, themselves fragile and subject to weather, growth and decay. Throughout The Excursion, the Wanderer reminds his companions that, inevitably, it is the natural process that endures, vanquishing all memorial effort:

So fails, so languishes, grows dim, and dies...
All that this World is proud of. From their spheres
The stars of human glory are cast down;...
Their virtue, service, happiness, and state
Expire; and nature's pleasant robe of green
Humanity's appointed shroud, enwraps
Their monuments and their memory. (VII, 986-1009)

The Wanderer's stance toward time approaches what Christopher Salvesen called, in Wordsworth's terms, a "wise passiveness." It indicates a disposition content with the dialectic of remembering and forgetting—free from nostalgia or the desire to fix, stabilize, or preserve consciousness—beyond time, in a sense.

This mode of "removal, tranquil though severe," affords a "Fresh power to commune with the invisible world...inaudible / To the vast multitude." (IX, 82-90) A character of both moral and memorial stability, the Wanderer sustains the possibility of memory's redemption, but only by its relinquishment to nature and a higher spiritual consciousness. This "higher power" is, in terms of my argument, a faith in the continuity of memory, its ultimate capability to withstand the disruptions of history, by virtue of the dialectics of remembering and forgetting.

Because the Wanderer's relationship to memory is itself representative, because this figure functions as a conceptualization of a disappearing mode of memory, he—unlike the other characters—is somewhat of a "site" in his own right. Conversely, the Solitary is more representative of Wordsworth's own problematic relationship to memory. "His life story is a generalized version of Wordsworth's, fleshed out with historical and literary analogs".

Perhaps it is more accurate to characterize the Solitary as representative of Wordsworth's skepticism, embodying his doubt of memory's redemptive power. Even before his appearance, the Solitary enters the poem as a memory. When the Wanderer and the Poet first believe him to be dead, the Wanderer recounts his friend's life in a rambling epitaph. Not coincidentally, the Solitary exhibits the most "memorial" consciousness in the poem, one in which the function of memory, under the extreme pressure of history, has overwhelmed all else.

In this sense, the Solitary is most clearly a negative figure for Wordsworth himself—portraying a sensitive imagination caught in the time-lapse between experience and remembrance, between feeling and articulation, unable to make the cognitive leap of faith which will grant him the privilege of "recollection in tranquility." Instead, the Solitary seeks solace in the sublimity of mountains and storms, which exceed imagination, memory, and everything subject to failure.

The poem begins its "meta-dialogue" on the power of memory, when the Wanderer attempts to reassure the Solitary that nature can redeem human life, even as it overwhelms and transcends it:

...living things, and things inanimate,
Do speak, at Heaven's command, to eye and ear,
And speak to social reason's inner sense,
With inarticulate language...

And further, by contemplating these Forms
In the relations which they bear to man,
He shall discern, how, through the various means
Which silently they yield, are multiplied
The spiritual presences of absent things. (IV, 1212-43)

Yet the Solitary remains mistrustful of "social reason," which has betrayed him. Ghostlike himself, his life is haunted by the presences of absent things—failed ideals, a dead family—and he is trapped in the narrative of his own history. His apartment is littered with cultural detritus, "sites of memory" in parvo—a telescope, fishing rod, scraps of poetry, musical instruments. Likewise, his memory is littered with lasting images he'd prefer to avoid, while transient figures of light and shadow in the vale still allow some respite for his imagination. When he denounces his companions' habits of conscious introspection and recollection, it is because such pursuits, for him, are occasions for remembered pain (V, l. 225). He sees little value in the memory's redemptive possibilities.

"Et in Arcadia Ego"

Despite the Solitary's apparent resistance, he too participates in the processes of individual rememoration, and his skepticism inscribes a new mode of cultural memory on the larger landscape of the poem. The Excursion's landscape figures for both cultural and individual memory on several levels. It is continually described in terms of gravesites or Arcadian recesses: a ruined cottage, the Solitary's little "urn-like vale," the children's abandoned play garden, an altar-like formation of rocks and vegetation, a series of marked and unmarked graves and monuments.

These "spots" as Hickey calls them, are not spots of time, but sites that are both "radical and radically ambivalent." The positioning of each "emphasizes the opening of the image for double interpretation" . The urn-like vale is, for instance, envisioned as a place of death for the old pensioner, a sign for death (the urn), and a refuge for the Solitary from his own memory. This resistance to fixed, allegorical meanings confounds efforts on the part of characters, or critics, to name any place as a definitive memorial site, to delineate and assign to it a stable and unambiguous meaning. Each of these locations generates a story: personal narrative, community history, or local legend. Midday rest at the ruined cottage was the occasion for the Wanderer's story of Margaret; the primeval nook to which the Solitary leads his friends in Book Three is the location for life story. It is also the scene of an extended conversation that chronicles a "history" of the world. In the graveyard, the Pastor recites his "oral histories" in order to persevere in the (already eroded) tradition of local memory in his village—to "bring to life" his community for the visitors. Throughout the poem, elegy and genesis often blend, suggesting that such narratives are analogous in The Excursion's system of memory. Origins beseech remembrance, as do departures.

Inviting his companions to rest upon "a slope of mossy turf," the Solitary begins his tale—primarily a history of crisis, for "times of quiet and unbroken peace...give back faint echoes from the historian's page". While his most sensational experiences are circumscribed by historically-relevant events or institutions such as the French Revolution and the Church, the "faint echoes" he refers to are traces of a more vulnerable, spontaneous memory, one that is inscribed in the landscape and that continues, for awhile, to reside there. Such is the recollection of the "low cottage" where the Solitary lived with his wife,

On Devon's leafy shores; —a sheltered hold...
See, rooted in the earth, her kindly bed,
The unendangered myrtle, decked with flowers,
Before the threshold stands to welcome us!...
—Wild were the walks on those lonely downs,
Track leading into track; how marked, how worn
Into the bright verdure, between fern and gorse
Winding away its never ending line...
...there, lay open to our daily haunt,
A range of unappropriated earth...

The "unendangered myrtle," mentioned twice in this tale, is a simple but telling metaphor. In light of her subsequent death, it can be read as an ironic figure for the Solitary's wife.

It also serves for a homespun "tree of life," and this passage is undeniably pastoral and Edenic in its associations. Indeed, the Solitary describes the Devonshire landscape as a biblical Eden; both locale and witness.

This particular landscape functions as a site of memory in several ways. The tracks that the Solitary and his wife made together are their life-story written into the ground. This inscription, on a figurative level, allows the Solitary to draw a "never ending line" of memory recycled in time. However, the Solitary's idealization of this landscape also suggests the utter irretrievability of the memory it records. What he has is the track, the mark on the land—only a representation. The Solitary's ideal life is no longer available to him as a re-livable experience in memory. Nor for that matter, is it possible to reanimate any of the portraits of ideal community in The Excursion, as David Simpson notes.

This passage also introduces, quite subtly, the process of land enclosure, as the couple wandered across what was notably "a range of unappropriated earth." By the time Wordsworth was writing The Excursion, "the enclosure of arable and pasture" had affected England's southern and Midland regions, but "did not apply to... [the Lake District] region of partially self-contained farms." Here, the Solitary recalls enclosure as a condition of his youth, and it exists wholly within the "continuity" of his memory.

However, the enclosure of common grazing lands "did affect these great open mountain wastes of the Lake District, though not seriously until the middle years of the nineteenth century" (MacLean, 92-93). I point this out because these later results of enclosure, as well as of subsequent economic developments that changed the face of the landscape, appear throughout The Excursion as both subject and subtext. Such man-made, physical, and long-lasting changes begin to put a new pressure on the memory—landscape relationship so fundamental to the poem's constructions of memory, and its historically-produced sites.

'Oh! that memory should survive to speak the word'

Frances Ferguson writes that "there is no tomb which does

not awaken the memory of the community from which the deceased sprang." Situated in a churchyard, the second half of The Excursion concerns members of the surrounding community, both living and dead. In the early passages of Book Five, Wordsworth also took the opportunity to include a detailed description of the church for, "As chanced, the portals of the sacred Pile / Stood open." This pile is conjectured by William Knight, the editor of the 1884 Paterson edition I used for this essay, to be St. Oswald's —"the Church at Grasmere".

The church's monuments, "sepulchral stones" and "foot-worn epitaphs" enumerated in this section are objects of the community's history. Such a history provides the context, the historical "pressure," for the Pastor's ensuing tales.

Cemeteries and sanctuaries are the obvious sites of communal memory, places of "spontaneous devotion" and unconscious tradition—funeral rites, for example. In Book Second, the Wanderer, spying the small funeral procession which bears the body of the old shepherd from The Solitary's steep valley home, observes that already, "Many precious rites / And customs of our rural ancestry / Are gone." As these customs disappear—such as the carrying of the dead past the doors of the living before burial—so does a community's means of integrating its tradition of memory into daily life.

This preoccupation with tradition —which is as integral to the identity of a culture as personal memory is to an individual—seems to have infected the editor William Knight. He notes that "The custom of mourners kneeling around the coffin was, till quite lately, in common use. It is still observed in some churches in Cumberland and Westmoreland, but is generally passing away"). I mention these editorial notes because they indicate the editor's present concerns, add an extra-textual layer of historical pressure to the poem, and affirm its status as a site of memory.

The shift to the churchyard in Book Fifth is more than a change of locale. The Pastor's retelling of his parishioners' lives "shapes these lives within the institutional context he represents" (Johnston, 292-3). His pastoral authority as a transmitter of community memory is what brings these lives into narrative, and as Johnston notes, just "telling the story of a life is not sufficient to give it meaning" (292-3). In Book Fifth, there is a noticeable shift in emphasis from storytelling that appeals to a more traditional or organic model of rememoration, to a memory narrative that exists only for its social and institutional usefulness as memory.

Possessing only a mental "map" of the churchyard, the Pastor guides his visitors around it, eulogizing the dead. It is important to note that these graves are unmarked, and it is the Pastor who "marks" them, representing them as sites of memory by which ideal virtues and communal values are defined.. The Wanderer enjoins him to

Epitomise the life; pronounce, you can
Authentic epitaphs of some of these
Who, from their lowly mansions hither brought,
Beneath this turf lie mouldering at our feet...
True indeed it is
That they whom death has hidden from our sight
Are worthiest of the mind's regard; with these
The future cannot contradict the past...
So begins the Pastor's narrative, one that moves back and forth between the
...heaving surface, almost wholly free
From interruption of sepulchral stones,
And mantled o'er with aboriginal turf
And everlasting flowers... (VI, 613-15)

to the undulating, aboriginal mountain landscape which surrounds them. Moreover, these histories in the poem incorporate the local oral history.

Ferguson makes the claim that such 'authentic epitaphs' serve to "recapture...past experience...uniting the present with the past, and the human with the natural". Hickey goes further, proposing that epitaphs become "a link in the metonymical chain, pointing to past and future but enclosing neither"). In light of Nora's discussion, however, I'd argue that these epitaphs are sites.

They are already representations, divorced from any

unconscious "living" tradition, and therefore make impossible any true reunion of past and present. Such "representations of truth in biographical form," as Kenneth Johnston terms them, are conceptualizations, narrative images made to serve a purpose. As such, they mark a reversal of the "spots of time," Wordsworth's celebrated mode of memory. "Instead of arresting visionary moments expanding into lifetime significance, these stories represent whole lifetimes compressed into a single summary account".

As Nora explains, sites are evidence of a society's nostalgia for itself, for "if what they defended were not threatened, there would be no need to build them"). Moreover, enclaves of memory—such as modern cemeteries—"originate with the sense that there is no spontaneous memory, that we must deliberately create archives, maintain anniversaries, organize celebrations, pronounce eulogies ... because such activities no longer occur naturally". These sites act metonymically as functional reminders or "translations" of past experience, but they cannot effect an unbroken continuum between past and present. The Pastor's invention of epitaphic narratives that order and preserve local memory admits that such memory is already "besieged by history."

This is true, at least, for the wandering threesome; being foreign, they are not participants in local memory, and request short epitomes in its place—representations. In other words, a truly "authentic" tradition of memory is somewhat proprietary, and therefore not available to these outsiders. This circumstance also suggests that, soon, such authenticity won't be available to anyone, and only increases the pressure of nostalgia, the "will to remember."

As the Wanderer's words suggests, epitaphs are brief, stylized representations of memory, not necessarily "links" to the memory itself. In his second Essay on Epitaphs, Wordsworth acknowledges the purely abstract, representative nature of the epitaph, as well as its "signifying" role, for

the writer of an epitaph is not an anatomist, who dissects the internal frame of the mind; he is not even a painter, who executes a portrait at leisure...The character of a deceased friend of beloved kinsman is not seen, no—nor ought to be seen, otherwise than as a tree through a tender haze or a luminous mist, that spiritualises and beautifies it; that takes away, indeed, but only to the end that parts which are not abstracted may appear more dignified and lovely; may impress and affect the more.

Rather than providing an authentic link to the past, an epitaph serves to "impress and affect" a graveside visitor, referring to a feeling or sense of memory which is not necessarily his own. Yet, Wordsworth suggests in the Essay that survivors of a deceased friend or beloved kinsman may trust the abstraction of the epitaph, for it is authentic if it is " truth hallowed by love—the joint offspring of the worth of the dead and the affections of the living!". Only if performed in the tradition of elusive and temporal "living memory," can epitaphs serve as links to the past.

As I suggested before, this section of The Excursion signifies an historical threshold, at which the epitaph soon ceases to serve such a tradition of memory. The Pastor's audience—and, we can assume, his parishioners—do not question the historical accuracy of what he has to say. His poetic epitaphs, they know, are at one with "those precious rites and customs" of his community. "These Dalesmen," observes the Poet, trust

The lingering gleam of their departed lives
To oral record, and the silent heart;
Depositories faithful and more kind
Than fondest [written] epitaph: for if these fail,
What boots the sculptured tomb?...

Yet, the Poet admits that "in less simple districts" where "stone lifts its forehead emulous of stone," the ground "all paved with commendations of departed worth," he finds security in more careful efforts to enclose, preserve, and fix memory. The Pastor is, in effect, the "author" of the community's sites of memory, in that he determines how and why people and events are remembered, and how memory itself is represented. His function in the community illuminates the complex relationship of memory and authority, demonstrating how sites of memory are manipulated and controlled by dominant cultural forces or social convention. Ironically, the Poet's "skepticism about the interpretation of narrative signs" suggests the absence, already, of a reliable tradition of memory in his experience; he cannot really understand it. Despite his assertion otherwise, I suspect the Poet would not trust his own epitaph to a country preacher.

Like Margaret's cottage, the sculptured tomb must eventually submit to weather and time, but its words are not so easily revised as 'oral record.' While the vulnerability of community memory to revision and reinterpretation may not disturb the dalesmen's confidence, the Poet speaks for those divested of such "living" memory. He is a modern individual, already besieged by a sense of history, and because he is not a member of any particular community, he can only appreciate graves as fixed sites, emblematic of the past and those who lived in it. Moreover, the Poet's preoccupation with the preservation of identity is an example of the "new economy and identity of the self" Nora describes—a shift from a tradition of memory to a history of memory.

These passages imply, as well, a nostalgia in the wake of history, for even " as traditional memory disappears, we feel obliged...to collect its remains, testimonies, documents, images, speeches, any visible sign of what has been". What is recovered serves to buttress identity and authority on both individual and cultural levels, for "recorded feelings and attitudes of people no longer living are remarkably effective in sanctioning and confirming one's own ways of living." This desire to confirm, validate and reinforce former and present "ways of living" against futurity is much of what drives The Excursion. In this sense the poem is both producer and product of nostalgia: an act of rememoration, more than a reenactment or "re-visioning" of poetic tradition, despite Wordsworth's and Coleridge's grand plans for the revolutionary philosophical poem called The Recluse, which included both The Prelude and The Excursion.

A relationship to the past is informed by "a subtle play between its intractability and its disappearance," and the emerging "question of... representation" [is]... radically different from the old ideal of resurrecting the past". In The Excursion, this difference is most evident in the story of the "flaming Jacobite" and "sullen Hanoverian"—enemies who, by degrees, became friends and whose latter "days were spent in constant fellowship".

There live who yet remember here to have seen
Their courtly figures, seated on the stump
Of an old yew...
They, with joint care, determined to erect,
Upon its site, a dial, that might stand
For public use preserved, and thus survive
As their own private monument. (VI, 486-504)

Knight notes that "of this 'dial'... there is no trace in Grasmere churchyard." While the sundial in the poem serves as a "private monument," it does not function as a monument to the past. It cannot reanimate the yew, neither does it memorialize the men's prior political relationship. Rather, it functions as an emblem of their recent "revised" friendship, and as such, it publicly revises and preserves both personal and community history (for only the Pastor can relate the "true" history of the friends).

The sundial is, literally and figuratively, a means of ordering and controlling time and futurity. As an example of extremely self-conscious memorializing, it also traces a shift from a memory entrusted to natural process to a memory produced by history, under the "pressure" of forgetfulness and time's passage.

Just as each of The Excursion's main characters represents a particular stance toward memory, the Pastor's epitaphs also demonstrate various stances or relationships between memory and history. His engagement with a more modern historical consciousness in the previous narrative is countered in Book Seventh with his "chivalric tale" of Sir Alfred Erthing. This sort of shift is demonstrative of what Hickey calls "deviations" or "unfulfilled promises" in The Excursion.

It also suggests that the poem is not structured by a single, stable paradigm of memory, but illustrates the historical threshold at which memory stands. In this "knight's tale," history is still recalled in the continuity of memory, "if belief may rest / Upon unwritten story fondly traced / From sire to son in this obscure retreat..." (VII, 952-54). The transformation, over generations, of Sir Alfred Erthing's mansion's ruins into dalesmen's cottages manifests the same process by which living memory is transformed and ceaselessly reinvented. Likewise, the memory of Sir Alfred Erthing is subject to new interpretations.

For the Wanderer, the knight is a figure of identification: an emblem of virtue and endurance in a time of political upheaval and social change, "conspicuous as our own / For strife and ferment in the minds of men," and a symbol of shifting cultural and economic realities, as his own "poor calling," once esteemed, grows increasingly obsolete (VII, 1064-66). Noting how these realities effect historical change and the technological usurpation of the bond between man and nature, the Wanderer observes that he has

...lived to mark
A new and unforeseen creation rise
From out the labours of a peaceful Land
Wielding her potent enginery to frame
And to produce, with appetite as keen
As that of war...
The foot-path faintly marked, the horse-track wild,
And formidable plashy lane...
Have vanished—swallowed up by stately roads,
Easy and bold, that penetrate the gloom
Of Britain's farthest glens. (VIII, 90-112)

While nature provides the raw material for this new and unforeseen creation, human endeavor is effacing the "slow rhythms of the past," and the shape of the landscape itself is being transformed. This is no integration of human and natural processes, but rather the imposition of industrial culture upon a rural or agrarian memory, diverting the streams of living tradition to power mills and factories, so that remaining springs and rivulets must be consecrated in memory's name.

Moreover, when the Wanderer complains that "whersoe'er the traveller turns his steps, / He sees the barren wilderness erased, or disappearing" (VIII, 129-31), he invokes the concept of "barrenness" in positive terms. The wilderness must remain wilderness—open and undeveloped— if it is to sustain the particular, topographical, nature—memory crucial to the survival of The Excursion's ideal rural community. Hickey corroborates The Excursion's "green thought"; the poem depicts a world "that is rapidly being overtaken by forces of industrialism and political and economic systematization—and by an accompanying mental machinery—that threaten to overwhelm the more modest process of cultivating the landscape as the ground for local and personal meanings". This ambivalence toward human impact on the land, and its "accompanying mental machinery," are symptomatic of a worldview that has ceased, or is ceasing, to comprehend the acts of human beings as natural. The physical effects of human endeavor—such as the Solitary's "never ending line" eroded into the landscape—are no longer folded into the concept of natural process. Rather, such changes are here conceived of as antagonistic to the landscape and its ground of "local and personal meanings."

"Even of the good is no memorial left"

As with the knight's history, the epitaph of Oswald provides a site of local memory that extends beyond the surrounding fell sides and achieves a greater cultural significance, opposing the social "erosion" coinciding with industrialization. The pairing of Oswald's story with Sir Erthing's, which follows it, also demonstrates the way memory narrative is generated in response to a group's or community's needs, and therefore, often repeats itself in different forms. Cultural memory does not exist to preserve a sense of "what happened," but works as a means of social instruction. Oswald, as a figure of cultural authority, appropriates and represents the same values as Erthing, but in a more contemporary form that would appeal to the young men of his own time. Likened to a Pan or an Apollo "veiled in human form," this "Child of Nature"—as he is described posthumously by the Pastor—is a paragon of rustic virtue and fortitude. Or, perhaps he is only such a paragon by virtue of his status as a site of memory.

...through the impediment of rural acres
In him revealed a scholar's genius shone;
And so, not wholly hidden from men's sight,
In him the spirit of a hero walked
Our unpretending valley... (VII, 743-47)

An adept hunter, and veteran of the Napoleonic wars, Oswald is the ultimate peasant-patriot, defender of "Albion's shores" and the ancient, indigenous, and sacred memory there enclosed. So pronounces the Pastor:

No braver Youth
Descended from Judean heights, to march
With righteous Joshua; nor appeared in arms
When grove was felled, and altar was cast down
And Gideon blew the trumpet, soul-inflamed...

Moreover, Oswald, once a participant in communal and national life, becomes via his epitaph, representative of everything that is "worth" remembering:

The old domestic morals of the land,
Her simple manners, and the stable worth
That dignified a low estate...
...the character of peace,
Sobriety, and order, and chaste love,
And honest dealing, and untainted speech,
And pure good-will, and hospitable cheer,
That made the very thought of country-life
A thought of refuge... (VIII, 235-45)

Wordsworth not only articulates what, in his view, is disappearing, but in doing so reifies an idealized notion of rural manners and morals, "the very thought of country-life" which informs his imagination and provides the foundation for his poetry. The Excursion is a multidimensional poem, in that it performs different "memorative" functions throughout its narrative. In this passage and those that follow, Wordsworth makes an earnest appeal that we not forget such values. The earnest panegyric on rural virtue in Oswald's story is set against Book Eighth's diatribe on the economic and social conditions that keep both the urban and rural poor from achieving an imaginative connection to the world—in short, that keep them from realizing their own tradition of "living memory:" Kenneth Johnston suggests that, for critics and citizens alike, this sobering portrait of an industrializing England really did serve a social purpose in representing the hardships of the poor. In this way, The Excursion strives to be memory, to represent its chosen truths, rather than question the act of memorial representation itself.

But the poem is too unstable, its irony makes a purely historical reading difficult. Such irony is most clearly expressed in the figure of an old logger. In the pursuit of his traditional occupation, he nevertheless participates in physical and social erosion. This issue— the effacement of the land and its "organic" values, by the very culture which depends upon them both—arises toward the end of Book Seventh, when

A team of horses, with a ponderous freight
Pressing behind, adown a rugged slope...
Came at that moment ringing noisily.
"Here," said the Pastor, "do we muse, and mourn
The waste of death; and lo! the giant oak
Stretched on its bier—that massy timber wain;
Nor fail to note the man who guides the team." (VII, 547-54) The Pastor, with no little hint of contempt, describes how this "peasant of the lowest class" has already outlived his life's "ordinary bounds" by ten years— and each year decreases the standing population of ancient oaks in the region. The Pastor admits his "motion of despite" toward this hardy old man,

...whose bold contrivances and skill...
bear such conspicuous part
In works of havoc; taking from these vales
One after one, their proudest ornaments.

Although he describes the logger in positive and vegetal terms—"green in age and lusty" —this indicates a deeper anxiety for the Pastor, who cannot reconcile this man's own simple manners and otherwise virtuous conduct with his repeated violations of nature, for which he reaps reward. Indeed, this logger makes his small living selling timber, and with the slow but "undaunted enterprise" of men such as he comes also the "acceleration of history."

Many a ship
Launched into Morecamb-bay to him hath owed
Her strong knee-timbers, and the mast that bears
The loftiest of her pendants; He, from park
Or forest, fetched the enormous axle-tree
That whirls (how slow itself!) ten thousand spindles:
And the vast engine laboring in the mine,
Content with meaner prowess, must have lacked
The trunk and body of its marvelous strength,
If his undaunted enterprise had failed
Among the mountain coves

Even in his tottering old age, the logger represents to the Pastor the ambition-driven, individualistic, modern man. Divorced from agrarian and communal ideals, this modern figure has begun make drastic changes in the landscape, interfering with natural cycles of time and threatening the cultural memory invested in those cycles. The Pastor even offers brief eulogies for some of the trees sacrificed to "progress." And, he argues, if one old tree is like the next, what is to stop the logger from felling "The Joyful Tree" (a site of community ritual) or "The Lord's Oak"?

"A Will to Remember"

Throughout The Excursion, and in much of his prose and shorter poetry, Wordsworth acknowledges the effects of a modernizing society and increasing industrialization on the landscape of the Lake District and those who lived there. The Excursion now functions as an important site of memory in several ways. It is the poetic "record" of an individual attempting to come to terms with the visible, surface transformation of landscape—with the recognition that what was once perceived as permanent is nearly as vulnerable as human memory. It also documents a traditional way of life in the Lake District and chronicles a communal, living memory under siege.

Like many of Wordsworth's other editors, William Knight included prolific textual notes to the Paterson edition, seventy years after the poem's initial publication—revealing his own interest in establishing and preserving an historical, stable context within and without the poem. But what emerges via these acts of recording is a sense of memory enshrined "under the sign of that which has already happened".

The Excursion's preoccupation with the past and its catalogue of "new and unforeseen creation" in the present imply a condition of discontinuity fast approaching, if not already present. In addition to its contrasting of rural and industrial economies, the poem emphasizes a struggle "between opposed economies of the imagination," and opposed modes of memory. This conflict is played out differently in the poem's various narratives. The story of Oswald, for example, is a site of "local memory" within the plot of poem, but stresses particularly memorable social values for readers of the poem as well. Other narratives, such as the story of little Margaret Green (VII), are "unmomentous"—recollections of unrepresentative lives that do not appear to formally signify anything but themselves). This sort of retelling is more illustrative of spontaneous "rememoration" than of conscious memorialization. It is an act that invokes a community's living, changing system of interrelated histories, and it speaks to a dying mode of social memory. The Solitary's skepticism interrogates both modes of memory. His inquiry, in Book Sixth, "into all the many lives that are never memorialized" is "generalized to the doubtful usefulness of all stories and myths".

This disturbing question, "what is the use of memory?" haunts The Excursion; it undermines Wordsworth's entire project, even as he seeks to answer it. Thus, the poem stakes out a critical territory in literary history, dramatizing the divorce of memory from history, and simultaneously seeking to intervene in this process. Once memory is "besieged" by history, according to Nora's argument, we can only seek to decipher our experience in terms of what we can no longer experience. And The Excursion—both text and notes—demonstrates just this act of decipherment, emerging from, and thereby defining, the remains of ancestral, customary traditions of rural English life and Lake District communities.

While The Excursion's concerted "will to remember" confirms that a shift from memory to history is irrevocable, before the poem begins, this has already happened.

Can literature ever be a legitimate form of memory, as Nora claims, or can it only function as a "site"? Wordsworth provides one answer in Book Ninth, in a dialogue between the Poet and the Pastor's wife. When the two spy a white ram, mirrored in a pool at sunset, the Pastor's wife exclaims

Ah! what a pity were it to...disperse,
Or to disturb, so fair a spectacle,
And yet a breath can do it! (IX, 454-56)
The Poet responds:
Ah! that such beauty, varying in the light
Of living nature, cannot be portrayed
By words, nor by the pencil's silent skill;
But is the property of him alone
Who hath beheld it, noted it with care,
And in his mind recorded it with love! (IX, 514-19)

This suggests that such visions, kept "alive" in the imaginations of living people, are vulnerable in the larger, social realm of representation. According to the Poet, art is inadequate to incorporate certain experiences, which might only survive as private, internal recollections. Like the twofold reflection, memory and narrative representation are joined, and yet remain "antipodes."

Perhaps all modern literature is created under historical pressure, produced by a fear of memory's erasure. Wordsworth's changing relationship to memory is demonstrated by what Kenneth Johnston terms the "apocalyptic discontinuity and the naturalistic continuities," of his poetry—the "fundamental poles of Wordsworth's imagination". Such a dialectic marks The Excursion as well as The Prelude's Book Fifth. In that famous passage, the Poet dreamed of a deluge that threatened poetry, a natural process that would, by extension, overwhelm memory. In The Prelude this fear remains a terrible fantasy; The Excursion suggests it is already reality. And in the wake of the flood, we are left with a will to remember.

Q. Discuss Wordsworth's Mother Tongue.

Or

Q. What were Wordsworth's Mourning, Language, and Identity in "The Emigrant Mother"?

Or

Q. Analyse William Wordsworth's The Emigrant Mother.

In Bearing the Word: Language and Female Experience in Nineteenth-Century Women's Writing, Margaret Homans argues persuasively that "romantic poetry... states most compellingly the traditional myth, as transmitted through literature, of women's place in language as the silent or vanished object of male representation and quest". Many critics, like Anne Mellor and Marlon Ross, have accepted masculine poets tendency to objectify women in romantic literature, and there are many obvious examples in the poetry which support the claim: the blessed babe section of book 2 of Wordsworth's Prelude, Keats's "La Belle Dames Sans Merci, "and Shelley's Alastor are just a few.

Critics often view William Wordsworth as particularly culpable in displaying insensitivity to gender issues and in objectifying women. For example, Ross argues that "Unlike Byron or Shelley, he never questions how the romantic poetic identity sustains sexual and political hierarchies". However, in several of his poems Wordsworth does represent women who have voices. In particular he represents mothers who are present subjects with powers of figuration and not silent or absent objects of quest.

Wordsworth presents one of his best examples of such a mother in "The Emigrant Mother" (1807), a poem about a woman who mourns the loss of her son. He explicitly appropriates a woman's voice to write his own poem; however, he gives his female representation all the narrative powers that he possesses, both receptive and creative, and the ability to recollect and reconstruct "her" story. Certainly, he controls the mother's song, but in representing the mother as telling her story and incorpo rating the words of others into her story, he constructs a woman who is much more than a silent object of quest.

Like the poet, she has the powers necessary to tell her story, to form her identity. When we see Wordsworth bestow the skills of the poet on a mother, our view must shift to a more complex understanding of his attitudes about gender, a view beyond the man-as-subject / woman-as-object scheme.

In the rest of my presentation, I will first explain several connections between mourning, language, and poetic composition. Then, I will show how the emigrant mother uses (or is constructed as using) the same methods to mourn her son and construct her voice that Wordsworth uses to create poetry. Because Wordsworth represents the mother as struggling to mourn her loss and to tell her story, he does represent a complex and dynamic subject who is more than a silent or absent object.

I believe that the act of mourning is structured like and can even represent language use and poetic creation. Building mostly on the work of Freud and Erikson, Robert J. Lifton defines mourning as a survivor 's struggle to reconstitute his psychic life in a way that can enable him to separate from the dead person while retaining a sense of connection with him, free himself from the deadness of that person and reestablish within himself, sometimes in altered form, whatever modes of immortality have been threatened by the death.

He stresses the significance of both separation and connection, of accepting the loss of the other but also maintaining a bond with that person. The means to maintaining connection with the absent other is symbolization. For Lifton, symbolization is "the specifically human need to construct all experience as the only means of perceiving, knowing, and feeling"(6 my emphasis). Through symbolization in mourning the survivor re-orders the experience of the other with enough difference to accept the real separation (the physical death) and with enough similarity to create continuity in life (the survivor's).Without building this continuity, Lifton argues that "psychic numbing"or stasis overwhelms the survivor.

A child's acquisition of language also appears to follow the pattern of mourning. Homans revises Lacan's model of language acquisition to explain how infants begin to use language and how this early language activity structures later activity. In her account children perceive separation from mothers as a "death"and use language as a means of reconnecting with their mothers; this dynamic of death and substitution ultimately structures all symbolic language.

This substitution appears to be a sort of mourning: a way for children to free themselves from their maternal figures while at the same time remaining connected to them. Since poeti c creation is a sophisticated form of early language activity, the death dynamic also structures this adult language activity. However, the dynamic is much more complicated in poetic creation than in early symbolic activity just as mourning carried out b y adults is more complicated than mourning carried out by children. As Lifton notes, "What distinguishes adult grief [mourning] and depression is symbolization around loss that is, compared to childhood counterparts, much more elaborate and more intensely focused".

While the parallel between mourning and language use is manifest in poetic practice, I believe that Lifton's definition of mourning and Wordsworth's definition of poetry are also very similar. Wordsworth says that poetry is

the spontaneous overflow of powerful feelings; it takes its origin from emotions recollected in tranquillity: the emotion is contemplated till by a species of reaction the tranquillity gradually disappears, and an emotion, kindred to that which was before the subject of contemplation, is gradually produced, and does itself actually exist in the mind. In this mood successful composition generally begins.

His formulation of poetry has two basic parts: 1) an original experience which he has been separated from by time—the actual experience is "dead"; and 2) his recollection, his re-ordering or re-collection, of that experience. The recollection is clearly not the same as the original, but it is "kindred" to the original; it is similar to and different from the original.

Mourning a dead person follows a similar pattern. Death separates the survivor from the absent other; eventually, the survivor reconstructs the other with enough difference to accept that person's actual death but also with enough similarity to establish a connection with him or her in order to affirm the continuity of life. To say that poetry equals mourning is of course too extreme. What I wish to suggest is that making poetry and mourning work are structured similarly and that both require separation from the original experience/other and a symbolic reconnection with th e original that accepts actual separation. Making poetry might be considered a subset of mourning work.

Wordsworth repeatedly represents separation and loss in the form of mourning as a significant part of the mother-child dyad from both the mother and child's point of view. In both situations, the subjects which are represented try to recreate the absent other. Psychoanalytic theory has shown us that infants "do this" when they begin to use symbolic activity: when the maternal figure, usually female, is absent, the child uses objects or language to try to replace her as in Freud's fort/da example.

What is interesting in Wordsworth's poetry is that he not only portrays this dynamic from the perspective of children, but that he also repeatedly portrays it from an adult mother's perspective. In poems like "The Sailor's Mother" and "The Force of Prayer"), Wordsworth represents mothers with powers of figuration based on separation from their children, but in "The Emigrant Mother" the voice is more sophisticated and complex.

In "The Emigrant Mother" Wordsworth presents a mother who has been separated from her son and tries to substitute another child for him. Like many other poems which represent the mother-child relationship (i.e., "The Norman Boy, ""The Sailor's Mother, "and "The Force of Prayer"), Wordsworth begins this poem very self-consciously with a speaker who meta-poetically reveals the source of the poem or "lay". In the introductory section, the speaker reveals that he is friends with a French emigrant who has been separated from her own child, that she has often shared her "griefs" with him, and that the poem that follows i s a song about what she "might say" to a neighbour child. At the end of the introduction he says, "My song the workings of her heart expressed" to stress his identification with her.

The song is a combination of the speaker's understanding of the emigrant mother's experience and the speaker's own imagination; it is based on what the speaker "heard and knew, or guessed "(3, 12-13). Just as in the Norman boy poems, I believe this detailed, meta-poetic introduction suggests that the poem is an example of Wordsworth's definition of poetry as the "spontaneous overflow of powerful feelings.... recollected in tranquility", an enactment of what Wordsworth describes in The Prelude when he characterizes the infant mind which is the model for the poetic spirit as "creator and receiver both. "The speaker "guesses" parts of the emigrant's story which is an overtly creative act; he separates what actually happened to the woman from what he individually "guesses "has happened.

To tell what he "knows" or has "heard" from her is a receptive act because he describes what has actually happened—what he knows has happened based on his relationship with the emigrant. In the song section which follows the introduction, the mother also relies on creative and receptive facets of her imagination to her story and to mourn her son. In the first stanza, the mother describes the "`Dear Babe[`s]'"separation from her real mother who is working in the fields The emigrant mother suggests that the child could comfort her if she would be her child for "`one little hour. '"She then explains her separation from her own child (a son) who is still in France, emphasizing the distance as "`a long, long way of land and sea'",.

Next, she tells of her possible complete separation from her son because he may be dead. Before leaving France the mother's tears fell on her son's face, and a nurse told her that such an act was "`"unlucky"'"; however, the mother then hyperbolically denies the act's unluckiness with a series of four no's. After vehemently denying that her tears killed him, she then says that he will die because, according to those who take care of the child in the mother's absence, "`"he pines"'.

Here we have the speaker outside the song representing the mother as doing exactly what he has done with his introduction: she bases some of the story on direct experience, but then guesses, to fill in the details about her child that she does not actually know, details which suggest a fantasy of identification. The mother hopes her son pines for her just as she obviously pines for him. Just as the speaker in the introduction, she bases the story both on information that she has received and which she creates; her experience of loss leads her to develop a v oice to construct a sense of reality (at least the speaker represents her as doing so).

However, the woman's creative imagination fails to satisfy when she realizes that the little girl's "`cheerful smiles'" and "`looks'" are not the same as her son's. Despite her efforts to make the girl into her child, by stanza five the illusion "`Tis gone—like dreams that we forget'". She sees the smiles of her son in her mind 's eye and then recognizes that the smiles of the girl do not correspond. The little girl "`troublest'" and "`confound[s]'"her to the degree that she "`must lay [her] down'". The receptive power of her imagination overcomes her creative impulse, knowing overcomes guessing. The mother consciously works through a fantasy o f reality as she would like it to be and the reality of her situation as it is.

In stanza six, her troubled state continues. She no longer tries to make the child into her son and explains that she loves the little girl for her own sake. She loves her even more than her sister's child who also lives nearby and "`who bears [the emigrant's] name'". The French woman even goes so far as to say that "`Never was any child more dear'" which suggests that she loves the infant girl more than any other child, even her own son. She tries to erase the son who she can only connect through memory and to replace him with an actual child who is present but not her own.

However, in stanza seven, the replacement strategy also fails. The verse paragraph begins with a very intrusive one-m dash which marks an abrupt shift in her thinking. The mother reveals that she "`cannot help it'" but that she must weep; she cannot replace her son. She fears that her tears and words do

He also represents th e mother as being able to represent other characters who tell stories: the mother tells of the nurse who told her: “`"Tears should not / Be shed upon an infant's face / It was unlucky"'". Certainly, his use of quotation marks and stanza numbers in each verse paragraph of the song remind readers that Wordsworth is very definitely in control (it is his song, and she is an "object of male representation") but in representing the mother as telling her story and incorporating the words of others into her story, she is not just a "silent" or "vanished" object of "quest". Just like the Wordsworth's self-representation in The Prelude, and all subjects represented in poetry, she is an object of Wordsworth's representation; however, she, unlike all poetic objects, is also given a complex voice to tell her story.

In several of his poems Wordsworth represents women who actively struggle to endure their losses and bring continuity to their lives. In portraying mothers who express desire and satisfy their desires to varying degrees, he represents women who are not simply objects of desire themselves. Indeed, their symbolizations or works of mourning are like the poet's constructions of poems.

Both the poet and the mothers strive to recollect or re-order an original experience or person to simultaneously accept their separation from it and maintain a sense of connection to it. This suggests that Wordsworth's view of women is, in some instances, more complex than many critics believe. To associate the same skills to a woman that he attributes to the poet breaks the binary system of man as subject and woman as object that is often attributed to him. What remains for critics is to uncover a pattern of when Wordsworth represents women as subjects an d when he represents them as objects and to speculate about why he shifts between these views.

Bibliography

See his poetical works, ed. by E. de Selincourt and H. Darbishire (5 vol., 1940–49);

His prose works, ed. by W. J. B. Owen and J. W. Smyser (3 vol., 1974);

Correspondence with his sister, ed. by E, de Selincourt (6 vol., 1967–82);

Biographies by *M. Moorman* (2 vol., 1965), *S. Gill* (1984), *K. R. Johnston* (1999), and *J. Barker* (rev. ed. 2005); studies by *M. Reed* (1967),

F. E. Halliday (1970), *R. Rehder* (1981), *J. K. Changler* (1984), *P. Hamilton* (1986),

A. J. Bewell (1989), and *D. Bromwich* (1999);

G. McMaster, William Wordsworth: A *Critical Anthology* (1973);

A. Sisman, The Friendship: Wordsworth and Coleridge (2007).